PROBLEM-ORIENTED POLICING

Soci 471

HV
9950
.G65
1990

PROBLEM-ORIENTED POLICING

Herman Goldstein
University of Wisconsin-Madison

06-12-00
31 20/31 16
Midwest

McGraw-Hill, Inc.
New York St. Louis San Francisco Auckland Bogotá
Caracas Lisbon London Madrid Mexico City Milan
Montreal New Delhi San Juan Singapore
Sydney Tokyo Toronto

This book was set in Times Roman by the College Composition Unit
in cooperation with Waldman Graphics, Inc.
The editors were Phillip A. Butcher and Ira C. Roberts;
the production supervisor was Louise Karam.
The cover was designed by Amy Becker.
R. R. Donnelley & Sons Company was printer and binder.

This book is printed on acid-free paper.

PROBLEM-ORIENTED POLICING

Copyright © 1990 by McGraw-Hill, Inc. All rights reserved. Printed in the United States of America. Except as permitted under the United States Copyright Act of 1976, no part of this publication may be reproduced or distributed in any form or by any means, or stored in a data base or retrieval system, without the prior written permission of the publisher.

13 14 15 16 17 DOC/DOC 9 9

ISBN 0-07-023694-1

Library of Congress Cataloging-in-Publication Data

Goldstein, Herman, (date).
Problem-oriented policing / Herman Goldstein.
p. cm.
Includes bibliographical references.
ISBN 0-07-023694-1
1. Criminal justice, Administration of—United States. 2. Police—United States.
3. Crime prevention—United States—Citizen participation. I. Title.
HV9950.G65 1990
363.2'0973—dc20 89-13681

To the memory of
GARY P. HAYES
1945–1985
whose vision and drive encouraged the
explorations on which this book is based.

CONTENTS

PREFACE xi

1 **Introduction** 1

2 **Progress in Policing** 5

DEVELOPMENT AND INFLUENCE OF THE PROFESSIONAL MODEL 6
THE FIRST CLUSTER OF RESEARCH: DOCUMENTING REALITY 8
NEW DEMANDS, AN ASSESSMENT OF NEEDS, AND THE BEGINNING OF A QUEST FOR NEW DIRECTIONS 9
EMERGENCE OF A NEW "COMMON WISDOM" ON THE POLICE 10
A SECOND CLUSTER OF RESEARCH: QUESTIONING THE VALUE OF STANDARD RESPONSES 12

3 **A Critique of the Current State of the Field: Considerations Leading to Problem-Oriented Policing** 14

THE PREOCCUPATION WITH MANAGEMENT, INTERNAL PROCEDURES, AND EFFICIENCY 15
THE PREDOMINANTLY REACTIVE POSTURE OF THE POLICE 18
THE NEED TO ENGAGE THE COMMUNITY 21
THE NEED TO MAKE FULLER USE OF RANK-AND-FILE POLICE OFFICERS 27
THE LIMITATIONS OF PIECEMEAL REFORM 29
The Resistance of the Police Subculture 29
The Lack of a Coherent Plan 30

4 Problem-Oriented Policing: The Basic Elements 32

GROUPING INCIDENTS AS PROBLEMS 32
FOCUSING ON SUBSTANTIVE PROBLEMS AS THE HEART OF POLICING 34
EFFECTIVENESS AS THE ULTIMATE GOAL 35
THE NEED FOR SYSTEMATIC INQUIRY 36
DISAGGREGATING AND ACCURATELY LABELING PROBLEMS 38
ANALYSIS OF THE MULTIPLE INTERESTS IN PROBLEMS 40
CAPTURING AND CRITIQUING THE CURRENT RESPONSE 42
AN UNINHIBITED SEARCH FOR A TAILOR-MADE RESPONSE 43
ADOPTING A PROACTIVE STANCE 45
STRENGTHENING THE DECISION-MAKING PROCESSES AND INCREASING ACCOUNTABILITY 47
EVALUATING RESULTS OF NEWLY IMPLEMENTED RESPONSES 49

5 The Early Experiences 50

BRIEF SUMMARIES OF SOME EARLY EXPERIMENTS 51
Madison, Wisconsin, Police in Collaboration with the University of Wisconsin 51
Baltimore County, Maryland, Police in Collaboration with the Police Executive Research Forum 52
London Metropolitan Police 53
Newport News, Virginia, Police in Collaboration with the Police Executive Research Forum 55
PROBLEM-ORIENTED COMPONENTS IN THE COMMUNITY-ORIENTED POLICING PROJECTS OF SEVERAL OTHER CITIES 57
Flint, Michigan 57
New York City 58
Los Angeles 58
Houston 59
Edmonton, Alberta 59
COMMON THEMES IN THE EXPERIMENTAL PROJECTS 61
CONTINUING EXPERIMENTATION 63

6 Identifying Problems 65

WHAT IS THE MEANING OF "PROBLEM"? 66
WHO IDENTIFIES PROBLEMS? 70
The Community 70
Police Management 72
Rank-and-File Officers 73

REDEFINING PROBLEMS AFTER PRELIMINARY INQUIRY 76
SELECTING FROM AMONG PROBLEMS 77

7 Analyzing Problems 80

TYPES OF INFORMATION TO BE ACQUIRED 82
SOURCES OF INFORMATION 84
RIGOR OF THE INQUIRY 88
CAUTIONS IN THE USE OF DATA FROM POLICE FILES 91
DIFFICULTIES IN TAPPING THE KNOWLEDGE OF RANK-AND-FILE POLICE OFFICERS 93
OBTAINING AN ACCURATE PICTURE OF THE CURRENT RESPONSE 94
ENSURING ADEQUATE DEPTH 98

8 The Search for Alternatives: Developing Tailor-Made Responses 102

MAKING THE SEARCH FOR ALTERNATIVES AN INTEGRAL PART OF POLICING 103
THE RANGE OF POSSIBLE ALTERNATIVES 104
Concentrating Attention on Those Individuals Who Account for a Disproportionate Share of a Problem 104
Connecting with Other Government and Private Services 106
Using Mediation and Negotiation Skills 111
Conveying Information 114
Mobilizing the Community 119
Making Use of Existing Forms of Social Control in Addition to the Community 121
Altering the Physical Environment to Reduce Opportunities for Problems to Recur 124
Increased Regulation, through Statutes or Ordinances, of Conditions That Contribute to Problems 127
Developing New Forms of Limited Authority to Intervene and Detain 128
More Discriminate Use of the Criminal Justice System 131
Using Civil Law to Control Public Nuisances, Offensive Behavior, and Conditions Contributing to Crime 139
CHOOSING FROM AMONG ALTERNATIVES 141
MEASURING THE EFFECTIVENESS OF ALTERNATIVE RESPONSES 145

9 Changes in Management: Creating a Supportive Organizational Environment 148

REDEFINING THE ROLE FOR RANK-AND-FILE OFFICERS 148
MANAGING THE USE OF TIME 151
A NEW LEADERSHIP STYLE 152
Articulating Values 152
Understanding Problem-Oriented Policing and Conveying Its Meaning to Subordinates 154
Changing the Relationship between Employer and Employee 155
DEVELOPING A NEW DIMENSION IN SUPERVISION 157
DECENTRALIZATION TO ENABLE OFFICERS TO CAPITALIZE ON THEIR KNOWLEDGE OF THE COMMUNITY 159
BROADENING RESEARCH AND PLANNING EFFORTS 161
REVISING THE CRITERIA FOR RECOGNIZING PERFORMANCE 163
RECRUITMENT AND SELECTION 165
TRAINING 167
DEVELOPING NEW SOURCES OF INFORMATION AND NEW KNOWLEDGE 168
Networking within and among Police Agencies 168
Professional Journals 171
A Research Agenda for State and Federal Agencies, Academics, and Research Organizations 171
GETTING GOING: SPECIAL UNIT OR DEPARTMENT-WIDE IMPLEMENTATION? 172

10 Reflections on Implementation Efforts 176

REFERENCES 181
INDEX 195

PREFACE

The police, especially in our large urban areas, are currently struggling with the overwhelming problems associated with the sale and use of drugs. They are under enormous pressure to deal with indiscriminate shootings of innocent citizens, an escalation of violence among drug sellers, frequent involvement of children in both drug use and sale, and the concern of whole neighborhoods terrorized by drug-related activities. A high percentage of all police business is now affected, in one way or another, by drug traffic and use. And all of this has occurred after at least two decades in which violence and street-order problems already ranked high among the nation's major concerns, and police have been under intense pressure to deal with them.

How can one, in such a stressful atmosphere, responsibly urge the police to take the time to consider, let alone implement, a somewhat theoretical concept for improving policing? Similarly, how can one responsibly suggest that the police give increased attention to seemingly petty behavior like panhandling, noise, and the nuisances created by the homeless and the mentally ill? And, at a time when police misconduct appears to be on the increase in some jurisdictions because of their role in controlling drugs, how can one responsibly propose changes, in policing that broaden the discretion of individual officers, encourage more informal relationships with the community, and develop a more relaxed working environment in police agencies?

These are difficult questions for anyone making proposals related to the police in the 1990s and beyond. Their importance is underlined by the strong, pragmatic strain that has always pervaded policing. One takes on a heavy burden in exploring theories, principles, and organizing concepts in a field in which there is an ever-present, urgent need to provide immediate relief from threatening problems. Police themselves often express impatience and even disdain when called upon to step back and analyze their work, because they live in a world of violence and disrespect for all the norms that govern our society—a world of guns and knives, of serious injury and death. The instinct for survival (both physical and in their careers) must be a primary concern. Likewise, citizens—and especially their elected officials—display understandable impatience with proposals that they perceive as not immediately responsive to problems about which they feel deeply.

Serious students of the police learn quickly that, despite many existing stereotypes, policing is an extraordinarily complex endeavor. And the more one learns about its complexities, the more puzzling it becomes. Working through this puzzle is a demanding challenge, requiring a unique blend of pragmatic considerations and intellectual capacity. It requires an understanding of the multitude of factors that influence the day-to-day behavior of police officers. It requires a solid understanding of our democracy and its values, and a commitment to their importance. It requires an understanding of our legislative process and the intricacies of the criminal justice system. It requires a realistic assessment of the capacity of the criminal justice system to meet public expectations. And it requires an in-depth understanding of the social, political, and behavioral problems that are of current concern in our society, and of the rapid changes that are occurring—especially in race relations.

Much of the complexity in policing stems from a myriad of conflicts and incongruities built into the police function—some inherent in the nature of the policing task and others created by the approach to policing we have taken over the years. I summarized the most fundamental of these conflicts in the introduction to an earlier work.

> The police, by the very nature of their function, are an anomaly in a free society. They are invested with a great deal of authority under a system of government in which authority is reluctantly granted and, when granted, sharply curtailed. The specific form of their authority—to arrest, to search, to detain, and to use force—is awesome in the degree to which it can be disruptive of freedom, invasive of privacy, and sudden and direct in its impact upon the individual. And this awesome authority, of necessity, is delegated to individuals at the lowest level of the bureaucracy to be exercised, in most instances, without prior review and control.
>
> Yet a democracy is heavily dependent upon its police, despite their anomalous position, to maintain the degree of order that makes a free society possible. It looks to its police to prevent people from preying on one another; to

> provide a sense of security; to facilitate movement; to resolve conflicts; and to protect the very processes and rights—such as free elections, freedom of speech, and freedom of assembly—on which continuation of a free society depends. The strength of a democracy and the quality of life enjoyed by its citizens are determined in large measure by the ability of the police to discharge their duties. (Goldstein, 1977)

Perhaps because these requirements seem so incongruous, and therefore difficult to meet, our society has been slow to work through all of the issues that arise in developing a policing institution that can be effective but not threatening to our way of life. Numerous conflicts continue to haunt the police: conflicts, for example, between public expectations and the reality of what the police can do; between the authority and resources that are needed and those that are provided; and between traditional practices and those that may be more effective.

But a crisis such as we are now experiencing with the use and sale of drugs forces us to face some of these conflicts. Thus, while the current problem of drugs appears, on the surface, to preoccupy the police, leaving no room for long-range planning, our efforts to deal with drugs are likely to have a major impact on the shape of policing in the future—just as efforts to deal with labor-management strife, racial conflict, and political protest helped work through complex issues in the past. The drug problem has made us newly aware of the limitations on the capacity of the police. At the same time, the pressure to deal with drugs has not stopped more general efforts to improve policing. To the contrary, major changes are actually occurring in the form of policing today, only some of which are shaped by the need to respond to the drug problem.

Thus, while I acknowledge throughout this volume the intense pressure on the police and the preemptive quality of the drug problem, I have guarded against the tendency for concern about drugs and related problems to unduly influence explorations about the future of policing. We need a broad conceptual framework in policing that helps the police build a strong, sensitive institution, with refined methods of operating, that can better transcend the crisis of the day, whether that crisis be labor-management strife, racial conflict, political protest, drugs, or some yet-to-be-identified social problem. In a democracy in which complex social problems will always place heavy demands on the police, we have an obligation to strive constantly—not periodically—for a form of policing that is not only effective, but humane and civil; that not only protects individual rights, equality, and other values basic to a democracy, but strengthens our commitment to them. The importance of meeting this need has nourished this effort.

ACKNOWLEDGMENTS

Work on this book was initiated with support from the National Institute of Justice, as part of its grant to the Police Executive Research Forum (PERF) for further experimentation with problem-oriented policing. I appreciate the confidence that this support reflects, especially on the part of James K. Stewart, the Director of the National Institute and Darrel W. Stephens, the Executive Director of PERF. Additional support was received from the Graduate School of the University of Wisconsin, the University of Wisconsin Law School, and the Evjue Foundation.

The central concept of this book—the focus on problems—grew rather naturally out of an approach that several of us on the Law School faculty adopted a long time ago in the teaching of criminal justice administration. My colleagues in this endeavor, Frank J. Remington and Walter J. Dickey, made the special contributions that come from frequent discussion and sharing of experience. I also greatly appreciate the support of two other colleagues, David E. Schultz and Orrin L. Helstad, who, through the Continuing Legal Education program, enabled me to start work on this project.

I am indebted to the leadership of the several departments that were among the first to experiment with problem-oriented policing: Chief Cornelius J. Behan and Colonel Phillip G. Huber, Baltimore County, Maryland; Commissioner Kenneth Newman and Chief Superintendent Tony Burns-Howell, London Metropolitan Police; Chief David C. Couper, Madison, Wisconsin; and Chief Darrel W. Stephens and his successor, Jay A. Carey, Newport News, Virginia. They afforded me numerous opportunities to learn from their experiences. I am especially indebted to the many officers of all ranks in these and other departments—especially those at the street level—who, through their participation, contributed so much to the development of the concept and provided feedback to me. My respect for their skill, experiences, and commitment makes me want to cite them by name, too, for their contribution is equally important to that of top management, but their number precludes my doing so.

The experimentation with problem-oriented policing that was undertaken in collaboration with the Madison, Wisconsin, Police Department resulted in a four-volume report, coauthored with Charles E. Susmilch. I drew heavily on segments of that report for use in Chapter 6 on the identification of problems and in Chapter 7 on their analysis.

Michael S. Scott, formerly my research assistant and now on the PERF staff, played a special collaborative role. In the conceptual stages, he helped outline the project, and he subsequently reviewed the relevant literature and organized the material then available. He prepared a first draft describing alternative responses, on which I have drawn heavily for Chapter 8. And he carefully critiqued each draft of the manuscript and assisted in filling gaps.

I benefited much from those who, at my request, took the time to provide detailed comments on draft material: Chris Braiden, Diane Hill, John E. Eck, Jay Meehan, William Saulsbury, Darrel W. Stephens, and Mary Ann Wycoff. Other reviews acquired by McGraw-Hill came from John A. Conley, University of Wisconsin–Madison; Donald J. Newman, State University of New York–Albany; and Samuel Walker, University of Nebraska at Omaha. The differing perspectives they brought to bear, reflecting their varied involvement in policing, sensitized me to the several audiences to which the book is addressed.

For editorial support, I was fortunate in enlisting two veterans whose skills appear to be in increasingly short supply. Elizabeth Uhr, with her exceptional editorial judgment and sharp pruning ability, greatly improved the manuscript. Lucille Hamre, with the painstaking care that spoiled all of us who ever worked with her, cleaned up earlier drafts of the manuscript and prepared the bibliography. I have been greatly aided throughout the project by the secretarial assistance of Diane Roessler and Lynda Hicks.

Herman Goldstein

PROBLEM-ORIENTED POLICING

CHAPTER **1**

INTRODUCTION

The police field has received more serious attention in the past three decades than in all the previous years of organized police service. This attention has resulted in many advances. Among these the most significant, in my opinion, is an increased openness within the field—a greater willingness to critique police work, to support research, to experiment, and to debate more freely the merits of new proposals for change.

In this welcome atmosphere of questioning and exploration, I have argued that the most commonly articulated proposals for improving policing do not go far enough (Goldstein, 1979). They concentrate on means rather than ends. They dwell on the structure, staffing, and equipping of the police organization, with the assumption that such efforts will eventually result in an improvement in the quality of policing. To develop a form of policing uniquely equipped to fulfill the complex needs of a free and diverse society, police reform must have a more ambitious goal.

Our society requires that the police deal with an incredibly broad range of troublesome situations. Handling these situations within the limitations that we place on the police is the essence of policing. It follows that efforts to improve policing should extend to and focus on the end product of policing—on the effectiveness and fairness of the police in dealing with the substantive problems that the public looks to the police to handle.

Serious in-depth exploration of these substantive problems opens many new doors for constructive change in policing. It often leads to new ideas for improving effectiveness; to ways of engaging both the police and the community more productively; and to dealing with conditions that have undermined efforts to improve the police in the past. Most important, it leads to a whole new perspective of policing.

The dominant perspective of policing is heavily influenced by the primary method of control associated with the work—the authority to enforce the criminal law. This influence is so strong that police officers are commonly referred to as law enforcement officers—a misnomer that uses only one of the methods they employ in their work to characterize all that they do. This common view has not only distorted our perception of the police role; it has disproportionately influenced the operating practices, organization, training, and staffing of police agencies. If, in a sharp departure from this traditional perspective, one begins with an analysis of each of the varied problems police handle and only then proceeds to establish the most effective response, one's perspective of policing is reversed. Rather than cling to the simplistic notion that the criminal law defines the police role, we come to realize that policing consists of developing the most effective means for dealing with a multitude of troublesome situations. And these means will often, but not always, include appropriate use of the criminal law.

The full significance of this change in perspective is illustrated by the current crisis relating to drugs. Because sale and possession of drugs are criminal, the traditional perspective of the police leads the public to look to the police as the agency having primary responsibility for the problem. The police, in turn, continue to depend most heavily on the criminal law in responding to the problem, though the pervasiveness of drug sale and use has overwhelmed their resources, and the process of detection, arrest, and prosecution is difficult and often futile. The current crisis is gradually forcing recognition—on the part of both the public and the police—that much more is required than simply law enforcement. Some police agencies recognized this long ago; others have yet to do so. With this new awareness, then, the challenge is to determine what use should be made by the police of the criminal law (given the difficulty of the process and limited resources); what other means are available to the police for dealing with the problem; and what the police (given their first-hand knowledge of the magnitude and complexity of the problem) should be urging others to do in responding to it. Thus, in its rough outlines, what is happening in reaction to the drug crisis, belatedly and somewhat clumsily, illustrates a larger need that exists with regard to each of the behavioral problems police are expected to handle.

A proposal for incorporating greater concern for the end product of police work into efforts to effect change in the police was initially outlined in the 1979 article cited above and has since been referred to as "problem-oriented policing." The label is a mixed blessing. It greatly facilitates communication among those who fully understand the concept, eliminating the need to define all of its elements in each interchange. But use of the phrase also creates the great risk that, when the concept is widely broadcast under the abbreviated label, it will be drained of much of its meaning. Concern about this risk was among the factors that stimulated the writing of this book.

While problem-oriented policing builds on the best of the past, it is obviously much more than just a new tactic or program to be added on to prevalent forms of policing. It entails more than identifying and analyzing community problems and developing more effective responses to them. In its broadest context, it is a whole new way of thinking about policing that has implications for every aspect of the police organization, its personnel, and its operations. With an ever-present concern about the end product of policing as its central theme, it seeks to tie together the many elements involved in effecting change in the police so that these changes are coordinated and mutually supportive. It connects with the current move to redefine relationships between the police and the community. Fully implemented, it has the potential to reshape the way in which police services are delivered.

This book describes problem-oriented policing as the concept has developed since it was first proposed. I have built on the points originally made in the 1979 article, expanding on the basic elements of the concept, demonstrating how these elements tie together, and explaining how they meet some of the long-term needs of the police. This effort has been greatly enhanced by the opportunity to observe and learn from the experiences of a number of police agencies that, in varying degrees, were among the first to implement the concept—especially those serving Baltimore County, Maryland; Newport News, Virginia; Madison, Wisconsin; New York City; and London. The large number of individuals who have been involved in the difficult task of introducing the concept into the "real world" of policing have contributed a great deal to its fuller development. If I fail to credit them at appropriate times, it is simply because—in the process of melding ideas and with the rapidity of developments in other cities—I can no longer distinguish who contributed what.

To lay a foundation for describing all the dimensions of problem-oriented policing, I first summarize briefly, in Chapter 2, the progress made in policing in recent years. Then, in Chapter 3, I critique the current state of the field, identifying the several factors that have contributed most directly to development of the problem-oriented approach to improvement. In Chapter 4 I set forth the basic elements of the concept as they have evolved, and in Chapter 5 I report on the early experiences in implementing the concept.

Building on these experiences, the second half of the book is devoted to exploring ways in which the police can develop their capacity for dealing with community problems. Chapter 6 considers what is involved in identifying problems—big and small. Chapter 7 outlines various approaches to analyzing problems. And Chapter 8, the longest chapter, identifies and critically examines a wide range of alternatives that police might consider in fashioning more effective tailor-made responses. Chapter 9 describes the numerous changes that will be required in the management of a police agency so that management policies and practices support—rather than impede, as they often now do—efforts to concentrate on the problems that constitute police business. And in Chapter 10, I reflect on the prospects for implementation.

Whether one views problem-oriented policing as a concept, a theory, a philosophy, or a plan, it obviously has a tentative character to it. It is open-ended. It invites criticism, alterations, additions, and subtractions. I stress this point lest the effort to be as specific as possible in communicating the idea is interpreted as unduly definitive of its shape. Throughout the book, I raise questions with the specific intent of stimulating others to contribute to further development of this overall approach to improving policing and to critique what is set forth here.

CHAPTER **2**

PROGRESS IN POLICING

In the past three decades significant insights have been gained into the police role—its complexity, what works and does not work, and how this knowledge can contribute toward shaping police operations in the future. Important as these new insights are, we have yet to develop a strong tradition for systematically building knowledge about the police and for tying new developments together. No common base is widely accepted as a point from which to "take off." And relatively few milestones exist in the development of new understanding regarding the police to which we can refer with any confidence that a wide audience will attribute common meaning to them. As a result, in an effort such as this one, in which the objective is to set forth a concept that looks to the future, it is necessary to summarize briefly those key changes in our understanding of the police and their functioning that contribute to an updated perspective of the field. (A more comprehensive, detailed summary—one of the best that has been produced—appears in Eck and Spelman et al. [1987, pp. 11–31].)

Of course, anyone with a serious interest in policing is well advised to go back much more than 30 years, if he or she has not already done so, and to become acquainted especially with the intense debates that preceded the first formal provisions for police service in England about 160 years ago. (An excellent summary that seeks to unsnarl the sometimes confused history of that period has recently become available [Reiner,

1985].) Those debates were extraordinarily rich in their intellectual quality; the principles that emerged from them are still relevant today.

Surely, too, one would want to have an overview of the history of policing in this country. But this history, until the 1950s, is, with a few exceptions (see Walker, 1977, pp. 79–106), almost devoid of any critical thinking regarding the really difficult issues in policing. It is, for the most part, an account of drift and responses to drift as the police always lagged behind in their capacity to meet the needs of a rapidly changing society. When the gap became too great, or when a scandal surfaced, efforts were made to "reform" the police. "Reform" occurred with such frequency that, to this day, the term has a kind of permanent meaning when associated with the police that it has lost with regard to most aspects of government.

DEVELOPMENT AND INFLUENCE OF THE PROFESSIONAL MODEL

Given the lag in attention to the police, it is abundantly clear why the dominant efforts to improve the police since the turn of the century focused on management of the police agency, and particularly on management designed to achieve more effective control. Under the best of circumstances, police agencies have several peculiar characteristics that make them especially difficult to administer. Police officers are spread out in the field, not subject to direct supervision. Individual officers exercise enormous authority, including the authority to deprive people of their liberty and, even more awesome, of their lives. Difficult and often unpredictable situations are inherent in policing. Many of the people with whom the police must deal are antisocial, frequently despicable, and sometimes violent. Failure to properly manage an organization with these characteristics has exceptionally high costs. The history of policing in this country is filled with examples of police agencies succumbing to favoritism and political influence. In such agencies, corruption, physical and other forms of abuse, callousness, discourtesy, and inefficiency were commonplace.

Faced with these problems, all of the major commentators on the police since the beginning of the century—Leonhard F. Fuld (1909), Raymond B. Fosdick (1915), August Vollmer (1936), Bruce Smith (1940), and O. W. Wilson (1950)—stressed the need to streamline the organization, upgrade personnel, modernize equipment, and establish more businesslike operating procedures. As anyone realizes who today takes on the responsibility for "straightening out" an inefficient, corrupt, disorganized police agency, gaining control over the actions of members of the organization must be the first priority. Given the sensitive nature of the police function, even those departments that enjoy a reputation for integrity and for operating within the law must continue to give high priority and disproportionate time to preventing wrongdoing and to dealing with complaints involving a relatively minute percentage of their total work force.

Upon implementation, the model that emerged from the work of Fuld, Fosdick, Vollmer, Smith, and Wilson—now referred to as the professional model—met the basic needs that had been identified. It did so by placing a high value on police being apolitical and by advocating centralized control, tight organization, pinpointed responsibility, strong discipline, efficient use of personnel and technology, and higher standards of recruitment and training. It sought to achieve a higher level of operating efficiency by emphasizing standard operating procedures, fast responses, efficient use of time, smooth flow of paperwork, and clean, modern facilities. The push toward greater operating efficiency gathered momentum as various new technologies (in motor vehicles, telephone systems, radio communications, data processing equipment, and ultimately computers) were adapted to police work. Thus, for several decades (especially 1940 through 1970), a concern with developing techniques to increase the control and efficiency of the police agency occupied those in the forefront of policing.

Because the professional model sought to project such a neutral, apolitical image, some got the impression that it attached little importance to the sensitive role of the police in our society. But the chief architects of the professional model viewed the improvements they advocated as making the police much more aware of the need to act lawfully, with appropriate protections for the rights of all citizens, including those accused of crimes. They sought to instill in officers a strong—some would even argue too rigid (''Just the facts, ma'am'')—commitment to the supremacy of the law and to the importance of equal treatment. The professional movement considered one of its major achievements to be the promulgation of the Law Enforcement Code of Ethics, adopted by the International Association of Chiefs of Police in 1957, which was significant in its exhortation to ''protect the innocent against deception, the weak against oppression or intimidation . . . and to respect the Constitutional rights of all men to liberty, equality and justice'' (O. W. Wilson, 1963, p. 6). And when O. W. Wilson brought his professional model to the Chicago Police Department in 1960, the operating policies he introduced—especially regarding recruitment, promotions, the allocation of personnel, and the handling of racial conflict—were seen by those concerned with racial equality and the protection of Constitutional rights as enormous advances for that era.

Not all departments were equally influenced by the professional model of policing. Some of the largest police agencies in the country were never "professionalized" in the sense of being subjected to a major reorganization to bring them into line with the characteristics of the professional model. They simply made changes as required by local conditions, new technology, and pressures from interest groups, governing bodies, and the courts, retaining many vestiges of older forms of policing. Or they went through periods in which they were committed to adopting the professional model, only to abandon the effort before it was fully implemented. The value of the professional model of policing was not seriously questioned until the late 1960s. (For a fuller, up-to-date critique of the professional model, see Kelling and Moore, 1988.)

THE FIRST CLUSTER OF RESEARCH: DOCUMENTING REALITY

Major research efforts that inquired into the nature of policing, and that were subsequently to have a major impact on the field, were first undertaken in the 1950s. Until then, both the public and the police had made certain assumptions about how the police ideally should operate, and these were often taken as descriptive of police operations even though practice differed sharply. Seven major empirical studies of the police penetrated beyond this facade: the early work of sociologist William Westley, completed in 1951 but not widely published until a later date (Westley, 1970); the ambitious studies of the American Bar Foundation, for which fieldwork was completed in 1957 (LaFave, 1965; Tiffany, McIntyre, and Rotenberg, 1967); the field observations of Jerome Skolnick (1966); the work of Egon Bittner analyzing the police function on skid-row (1967); Raymond Parnas's study of the police response to domestic disturbances (1967); James Q. Wilson's analysis of different policing styles (1968); and the studies of citizen–police contact by Albert Reiss (1971).

In their descriptions of what was happening on the streets and in police stations, these studies documented the enormous gap between practice and the image of policing. They identified problems in policing that were not simply the product of poor management, but rather reflections of the inherent complexity of the police job. Here, for purposes of illustration, are a few of the major findings, summarized from a previous work by this author:

- Informal arrangements for handling incidents and behavioral problems were found to be more common than was compliance with formally established procedures.
- The pressures of volume, public pressures, interagency pressures, and the interests and personal predilections of functionaries in the criminal justice system were found in many instances to have more influence

on how the police and the rest of the criminal justice system operated than the Constitution, state statutes, or city ordinances.

• Arrest, commonly viewed as the first step in the criminal process, had come to be used by the police to achieve a whole range of objectives in addition to that of prosecuting wrongdoers: for example, to investigate, to harass, to punish, and to provide safekeeping.

• A great variety of informal methods outside the criminal justice system had been adopted by the police to fulfill their formal responsibilities and to dispose of the endless array of situations that the public—rightly or wrongly—expected them to handle.

• Individual police officers were found to be routinely exercising a great deal of discretion in deciding how to handle the tremendous variety of circumstances with which they were confronted (Goldstein, 1977, pp. 22–24).

Together, these and similar findings introduced a new ''realism'' about policing, although it was not quickly accepted. Discrepancies between the ideal and the reality were more often seen as local aberrations or as deviations that ought to be corrected through intensified efforts to implement the best of then current practice. Acceptance of some of these conditions as inevitable did much violence to prior notions, introducing uncertainty and ambiguity into areas in which precision and clarity had previously been a source of some comfort.

NEW DEMANDS, AN ASSESSMENT OF NEEDS, AND THE BEGINNING OF A QUEST FOR NEW DIRECTIONS

Crises stimulate progress. The police came under enormous pressure in the late 1960s and early 1970s, confronted first with a sharp increase in concern about crime and then by a steady increase in the number and intensity of civil rights demonstrations, racial conflicts, riots, and political protests. If police practices were not already a subject of grievance, police responses to the demonstrations and riots raised new concerns among a much larger segment of the public. Both the underlying problems (i.e., crime, racism, the Vietnam war) and the practices of the police generated five national studies, each with a different focus, that included assessments of the state of policing: the President's Commission on Law Enforcement and Administration of Justice (1967); the National Advisory Commission on Civil Disorders (1968); the National Advisory Commission on the Causes and Prevention of Violence (1969); the President's Commission on Campus Unrest (1970); and the National Advisory Commission on Criminal Justice Standards and Goals (1973).

Although these studies were highly critical of many aspects of policing, the vast majority of the specific recommendations that emerged from them reflected a continuing belief that the way to improve policing was to improve the organization, staffing, education, training, and equipping of the police. But in their analysis and criticism, the various studies began to raise questions about the police that had never been raised in the past—about their function, their accountability, and their relationship to the community. Interest in these questions was pursued by the institutions newly created, and the individuals newly involved in the field because of increased concern about the police—the federal research and assistance program (the Law Enforcement Assistance Administration); state planning and coordinating councils; local post-riot study commissions; the Police Foundation, established by the Ford Foundation to support research and improvement in policing; academics newly attracted to conducting studies in the field; and students enrolled in freshly established college programs for police personnel. And this questioning was further energized by minority, civil rights, and protest groups whose concerns about the police did not end with publication of the national studies.

As the questioning gained momentum, the limitations and some of the negative consequences of the professional model became increasingly apparent. Like many who are enthusiastic about new movements, those who implemented the professional model often went too far to achieve its objectives. In the effort to make the police apolitical, the police were sometimes cut off from all accountability to the public. In the desire to achieve effective controls over their personnel, administrators often destroyed important contacts with members of the community, stifled initiative, and created a negative, distrustful working environment. And to achieve a high level of efficiency, operating procedures were adopted that, in retrospect, irritated citizens on whose cooperation the police depend and reduced the effectiveness of the police in meeting community expectations (as, for example, in dealing with less serious conduct or with fear). Additional limitations of the professional model, stemming from a lack of sufficient attention to the substantive problems that create the need for police services, began to surface. They will be described in Chapter 3.

EMERGENCE OF A NEW "COMMON WISDOM" ON THE POLICE

The questioning that started with the nationwide studies of the police role in relation to crime, racial conflict, and political protest stimulated serious students of the police to take fuller advantage of the relatively small body of knowledge that had been acquired up to that time. The results of the "first cluster" of research on the police now received much more careful and wider reading. Gradually, the insights acquired in those earlier studies were accepted and incorporated into our thinking about the police. The following points are now, in most quarters, considered part of the common wisdom of the police.

- The police do much more than deal with crime; they deal with many forms of behavior that are not defined as criminal.
- The wide range of functions that police are expected to perform, including dealing with fear and enforcing public order, are appropriate functions for the police; from the perspective of the community, they may be as important as the tasks the police perform in dealing with behavior labeled criminal.
- Too much dependence in the past has been placed on the criminal law in order to get the police job done; arrest and prosecution are simply not an effective way to handle much of what constitutes police business. And even if potentially effective, it may not be possible to use the criminal justice system in some jurisdictions because it is so overloaded.
- Police use a wide range of methods—formal and informal—in getting their job done. "Law enforcement" is only one method among many.
- Police, of necessity, must exercise broad discretion, including discretion in deciding whether to arrest and prosecute in situations in which there is ample evidence that a criminal law has been violated.
- The police are not autonomous; the sensitive function they perform in our society requires that they be accountable, through the political process, to the community.

Pulling out these observations and reflecting on the degree to which they have been accepted by practitioners not only establishes a common base from which to proceed; it attests to the fact that substantial progress has in fact been made in our thinking about the police. Furthermore, the police have acted upon this new common wisdom. Major programs for improving policing are based on it, such as, for example, the widespread move to develop operating policies to help guide police officers in the exercise of their discretion (Walker, 1986); the move to equip police with alternatives to the criminal justice system for getting their multifaceted job done (see Chapter 8); and the variety of programs for involvement with the community (see, e.g., Skolnick and Bayley, 1986, 1988a, 1988b; Kelling, 1988). This progress belies some of the criticism commonly directed at the police field as being totally resistant to change. Acceptance of these altered perspectives has required a radical change in perceptions of the role of the police.

A SECOND CLUSTER OF RESEARCH: QUESTIONING THE VALUE OF STANDARD RESPONSES

It was only natural that, as police practitioners themselves became involved in establishing a research agenda, questions would gradually be raised about the value of the standard operating procedures that were an integral part of the professional model. These procedures evolved from several assumptions. A high value was attached to maximizing the number of police officers assigned to motorized patrol, in the belief that random patrol was the most effective way to reduce crime. High priority was given to responding quickly to calls for police assistance, in the belief that speed was necessary to apprehend criminals, deter criminal conduct, and reassure citizens that help was quickly available when needed. And detective operations were organized so that all reports of crimes were followed up, in the belief that this would contribute to their solution and thereby add to the atmosphere of deterrence that the police were committed to creating.

First among these inquiries was the Kansas City Preventive Patrol Experiment, which now ranks as a milestone in the development of policing in this country (Kelling et al., 1974). It not only brought into question the value of the dominant form of policing—random, motorized preventive patrol—in which an enormous investment had been made; as the first major controlled study, it also demonstrated that experiments could be conducted in an ongoing police operation.

In a relatively short period of time (1972–1982) following the Kansas City study, several other experiments and research projects, more modest in their goals, raised similar questions about the value of standardized operating procedures in which the professional model had placed great faith. Succinct, fully cited summaries of the results of these studies are incorporated in most recent works on the police and, therefore, need not be repeated here (see, e.g., Skolnick and Bayley, 1986, pp. 4–5). Eck and Spelman conveniently summarize the major findings that resulted from the rapid sequence of studies in this paragraph:

> First, the Kansas City Preventive Patrol Experiment questioned the usefulness of random patrol in cars [Kelling et al., 1974]. Second, studies of response time undermined the premise that the police must rapidly send officers to all calls [Kansas City, Missouri, Police Department, 1978; Spelman and Brown, 1984]. Third, research suggested, and experiments confirmed, that the public does not always expect fast response by police to nonemergency calls [Farmer, 1981; McEwen, Connors, and Cohen, 1984]. Fourth, studies showed that officers and detectives are limited in their abilities to successfully investigate crimes [Greenwood, Petersilia, and Chaiken, 1977; Eck, 1982]. And fifth, research showed that detectives need not follow up every reported unsolved crime [Greenberg, Yu, and Lang, 1973; Eck, 1979]. In short, most se-

rious crimes were unaffected by the standard police actions designed to control them. Further the public did not notice reductions in patrol, reduced speed responding to nonemergencies, or lack of follow-up investigations (Eck and Spelman, 1987, p. 35).

What does this mean for policing? Was the professional model all bad? No. A new police administrator would still be well advised to implement many of its features in a police agency lacking in organization, efficiency, control, and integrity. It is a tribute to the enduring value of many of the changes associated with the professional model that, even in the 1980s, they continue to be important ingredients in the prescription for treatment of seriously ailing police agencies. Since 1979, the Commission on Accreditation for Law Enforcement Agencies has taken responsibility for establishing professional standards and creating new standards to reflect more recent developments in policing. It seeks to upgrade the policies, procedures, and practices of police agencies by giving recognition to those agencies that meet its standards. (For a description of the Commission and a critique of its work, see Mastrofski, 1986.)

The lesson drawn from the studies that questioned the value of standard procedures is that the police erred in doggedly investing so much of police resources in a limited number of practices, based, in retrospect, on some rather naive and simplistic concepts of the police role. They sought to deal in a generic way with a wide variety of quite different tasks for which the police are responsible. It became increasingly apparent that the design of improvements in policing must be based on a fuller recognition of the complexity of the police task as that complexity was recognized starting with the research of the 1950s. Although it brought many of the steps that had been labeled as progress into question, this recognition, itself, may in retrospect mark the most progressive step that the field has taken.

CHAPTER **3**

A CRITIQUE OF THE CURRENT STATE OF THE FIELD: CONSIDERATIONS LEADING TO PROBLEM-ORIENTED POLICING

The developments, new insights, and research findings briefly summarized in the preceding chapter have brought us to a new era in policing. Not everyone in the police field has been affected by them. But among progressive police, more questions are being asked; more research is being conducted; and new approaches to policing are being tried. Practitioners, often under pressure to achieve more with less, are groping for novel ways in which to carry out their job. This is a painful and sometimes frustrating process, but it is also a healthy and exciting one. It creates an atmosphere that encourages constructive criticism.

From among the various critiques of the most advanced forms of policing, I have chosen five points to explore in this chapter. They are not of equal significance, nor have they received equal attention in the literature. I have selected them for detailed examination here because, together, they account for many of the frustrations in policing and because they are the five concerns that have most strongly influenced the development of problem-oriented policing.

1 The police field is preoccupied with management, internal procedures, and efficiency to the exclusion of appropriate concern for effectiveness in dealing with substantive problems.

2 The police devote most of their resources to responding to calls from citizens, reserving too small a percentage of their time and energy for acting on their own initiative to prevent or reduce community problems.

3 The community is a major resource with an enormous potential, largely untapped, for reducing the number and magnitude of problems that otherwise become the business of the police.

4 Within their agencies, police have readily available to them another huge resource: their rank-and-file officers, whose time and talent have not been used effectively.

5 Efforts to improve policing have often failed because they have not been adequately related to the overall dynamics and complexity of the police organization. Adjustments in policies and organizational structure are required to accommodate and support change.

THE PREOCCUPATION WITH MANAGEMENT, INTERNAL PROCEDURES, AND EFFICIENCY

The majority of changes that have been advocated in policing over the past several decades reflect a continuing preoccupation with means over ends; with operating methods, process, and efficiency over effectiveness in dealing with substantive problems; with the running of the organization rather than with the impact of the organization on community problems that the police are expected to handle. Concern over this imbalance led to development of the concept of problem-oriented policing (Goldstein, 1979).

The distinction I draw can be illustrated by an analogy to the medical field. The concerns of health care professionals in running hospitals, in employing doctors and nurses, and in financing health care are all of great importance, but they have relevance only as they affect the treatment of diseases and injuries. The substantive problems in the medical field are the diseases and injuries that doctors and other health care professionals are expected to handle, and the end product in medicine is the treatment provided. By substantive problems in policing I mean the behavioral problems that the public expects the police to handle, such as sexual assaults, speeding, shoplifting, burglaries, sales of drugs to minors, the homeless, street robberies, and disputes among neighbors. And by end product I mean the response the police make to these problems.

Relatively little in the current organization and staffing of police agencies reflects a regular, continuing institutionalized concern for substantive matters. Some agencies and administrators get closer than do others. Some get involved when a problem becomes a crisis. But the field as a whole has seldom taken a serious, inquiring, in-depth interest in the wide range of problems that constitute its business, nor does it have a tradition of proceeding logically from knowledge gained about a particular problem to the fashioning of an appropriate response.

Evidence of the imbalance between procedural and substantive concerns abounds. It can be seen in the way police administrators spend their time. It can be seen clearly in the leading texts in the field, the journals, and the subjects listed in the advertisements of upcoming training conferences. It is reflected in the topics scheduled for discussion at professional meetings. It is mirrored in the content of the many college courses established to prepare students for a career in policing. And it is painfully apparent in the matters that occupy those involved in planning and research—the specialized sections of police agencies in which one would expect to find evidence of some in-depth concern with the problems on which the police apparatus is supposed to have an impact.

Just as the efficient running of a hospital is of crucial importance to the effectiveness of the medical field in treating illnesses, all of the considerations that go into running a police agency are of the utmost importance in determining the quality of the end product: the service delivered to the community. One should not, therefore, disparage the tremendous effort that has gone into creating and maintaining a well-organized, adequately staffed, efficient police agency.

What is troubling in policing, when compared to these other fields, is the extent of the imbalance. It is not only that substantive concerns have been neglected, with the result that community problems have not received the kind of careful attention they require. The skewed, almost perverse obsession with the running of the organization has often resulted in implementing changes that have decreased, rather than improved, the capacity of the police to deal effectively with these problems. The high priority given to organizational matters gets in the way of delivering police services.

A number of factors inherent in police functioning explain the lack of adequate attention to substantive matters. Already cited, in the earlier discussion of the professional model of policing, was the principal factor—the enormity of the task of managing police agencies and the way it preempts the time and energies of police administrators. Other factors include the following:

- The diverse, poorly defined, and sometimes overwhelming character of the police job makes it difficult to establish what, precisely, is the end product of policing. Appeals to focus on the end product therefore understandably meet with some confusion and apprehension.
- Police are commonly viewed as palliators—as being concerned primarily with meeting immediate, emergency needs. It follows that greater rewards are attached to alleviating problems than to solving or curing them.
- Many of the problems that police must deal with are insolvable. This is the very reason they come to the attention of the police. The potential

for doing anything about an age-old problem like prostitution or shoplifting is limited. Improving a communications system or establishing a new operating procedure, in contrast, is much more satisfying. Nonsubstantive matters are more self-contained within the agency, and the police are therefore less dependent on outside forces for their success in dealing with them.

• The constraints under which police operate in a democracy make police reticent to take the initiative in addressing problems. Many officers view their function as simply doing what is formally required of them, even if it is widely recognized that this may be ineffective.

The professional model of policing not only reflects the preoccupation with running the police organization, it perpetuates the imbalance between the concern for operating efficiency and the concern for substance. In retrospect, it seems ironic that a model bearing the label "professional" should be so narrow. Although it was a major advance when first put into practice, the managerial streamlining known as professional policing put a low ceiling on the meaning of "professionalism" in the police field. When used in other occupations, the term usually implies concern with the conditions or behavior with which the professional must deal. Drawing once again on the medical model, physicians are assumed to know a good deal about diseases and the nature of injuries to the human body; what they do in treating patients is based on the collective knowledge about an illness and the accumulated experience in its treatment. The police do not have an established body of knowledge about the various behaviors and conditions that they are expected to prevent and treat. And there is little commitment to developing such a body of knowledge. Is it any wonder, then, that the field often flounders when attempting to determine what the police should do in responding to community problems? The arrangements in place for policing—including those relating to recruitment, training of officers, and management of the police agency—have been designed without much understanding of the problems that those who are recruited, trained, and managed are expected to handle.

The analogy to the medical field obviously has its weaknesses. The behavior and conditions that are police business are not subject to the same scientific analysis and treatment as are medical problems. But much is already known and much more can be established if a more systematic effort is made to study specific aspects of police business. For the police to develop beyond their present state (and coincidently to establish a stronger foundation for professional status), they must devote more effort to understanding the conditions and behaviors they are expected to prevent and treat and, using this knowledge, develop and improve methods for dealing effectively with them.

Some progress has been made. In recent years, practitioners and commentators on the police have taken a great interest in the problems of spousal abuse and sexual assault and in the police response to them. Arson and missing children have also received concentrated attention. A national conference on the police included sessions on the police response to the mentally ill and the homeless (U.S. Department of Justice, National Institute of Justice, 1987). Significantly, however, most of these problems were examined as a result of outside pressures, not at the initiative of the police who deal with them all the time.

THE PREDOMINANTLY REACTIVE POSTURE OF THE POLICE

When Albert Reiss conducted one of the first systematic observations of police street activity in the late 1960s, his primary interest was in observing police-initiated interactions with citizens. His staff soon realized that the vast majority of police contacts were initiated by citizens through a telephone request for service (Reiss, 1971). It has taken all of us (researchers and practitioners alike) a long time to recognize what should have been obvious: Urban police agencies spend most of their time reacting to citizen demands for service. And it has taken even longer to recognize the full implications that this reactive stance has for police organization and the form of police services.

Some elements within most police forces are proactive, such as units to ferret out drug sales, commercial gambling, and other forms of organized crime. Traffic enforcement, especially if assigned to a special unit, is predominantly proactive. In an effort to increase their effectiveness in controlling crime, police agencies have assigned more officers to such proactive activities as decoy operations designed to apprehend street robbers or sting operations designed to identify those who trade in stolen merchandise. It does not follow, however, that all officers taken away from regular patrol operations and placed in specialized units are engaged in proactive work. Especially in big cities, some of the largest special units reflect, in their daily work, simply a different way of responding reactively to the larger and more persistent demands for police service. If all the operations in a police agency that are clearly committed to proactive work are aggregated, they account for a relatively small percentage of police resources.

It is now common to hear yearnings for "the good old days"—before police agencies were motorized—when police officers are described as having spent most of their time on the streets, walking a beat, in contact with citizens. It is not clear if this is an accurate portrayal of policing in the past or a romanticized version evoked by nostalgia. Whether police are more or less reactive today than they were years ago, it is important to understand some of the factors that have perpetuated and reinforced the reactive posture of the police.

• The switch to motorized patrol, coupled with dramatic improvements in communications, enabled the police to greatly increase their readiness to respond to calls for help, especially from areas not previously served by foot patrols.

• As late as 1940, only 37 percent of all households in the United States had a telephone (U.S. Department of Commerce, 1969, p. 495). This meant that many city dwellers who wanted police help had to cry out to neighbors, locate a telephone, find an officer on patrol, or go to a police station. By 1968, 90 percent of all households had a telephone (ibid.). The telephone has since become a standard piece of household equipment, and with it, each citizen automatically acquires the enormous, usually unchallenged power to summon a police officer to his or her doorstep. The police have become enslaved by the telephone.

• The professional model of policing included a commitment to respond to *every* call for police service and to do so quickly. This became one of the most distinctive standards of high-quality police service. And in the absence of other ways to measure the police job, calls made to the police had the added attraction to the "scientific" managers of the era of being a very specific, quantifiable way to assess the need for police services.

• A reputation for responding quickly to all calls for police assistance became a way to give citizens a feeling of increased security. Police sought to put citizen fears to rest by conveying the message that "a police officer is only as far away as one's telephone." This message was often promoted through advertising campaigns to reassure citizens when police stations were closed as part of the move toward centralization and when central communications systems were installed, depriving citizens of the opportunity to call their local station. Responding to citizen concerns about crime, John Lindsay, when he campaigned for mayor of New York City in 1965, advocated making it possible for citizens to call the police from any phone booth without having to use a coin—an arrangement now common throughout the country.

• Much of the attraction in the universal 911 system is that it gives citizens a greater sense of security by making it easier to contact the police. Indeed, "911" has taken on great symbolic value, now commonly referred to within police circles as a "tyrannical force" that places an increased preemptive demand on police resources. It has given new life to the widespread assumption that calls made to the police have first claim on police resources.

In the vast majority of police departments, the telephone, more than any policy decision by the community or by management, continues to dictate how police resources will be used. These agencies are vulnerable to having all of their resources consumed in reacting to calls for help. This siphons personnel away from other equally important or perhaps more important tasks. It fosters the notion among operating personnel that policing consists simply of responding to incidents. As Robert Force put it, police are often responding to little more than the most overt, one-time symptom or manifestation of a problem rather than to the problem itself (Force, 1972, pp. 406–407). Police are not part of the solutions to the problems they are called on to handle. They may actually make some problems more difficult to resolve (Force, 1972, p. 434).

Clearly, the reactive posture encourages superficial responses, placing a higher value on "getting there" and on "getting out" than on what actually happens in the handling of the incident. Officers frequently judge one another by the speed with which they handle a call. This is so ingrained in police thinking that it has been astutely observed that police routinely describe the time they spend handling calls as "being out of service" and feel under constant pressure to dispose of calls quickly so that they can "get back in service." Based on their comprehensive analysis of the whole phenomenon and its negative consequences, Eck and Spelman have introduced the helpful phrase "incident-driven policing" to describe it (see Eck and Spelman et al., 1987, pp. 1–2).

The phenomenon, however, cuts even more deeply. It erodes the strength and self-image of the police. The agency commonly viewed by the outside world as so powerful, and frequently criticized as having too much autonomy, is often viewed by its own personnel as extraordinarily weak, as not having a direction of its own, as buffeted about and responding, in a feeble fashion, to the demands of every Tom, Dick, and Harry. Operating almost exclusively in a reactive mode results in the police resigning themselves to providing a very limited type of service; to responding repeatedly and inadequately to the same calls, often from the same persons or addresses. Officers become frustrated and cynical, and the public is left unsatisfied.

Is this situation inevitable? No. Recent experiments with "call diversion" and "differential response" have demonstrated that the police can exercise a good deal of control over their work load (Cahn and Tien, 1981; Farmer, 1981; McEwen, Connors, and Cohen, 1984). Under these arrangements, those receiving calls for police service are expected to determine if it is necessary to dispatch a police officer and to assign priorities to those calls requiring a field response. A variety of procedures are used to meet the needs of citizens to whom an officer is not sent. All indications are that these systems save an enormous amount of time, reduce officer frustrations, and are equally satisfactory to the callers. A well-informed, pleasant, helpful clerk on the telephone may be even more satisfying to an agitated citizen than an uninterested police officer who resents dealing repeatedly with a matter that he or she considers petty.

Commendable as these advances are, they represent only a small beginning in restoring a better balance between the reactive and proactive roles of the police. Much more has to be done to equip police to make the crucial judgments about cases at the earliest screening stage. Richard Larson (1988), in his ongoing work, draws attention to the dispatcher as the real manager of scarce police patrol resources. (Appropriately concerned about the continuing need to respond quickly to some calls, Larson outlines a number of other proposals for reconciling this need with the need for more proactive work.) As categories of cases are identified that do not require a field response, careful consideration must be given to the quality of the response that is provided over the telephone. This leads directly to the need for increased concern with the substantive problems reflected in the calls that are received—a need that problem-oriented policing is designed to meet.

Through systematic analysis of all calls to the police, the problems that give rise to them can be better addressed. Such an approach has the potential for producing three major benefits: (1) The number of calls received by the police could be reduced significantly, thereby making more time available for proactive work; (2) the effectiveness of the police in responding to citizen concerns could be improved greatly by addressing an underlying problem directly rather than dealing repeatedly with the symptoms of that problem; and (3) the negative consequences for both the police organization and police officers of being incident-driven could be greatly reduced.

THE NEED TO ENGAGE THE COMMUNITY

The police must do more than they have done in the past to engage the citizenry in the overall task of policing. In a field in which resources are so often strapped, the potential of this relatively untapped resource is enormous. The police have erred in pretending for all these years that they could take upon themselves—and successfully discharge—all of the responsibilities that are now theirs. A relatively small group of individuals (whether 10 in a community of 5,000, or 28,000 in a city, such as New York, of 7.5 million), however powerful and efficient, simply cannot meet those expectations. (In the city of Edmonton, Alberta, for example, with a population of approximately 500,000, only 24 police officers are on duty during the early morning hours.) A community must police itself. The police can, at best, only assist in that task.

In exploring this need, as in critiquing reactive policing, some commonly hark back to the "good old days" when, it is widely assumed, neighborhoods and whole cities had a greater sense of community; residents did more to control their own conduct; and the police enjoyed a closer relationship with residents. There probably were (and still are) neighborhoods and cities with strong community norms that served as a curb on behavior. People did not do certain things because they were concerned about what the neighbors would think or do. But accounts of urban areas and of policing more than a century ago remind us that these conditions were by no means universal. On the contrary, a lack of a sense of community, a mixture of life-styles, and anonymity have always been a part of city life. And relationships between the police and various classes of citizens were often very strained. The police were seen as the representatives of the upper class, enforcing laws upon the workers, the minorities, and the poor in ways that were designed to protect the interests of the wealthy. (See, e.g., Harring, 1983.)

Despite sometimes strained relationships, the public looked to the police for solutions to their most troublesome problems. And the police, in taking on the incredibly broad range of functions that now constitute their business, not only relieved the citizenry of responsibility for policing themselves, they went further: They adopted operating procedures that had the effect of divorcing them from the communities they policed. The "professional" commitment to enforcing the law "without fear or favor, malice or ill will" was accompanied by a commitment to keep personal feelings from influencing decisions. These commitments, which extended to all functions of the police—not simply those incidents in which law enforcement was involved—resulted in all citizens being seen as having the same needs, wherever they lived, with little allowance for different life-styles and cultural backgrounds; and all police officers were likewise seen as having uniform technical skills that could be applied to whatever problems arose. No value was attached to maintaining ties with members of the community. Officers in some cities were even prohibited from talking with citizens "except in the line of duty." They were often prohibited from working in the areas in which they resided. Assignments were made without regard for an officer's familiarity with a neighborhood. What the police did was done *to* a community rather than *for* it. Thus, efforts to meet more efficiently and objectively the need for services that citizens could not provide for themselves led to operating procedures that increased the gulf between citizens and the police.

It took the racial disturbances of the 1960s to call this trend into question. The outpouring of hostility toward the police, evidenced in the riots and documented in the studies that were subsequently conducted, awakened the police and the citizenry generally to just how removed the police had become from minority communities. The police were commonly characterized as "an occupation army" whose practices offended the residents living in these areas.

The new awareness of the acute nature of the we–they syndrome in minority communities led to the establishment of programs to improve relationships between the police and the community. In retrospect, many of these were incredibly naive; they did not get at the problems of concern to residents. They were often limited to getting a greater number of people to like the police. And they frequently failed in achieving even this limited objective.

Some police agencies, however, moved well beyond these initial efforts, identifying and acting upon sources of concern; developing greater sensitivity of officers to minorities; and seeking, in various ways, to promote greater cooperation and understanding between the police and the community.

The research findings of 1972 through 1982, beginning with the Kansas City study, altered significantly the way in which the police viewed their relationship with the community. Upon discovering that their traditional methods were nowhere as effective as previously assumed, the police realized the need to enlist the community in preventing and controlling crime. But it was clear that this would not be accomplished simply by renewing the old campaigns—e.g., educating people to lock their cars—or even through ambitious efforts to organize neighbors into blockwatch programs. The police were going to have to cultivate an entirely different type of relationship with the citizens they served. And this need for redefining the relationship between the police and the community was no longer limited just to neighborhoods inhabited by minorities. With a goal that went well beyond reducing tensions and being liked, it was recognized that getting the police job done required the greater involvement of all citizens.

Increased concern about the police role in handling public order problems and in responding to fear of crime added impetus to this movement. In their widely cited article, "Broken Windows," Wilson and Kelling link physical deterioration with the breakdown in public order and crime (1982). They argue that signs of deterioration in a neighborhood, whether physical or in the form of disorder, if uncorrected, lead ordinary citizens to reduce their own efforts to maintain their homes and to control unruly conduct. (For a comprehensive analysis of the relationship between communities and crime, see Reiss and Tonry [1986].) What the police can do in dealing with crime, public order, and fear is heavily dependent on the kind of partnership they develop with the community (see Moore and Trojanowicz, 1988; Moore, Trojanowicz, and Kelling, 1988).

Based on all of these considerations, the police recognize that they must enlist the citizenry to do more to police themselves. How best to do this is not clear. Current efforts, in their embryonic state, are taking many different forms, influenced by a variety of local factors and serving diverse purposes. Eliciting the help of the community is usually a major objective, but equal importance in some jurisdictions may be attached to reducing tensions, to reducing fear, and to facilitating the work of the police. We now make wide use of "community policing" to categorize these efforts, but the term does not yet have a uniform meaning. (Because of its current importance, the concept of community policing has been the subject of study by an Executive Session at Harvard's John F. Kennedy School of Government. In a series of meetings spread over a period of three years, a group of police chiefs, mayors, academicians, and others explored the use and promise of such strategies as community-based and problem-oriented policing. These meetings resulted in a series of reports, most of which have been published and are cited in this book. For an interesting collection of papers on the evolving concepts of community policing and the issues they raise, see Greene and Mastrofski, 1988.)

When translated into operational terms, police efforts to engage the community make use of a variety of tactics, such as foot patrol, storefront offices, and sponsorship of recreational programs. More ambitiously, police have sought to mobilize communities to, for example, report certain types of behavior, press neighbors into correcting annoying conditions, and make demands on the management of apartment complexes, on employers, on businesses, or on other agencies of government. In describing community-oriented innovations in six cities, Skolnick and Bayley (1986) report that the efforts of each of the six police agencies that launched ambitious community-oriented policing projects made the community a co-producer of police service. (The term "co-producer" was first used in policing by Ostrom et al. [1978].) Persistent, carefully cultivated engagement by the police with communities does result in communities subsequently taking initiatives for themselves.

From among the wide range of programs to engage the community, two quite different patterns are emerging. The first is a rather broad, ambitious, but somewhat amorphous effort to develop a new relationship with all or designated parts of the total community, in hopes that this will reduce tensions, create a reservoir of goodwill, and ultimately enable the police and the community to work together to solve community problems. The second is a narrower effort in which the initial objective is to deal with a specific problem. If, in exploring the problem, the police conclude that it could be eliminated or significantly reduced by some form of community involvement, they then set out to bring about such involvement.

Because the programs that fall into the first pattern are so much more ambitious and comprehensive, calling for major institutional adjustments, they raise many complex issues. What is meant by "community"? Is the community the entire city, a portion of the city, a neighborhood, a city block, or the residents of a specific apartment house? Are the assumptions made about the degree of consensus that exists within a community, once it is defined, correct? Is it recognized that there are communities within communities? A comprehensive, institutional effort to build new relationships with the "community" carries with it some uniform expectations of what the police should elicit from a community. But a division of a precinct into areas will not necessarily produce groups of individuals with shared values that can be reinforced in ways that help control behavior. Areas of cities requiring the greatest amount of police attention are usually those in which there are no shared norms and little sense of community. Does it make any sense to talk of strengthening the "informal mechanisms of social control" in such areas? Other questions arise as well. Are the police, by engaging with the community, prepared to share decision making and power with the community? Is this desirable? Will the community make demands that result in the police exceeding their authority? Will the police use their new-found support from different communities to become an overly powerful force in the larger community? And what happens when community interest fades because there is no problem of sufficient magnitude to bring the citizenry together?

In contrast, the more limited pattern of police–community engagement does not raise these complex issues. In what I have observed of the practice, as distinct from the rhetoric of community policing, police tend to engage the citizenry in a very pragmatic and more relaxed manner. They use "community" rather deftly to describe those affected in any way by the specific problem they are attempting to address, or the program being launched in response to the problem. There is no expectation that they have identified a community with shared values. On the contrary, the problem of concern may be one of tension between groups living or doing business within the same area. In identifying the community or communities concerned with a problem, it is taken for granted from the outset that the people to whom one seeks to relate will vary a great deal. In a middle-class area, a well-functioning neighborhood organization may already exist. Police are not so naive as to expect that they can develop an equivalent community force on a crime-ridden skid-row. They may, however, be able to reduce the problems even there if they can elicit a greater sense of community by encouraging the inhabitants to look out for one another—protecting against assaults, robberies, and harm caused by alcohol, drugs, or the elements. The most severe problems associated with street prostitution can be reduced if prostitutes can be encouraged to bring juvenile prostitutes to police attention, expose those who rob their customers, and respect each other's turf. From a practical standpoint, "community" is not synonymous with "law-abiding."

Although the police will, in this more limited form of police–community engagement, extend themselves to a community, expressing a desire to learn about their needs and problems and to respond to them, this does not carry with it any sharing of decision making. The police clearly reserve for themselves the ultimate decision of how to deal with the situation. And if the police or the community, or both together, conclude that, for example, more resources or a change in law are needed, they seem to turn comfortably to the established political process, i.e., to city council members, mayors, and state representatives. The community policing projects with which I am familiar, by involving elected officials in dealing with problems, have actually strengthened existing systems of political control over the police.

The links that are established between the police and the community in the more limited pattern are not expected to be permanent; they are maintained as long as the problem that required their development exists. The community may be left stronger, but the measure of police success does not depend on a continued tie with the police—on, for example, the number of subsequent meetings held and the participation in these meetings. Communities are shifting groups, defined differently depending on the problem that is addressed. Yet, out of this total effort, maintained over a long period of time, one would expect the total community, eventually, to view the police in a different, more positive light and to recognize increasingly that the effectiveness of the police depends on community involvement.

I have developed this rough and perhaps exaggerated distinction between two patterns of police–community engagement in an effort to clarify the relationship between the popular movement toward community-oriented policing and what is proposed in this book. The first pattern—setting out in a general manner to engage the total community—is reminiscent of past police reforms. It risks perpetuating the imbalance of means over ends. If one is concerned about *both* the need to make fuller use of the community in seeking to control behavior and the need to focus on substantive problems rather than the organizational and institutional arrangements for providing police service, the second pattern—involving the community as needed in dealing with specific problems—is preferred. It attaches highest priority to improving the quality of the end product of policing, calling for changes in the police organization only as they contribute toward achieving that goal.

Given the current state of policing, the police, in my view, are most likely to engage productively with the community if they (1) assign officers to areas for long enough periods of time to enable them to identify the problems of concern to the community; (2) develop the capacity of both officers and the department to analyze community problems; (3) learn when greater community involvement has the potential for significantly reducing a problem; and (4) in such situations, work with those specific segments of the community that are in a position to assist in reducing or eliminating the problem.

THE NEED TO MAKE FULLER USE OF RANK-AND-FILE POLICE OFFICERS

Although much attention is now focused on the potential in developing new forms of relationships with the community, we have been slower to recognize what might be realized from making fuller use of the skills, brains, and time of rank-and-file police officers.

Of all of the individuals who are employed in policing in this country and who are authorized to exercise police powers, the vast majority are patrol officers—the lowest rank in a police agency. These are the men and women who provide police service to the public. Some of these men and women will move up in the ranks, taking on responsibilities for the supervision and direction of their fellow workers. But most will serve out their careers as patrol officers.

As one of its prime objectives, police management has sought to make maximum use of rank-and-file officers, but these efforts have concentrated on making more efficient use of an officer's time. Management has not given much consideration to the possibility of realizing a higher return on the enormous investment in rank-and-file officers by making fuller use of their knowledge, talents, and skills.

The dominant form of policing today continues to view police officers as automatons. Despite an awareness that they exercise broad discretion, they are held to strict account in their daily work—for what they do and how they do it. Officers constantly complain that they are treated like children; they want desperately to be recognized as mature adults. Especially in procedural matters, they are required to adhere to detailed regulations. In large police agencies, rank-and-file police officers are often treated impersonally and kept in the dark regarding policy matters. Officers quickly learn, under these conditions, that the rewards go to those who conform to expectations—that nonthinking compliance is valued.

This attitude on the part of administrators is understandable, given the factors that have influenced the development of policing in this country. To this day, an incident that exposes wrongdoing on the part of police officers frequently results in a reassertion of controls—a tightening of administrative procedures for holding officers accountable so that the type of incident that occurred will not occur again.

By placing so much emphasis on control, we have stifled many attributes of rank-and-file officers that, if given the opportunity to develop, could contribute enormously to the quality of police service. Policing is denied the benefits of their constructive thinking, creativity, and resourcefulness. And it is denied the benefit of the vast amount of knowledge, insight, experience, and just plain street savvy that officers acquire. This loss is all the more tragic because substantial efforts have been made within the past several decades to attract into policing officers who have broader perspectives and more education.

The police field can be the beneficiary of a flood of new ideas, new energy, enthusiasm, and commitment by modifying some of the constraints under which rank-and-file police officers now function. This means, quite simply, making it legitimate for rank-and-file officers to think and be creative in their daily work; and making it legitimate for them to help develop better ways for their agency to deal with community problems. It means giving officers much more freedom, within appropriate restraints, in carrying out their job. The potential benefits are of two kinds. The most important is the improvement that this could produce in the quality of the responses that the police make to oft-recurring community problems. In addition, such a change would be directly responsive to some critical needs in the police organization—the need to treat rank-and-file police officers as mature men and women; to demonstrate more trust and confidence in them; to give them more responsibility and a stake in the outcome of their efforts; and to give them a greater sense of fulfillment and job satisfaction.

In recent years, there has been modest experimentation within policing with various forms of participative management and specifically with the use of task forces and quality circles—the latter being small groups that meet regularly to figure out better ways in which to get the job done. Although significant, these efforts have evolved primarily in response to demands from rank-and-file officers for a greater role in influencing decision making related to working conditions—hours, uniforms, equipment, and reporting procedures—and from a desire on the part of management to reduce resistance to proposals for change. Thus, so far, the limited participation of rank-and-file officers in management mirrors the preoccupation of management with the running of the agency.

Few efforts have been made to involve the rank and file in ways that would take advantage of their rich storehouse of information about substantive community problems and the effectiveness of police responses to them. Some of these exceptions can be found in the early experiments in community policing (see, e.g., Trojanowicz, n.d.; Kennedy, 1986;

Skolnick and Bayley, 1986). The results of these modest efforts, augmented by the results of the early experiments in problem-oriented policing (described in Chapter 5), are an incentive to look to problem-oriented policing as the vehicle by which we can achieve three important, mutually supportive objectives: (1) tapping the accumulated knowledge and expertise of police officers; (2) enabling officers to realize a higher level of satisfaction in their jobs; and (3) enabling the citizenry to realize a higher return on their investment in the police.

THE LIMITATIONS OF PIECEMEAL REFORM

Many past efforts to bring about change in the police suffered because they were undertaken in isolation. The architects of change have failed to recognize the power of the police subculture, the effect it has on any change, and the need, therefore, to deal with some of the factors that contribute to its strength. Likewise, in a more general fashion, proposals for change in the police were advanced without any regard for how they related to or were supported by other conditions and changes in the police organization.

The Resistance of the Police Subculture

Those who study the internal dynamics of police agencies have a heyday in demonstrating the naivete of so-called police reformers. Police departments have a life of their own. Powerful forces within the police establishment have a much stronger influence over the way in which a police agency operates than do the managers of the department, legislatures and courts, the mayor, and the members of the community. We now have a substantial literature on the inner workings of police agencies, documenting the ease with which rank-and-file officers dismiss efforts to influence their behavior. (See especially the works of Rubinstein, 1973; Van Maanen, 1974; Manning, 1977; Punch, 1979; and Reuss-Ianni and Ianni, 1983.) Against this background, many of the exhortations for change in policing do, indeed, look naive, and the elaborate schemes for "improving the police" unlikely to succeed.

The strength of the subculture grows out of the peculiar characteristics and conflicting pressures of the job: the ever-present physical danger; the hostility directed at the police because of their controlling role; the vulnerability of police officers to allegations of wrongdoing; unreasonable demands and conflicting expectations; uncertainty as to the function and authority of officers; a prevalent feeling that the public does not really understand what the police have to "put up with" in dealing with citizens; a stifling working environment; the dependence that officers place on each other to get the job done and to provide for their personal safety; and the shared sense of awareness, within a police department, that it is not always possible to act in ways in which the public would expect one to act.

If a proposal for change is to have any chance of succeeding, it must be reviewed with an eye to considering how it relates to the police subculture and how it can best be introduced. What this means, specifically, is that proposed changes in policing must be designed so that they are not perceived by rank-and-file police officers as further complicating their job or as reflecting a lack of understanding of their job and the conditions under which they operate. But that is only the minimal requirement. Changes in policing should also be designed to reduce the factors that contribute to the strength of the police subculture. Thus, for example, proposals for giving police added resources and appropriate limited authority to get their job done do more than improve the quality of police service. They also relieve the police of a major frustration—the lack of appropriate resources and authority. The same can be said for other proposals that eliminate the need for the police to operate in ways that are subject to criticism because they are not in accord with formal directions. The more that can be done to enable the police to do their job forthrightly, in line with formal public expectations, the less likely it becomes that police officers will separate themselves from the community and look exclusively to their peers for support. And the more comfortable police are in engaging with the community, the more likely it is that they can encourage the community to deal with matters that are currently the exclusive concern of the police.

The Lack of a Coherent Plan

The vast majority of changes that have been promoted in policing in recent years have been fragmentary. They have not been part of a coherent scheme and have not altered those aspects of the organization on which they depend for their success. Some of these changes have been large and costly, such as the enormous investment in educating police personnel without comparable changes in the working environment of police departments to accommodate and take full advantage of educated officers. Other changes have been more modest, such as expecting team police units to exercise independence in providing a form of police service specially suited to a given neighborhood, but maintaining tight administrative controls that prevented them from doing so. Currently, officers in some agencies are being urged to commit themselves to community policing programs, but with no changes in the traditional criteria on which rewards and promotions are based, thereby reducing the likelihood that they will increase their eligibility, during their period of service, for the few rewards available in a police department.

Changes in large bureaucracies grow out of a variety of developments, many of which are not predictable. It follows that change more often is a matter of skillfully taking advantage of opportunities than systematically executing a detailed plan. An awareness of these dynamics, however, does not eliminate the need to consider how any single proposal will fit into the complex framework that is current-day policing. Nor does it eliminate the need to have in mind a coherent vision of the ideal arrangement for providing police services so that, despite the messy way in which change occurs, each change will move the agency a little closer to achieving the ideal. Complex as it is to achieve significant, lasting change in a police organization, the chance of doing so is greatly increased if it is appropriately related to a larger scheme. That is why, in urging that the police field redirect its improvement efforts to focus on community problems, it is important not only to outline a process for doing so, but to set forth, as well, the implications this will have for the police organization.

CHAPTER **4**

PROBLEM-ORIENTED POLICING: THE BASIC ELEMENTS

Problem-oriented policing grows out of the critique of the current state of policing set forth in Chapter 3. In a narrow sense, it focuses directly on the substance of policing—on the problems that constitute the business of the police and on how they handle them. This focus establishes a better balance between the reactive and proactive aspects of policing. It also creates a vehicle for making more effective use of the community and rank-and-file officers in getting the police job done. In its broadest context, problem-oriented policing is a comprehensive plan for improving policing in which the high priority attached to addressing substantive problems shapes the police agency, influencing all changes in personnel, organization, and procedures. Thus, problem-oriented policing not only pushes policing beyond current improvement efforts, it calls for a major change in the direction of those efforts.

To initiate the exploration, I set forth, in this chapter, the fundamental elements of problem-oriented policing. Taken together, these constitute the core of the changes that are required in the way we think about the police job. Subsequent chapters describe in greater detail how these key elements fit together and evolve; how they can be implemented; and the implications their acceptance has for the staffing and organizing of police agencies.

GROUPING INCIDENTS AS PROBLEMS

The primary work unit in a police agency today for the officer assigned to general patrol is the incident. In the course of a typical day, a police officer will usually handle several incidents, such as the theft of a car, a barking dog, a dispute among neighbors, a robbery, a request for information, a report of suspicious circumstances, or a traffic accident.

As noted earlier, the professional model of policing is designed to increase the efficiency with which incidents are handled. Much of the success of police officers is judged by how speedily and efficiently they handle the incidents to which they are assigned.

In handling incidents, police officers usually deal with the most obvious, superficial manifestations of a deeper problem—not the problem itself. They may stop a fight but not get involved in exploring the factors that contributed to it. They may disperse a group of unruly juveniles but not feel under any obligation to inquire into what brought the youths together in the first instance. They may investigate a crime but stop short of exploring the factors that may have contributed to its commission, except as these are relevant to identifying the offender. In handling incidents, police are generally expected to deal with the disruptive, intolerable effects of a problem. That requires a response quite different from what might be involved in dealing with the underlying conditions or problem. Clearly, some officers go further, dealing with the problem itself. But most policing is limited to ameliorating the overt, offensive symptoms of a problem. To go beyond that is considered extra.

It follows that incidents are usually handled as isolated, self-contained events. Connections are not systematically made among them, except when they suggest a common crime pattern leading to identifying the offender. This is so even though the incidents may involve the same behavior, the same address, or the same people and may recur frequently. One often gets the feeling that police, conditioned by the strong commitment to reactive policing described in the last chapter, are resigned to dealing with incidents as isolated events—until some other force comes along that will treat the underlying problem. (The situation is perhaps best illustrated by an incident in which a police dispatcher assigned a newly hired officer to respond to a burglar alarm. The officer, unfamiliar with the area, asked for directions. His sergeant provided the directions and, aware of a long history of false alarms from this address, advised the officer: "Get used to it. It goes off all the time.")

The first step in problem-oriented policing is to move beyond just handling incidents. It calls for recognizing that incidents are often merely overt symptoms of problems. This pushes the police in two directions: (1) It requires that they recognize the relationships between incidents (similarities of behavior, location, persons involved, etc.); and (2) it requires that they take a more in-depth interest in incidents by acquainting themselves with some of the conditions and factors that give rise to them.

FOCUSING ON SUBSTANTIVE PROBLEMS AS THE HEART OF POLICING

The public expects the police to deal with such varied problems as the sexual abuse of children, widespread sales of drugs, robberies of store clerks, and destruction of public property. The public also expects the police to handle problems such as fights that break out in taverns, domestic disputes, missing children, complaints about unreasonable noise, disruptive gatherings of juveniles, and troublesome situations that involve the homeless, the mentally ill, and those incapacitated by alcohol. These are among the many substantive problems—i.e., groups of frequently recurring incidents—that constitute police work.

These substantive problems can be defined at different levels and in different ways. Shoplifting, for example, can be viewed as a citywide problem, raising questions about how the entire police agency copes with it. Or it can be viewed as a problem within a specific shopping area or even within a specific store, raising questions about how the police and the merchants who are directly involved deal with it. Likewise, one can profitably explore theft from residences as a citywide problem, or one can examine theft from residences in a given precinct, neighborhood, or housing complex. It may even be profitable to zero in on a specific apartment house or even a single private residence if repeated thefts have been reported. The choice of the most appropriate level depends on an initial analysis of the problem.

But not all substantive problems need to be defined in behavioral terms descriptive of alleged wrongdoing. They may be defined more helpfully as troublesome areas (e.g., a park or housing complex), specific businesses (e.g., a tavern), specific people (e.g., a mentally ill person who harasses passersby), or groups of people (e.g., a juvenile gang) around which a variety of incidents might cluster. Thus, for example, if initial analysis led one to focus on a concentration of liquor-serving establishments and adult entertainment on a city block, one might bring together incidents that otherwise might be routinely classified as disorderly conduct, assaults, prostitution, drunkenness, runaways, parking violations, and liquor license violations.

Because the police—as the "hired hands"—are available to deal with the unsavory aspects of life in the community, the citizenry tends to define substantive problems as *police* problems. But it would be more accurate to define substantive problems as *community* problems. The emphasis on community has two implications. It means looking to the community to define the problems that should be of concern to the police, rather than succumbing to the tendency of the police on their own to define the problems of concern to the community. And it means gaining an understanding of all of the dimensions of a problem in the total community. What the police are seeing is often but a part of the total problem. Thus, for example, in a study of the drinking driver, it was found helpful to consult with prosecutors, judges, alcohol-treatment personnel, insurance executives, tavern keepers, liquor-licensing authorities, victims, the survivors of victims, physicians, nurses, driver-education instructors, and driver-improvement personnel (Goldstein and Susmilch, 1982a, p. 93). The picture that emerged was radically different from the picture one gets of the drinking-driver problem by focusing exclusively on the arrest and prosecution of such drivers.

Typically, when police speak of problems in policing, they refer to problems in the internal management of the police agency: e.g., lack of adequate personnel, limited promotional opportunities, nonfunctioning equipment, poor morale, or—reaching a little beyond—frustrations in the prosecution of alleged offenders. But even when police are instructed in the meaning of "substantive" problems and are then asked to focus on them, they are apparently so conditioned to thinking in terms of the problems of the organization that they frequently slip back to identifying concerns in the management of the agency. *Thus, focusing on the substantive, community problems that the police must handle is a much more radical step than it initially appears to be, for it requires the police to go beyond taking satisfaction in the smooth operation of their organization; it requires that they extend their concern to dealing effectively with the problems that justify creating a police agency in the first instance.*

Viewed in this manner, a "problem" becomes the unit of police work. This serves as a useful, constant reminder of the underlying premise—that the job of policing consists of much more than dealing with crime and enforcing the criminal law. To describe police work as consisting of the handling of problems is a more accurate definition of the police function. It has the added value of avoiding the confusion that arises from using the manner in which the police *may* respond to a task to describe that task, as occurs when the job of the police is described as law enforcement. It is a more neutral way of describing the police work unit, helpful to further analysis because it avoids any implication of a premature judgment as to how the police may deal with it.

EFFECTIVENESS AS THE ULTIMATE GOAL

The need to go beyond handling incidents and to become more concerned with the substantive problems the police must handle leads directly to a concern for *effectiveness* in dealing with these problems. Lack of concern with effectiveness has been a source of great frustration with the many changes that have occurred in policing in the past several decades. Because most of these changes have related primarily to the running of the organization, it has been difficult to assess their impact, if any, on substantive problems. Too often, after an enormous investment in a major change, we have been left wondering what value the change had for the quality of police service.

An intensified effort to focus on the effectiveness of the police raises difficult questions about the meaning of "effectiveness" as that term applies to the substantive problems the police handle. Many of these problems, by their very nature, are intractable. It makes no sense, therefore, to equate effectiveness to solving problems, for the problems are seldom eliminated.

Eck and Spelman, having struggled with the meaning of "effectiveness" in the context of problem-oriented policing, developed a helpful formulation by identifying five varying degrees of impact that the police might have on a problem: (1) totally eliminating it; (2) reducing the number of incidents it creates; (3) reducing the seriousness of the incidents it creates; (4) designing methods for better handling the incidents; and (5) removing the problem from police consideration (Eck and Spelman et al., 1987, pp. 5–6). Number five is obviously unsatisfactory unless it results in the problem being dealt with more effectively than it would have been if handled by the police.

Some probiems can be eliminated. If this can be achieved, given the nature of most police work, both the police and the community have a great sense of accomplishment. For much of police business, however, a more realistic goal is to reduce the number of incidents that a problem creates and to reduce the seriousness of these incidents. That is why it is helpful to characterize the police role more realistically as *managing deviance* and then concentrate on equipping the police to carry out this management role with greater effectiveness. But this does not mean that the police should simply resign themselves to ameliorating the most superficial, offensive aspects of the incidents they handle.

THE NEED FOR SYSTEMATIC INQUIRY

Once police clearly identify a problem by grouping together similar or related incidents, further progress in dealing with the problem requires the systematic collection and analysis of information about it. This means an in-depth probe of all of the characteristics of a problem and the factors that contribute to it—acquiring detailed information about, for example, offenders, victims, and others who may be involved; the time of occurrence, locations, and other particulars about the physical environment; the history of the problem; the motivations, gains, and losses of all involved parties; the apparent (and not so apparent) causes and competing interests; and the results of current responses. (For a full exploration of what is involved in the analysis of problems, see Chapter 7.)

Police know a lot about the categories of incidents they handle. Experience indicates that much of this knowledge is of great value in fashioning a more effective response. But experience also reveals that the police have not invested in establishing the validity of their conclusions about problems and of their effectiveness in handling them, and that they do not have the answers to many questions that one would want answered before deciding what constitutes the most helpful response.

Crime analysis, which has been an important part of the professional model of policing, is a base on which police can build in meeting the much wider and deeper demands for inquiry associated with problem-oriented policing. In a police agency in which individual officers may not know what has occurred outside the areas in which they work or during periods when they are not on duty, crime analysis has been the primary means for pooling information that may help solve crimes. Initially, it consisted of a review of reports on similar crimes to identify those that may have been committed by the same individual or group, with the hope that the sum of information from a number of reports might better enable the police to identify and apprehend the offender(s). If an offender was apprehended, similar analysis might enable the police to solve other crimes for which the offender was responsible and to increase the strength of the case against him or her. As crime analysis developed, attention focused on discovering patterns of criminal activity, enabling analysts to alert patrolling police officers to individuals suspected of committing a particular type of crime and to the area in which they might commit it. Anticipating where the offender was likely to strike also enabled the police to set up surveillance and undercover operations.

At its best, crime analysis has been used to identify offenders and interrupt crime patterns rather than to gain the kind of knowledge and insights that might be used to affect the conditions that accounted for the criminal conduct. The Integrated Criminal Apprehension Program (ICAP), in which the Law Enforcement Assistance Administration invested heavily in its final years, came close, in some of its multifaceted operations, to developing basic crime analysis techniques to a level at which they might have been used more effectively to analyze substantive problems (Gay et al., 1984). As a broad management system (usually computer-based), ICAP lent new emphasis to some of the key features of the professional model of policing, with its stress on operating efficiency, but some departments conducted studies that contributed significantly to the analysis of substantive problems in the manner contemplated here.

Problem-oriented policing actually provides an incentive to make much more effective use of the data typically collected as part of crime analysis and to expand beyond the current limited objectives of the most advanced crime analysis models. This would first require focusing more broadly on all of the problems police handle rather than on just traditional categories of crime. It would require trying to understand the nature of these problems as a basis for critical review of the agency's response, rather than limiting inquiries to narrower operational goals. It would use more sources of information than just the reports filed by police officers. To understand all aspects of a problem, police would have to become adept at conducting literature searches, using telephone and door-to-door surveys, interviewing those having the most direct knowledge about a problem (including citizens, officers, representatives of various government agencies and private services, and ex-offenders), and making use of data collected by other government agencies and in the private sector. Finally, the type of systematic inquiry contemplated as part of problem-oriented policing would place a much higher value on the accuracy and preciseness of the data used and the conclusions reached than has been characteristic of studies conducted within police agencies.

The range and depth of each inquiry will obviously depend on the magnitude of the problem and the level at which it is examined. An inquiry made by personnel at the operating level cannot possibly be conducted with anything approaching the care and precision that can be brought to bear in a more ambitious study, conducted with more resources and research skills. But even at the lowest levels of inquiry, progress will have been made if the agency is committed to the value of systematic inquiry as a prerequisite to the development of an intelligent response and if officers are made sensitive to the need to be as objective as possible in establishing the facts regarding a problem, much as they are trained to do in a criminal investigation. (See Chapter 7.)

DISAGGREGATING AND ACCURATELY LABELING PROBLEMS

Having dwelled on the need to bring isolated incidents together and begin to view them collectively as problems, it seems, at first blush, contradictory to urge that problems be taken apart. But that is, indeed, an important component of problem-oriented policing and an important stage in the analysis of problems. The seeming contradiction stems from the tendency of the police, once urged to think in terms of problems, to use labels that are overly broad, too influenced by legal definitions, or reflecting an acceptance of the community's perspective of a problem without benefit of the information that the police develop as a result of systematic inquiry. Use of overly broad or inaccurate labels impedes efforts to develop more effective, customized responses to discrete problems.

At the most elementary level, citizens, as well as the police and others who work within the criminal justice system, overuse miscellaneous terms such as "crime," "street crime," "disorder," "delinquency," and "violence." Surprisingly, many police agencies continue to use generic terms to categorize portions of their business. Researchers interested in specific types of police calls are often still required, in this day of elaborate computer capacities, to "dig out" by hand those cases that constitute a substantial, distinctive portion of a police agency's regular work load. Overly broad categorizations of incidents impede efforts to gain insight into a discrete substantive problem.

For obvious reasons, police commonly use labels tied to the criminal code, such as robbery, burglary, and theft, to categorize incidents. The terms have meaning in the community beyond the use ascribed to them by the law. Because much police business consists of dealing with these common problems, use of the terms is essential in organizing a police agency's response to them. But use of the statutory labels to describe substantive problems may mask important distinctions when the ultimate objective is to develop a more appropriate response to a specific form of behavior. It is not helpful, for example, to collect incidents under the label "sexual assault" and then proceed to address the problem of sexual assault without distinguishing the very different types of sexual assaults. The challenge presented by street attacks on strangers is quite different from that presented by sexual assaults within the family, which, in turn, differs from sexual contacts between adolescents.

Another drawback to the use of criminal labels is that they perpetuate the impression that police interest in a problem is limited to arrest and prosecution. In fact, police concern about a problem labeled as burglary or street prostitution goes well beyond just arresting and prosecuting the offenders. It extends to many of the side effects and consequences that the behavior produces. In the case of street prostitution, the problem would exist for the police whether or not it was defined as a criminal offense (see discussion on pp. 40–41). Thus, there is a big difference between speaking narrowly about dealing with burglars and prostitutes from a legal perspective and dealing with burglary or prostitution as those problems exist in the community.

Experience in developing problem-oriented policing has taught us that one must also be cautious about accepting the label initially placed on problems, whether by the public or by the police. Inquiry may reveal that the problem is significantly different from first descriptions (see Chapter 6).

The ultimate objective of problem-oriented policing—the development of a more effective response—underlines the importance of disaggregating problems. Problems with the same generic label may in fact require radically different responses. Systematic thefts from cars parked in shopping malls and at motels present a radically different problem than the random theft of items from cars parked in residential areas. Fires set by teenagers as a form of vandalism call for a different response from that required for fires set by persons intent on collecting insurance. Complaints about noise emanating from the apartments of neighbors present a radically different problem from complaints about the noise made by racing automobiles or industrial operations.

ANALYSIS OF THE MULTIPLE INTERESTS IN PROBLEMS

If the police were asked, in the past, why they were concerned about a particular problem, they would often explain that the conduct involved was against the law. That response would not have been unsatisfactory so long as one adhered to the old notions that the primary job of the police was to enforce the law and that the police had no discretion in deciding how the law was to be enforced. But with increased awareness that the job of the police is much broader and that police must, of necessity, exercise discretion in using the law to deal with community problems, one must examine more critically the nature of the police concern with each of the problems the police are expected to handle. More penetrating analysis of a problem requires examination of some of the interests served in making the conduct illegal. And even if the conduct is not legislatively proscribed, the same need exists to identify the various interests in controlling a problem. The nature of the community's concern and interest in a problem is of critical importance in deciding how best to respond to it.

This point is nicely illustrated by examining the multiple interests in a common problem such as street prostitution, which is clearly illegal. Narrowly, one could assert that police are in the business of dealing with street prostitution because it is against the law. But large numbers of street prostitutes—both male and female—can usually be found in our urban areas. Other problems compete for police time. Enforcement is difficult. Simply viewing the conduct as illegal is not helpful in formulating a response. The challenge to the police is to develop a program that will deal with the most troubling aspects of prostitution in the fairest and most effective manner. Development of a rational plan requires careful analysis and the answer to some specific questions: Why is the community concerned? What are the social costs? Who is being harmed and to what degree? In an effort to answer these questions, one might identify as many as 13 different and often competing interests:

1 The behavior constitutes an offense to the moral standards of some segments of the community.

2 It creates a nuisance to passersby and to adjacent residents and business establishments.

3 Uninvolved individuals who must frequent the area are offended if they are solicited.

4 Juveniles may become prostitutes.

5 A prostitute may be harmed by her or his customers.

6 Those who patronize a prostitute may be assaulted, robbed, or defrauded.

7 Prostitutes may be exploited financially and physically by their pimps.

8 Street prostitution may provide the seedbed for organized criminal interests in the community.

9 Prostitution is usually linked to drugs, with the possibility that the prostitutes make extensive use of drugs.

10 Prostitutes as citizens have rights that need to be protected.

11 Street prostitutes create parking and traffic problems in the areas where they congregate.

12 The presence of prostitutes may have a deleterious effect on the economy of the area, reducing the value of buildings and limiting their use.

13 Prostitutes may spread sexually transmitted diseases such as syphilis, herpes, and AIDS.

The results of systematic inquiry should provide facts that make it possible to quantify the basis for these concerns so that their significance may be better assessed. How often are juveniles involved? What evidence is there of organized criminal interests? How often are prostitutes injured? Are the values of property in the area changing? And what do we know about the role of prostitutes in spreading various diseases? The answers to these questions, among others, would help clear away some of the brush, producing a much sharper understanding of the problem and identifying more clearly the policy decisions that must be made.

After identifying competing social interests and gathering facts that enable an assessment of the relative importance of each interest, value judgments must be made in ranking their importance. Ideally—and this is admittedly a very difficult step—the police will be able to work out a consensus within the community. Engaging in open discussion of the competing social interests is itself a healthy exercise for a community. And having the facts available to help the citizenry weigh the significance of each interest greatly advances such discussions. For the police, a clear determination of why they are concerned about a particular problem is an essential prerequisite to their fashioning a sensible strategy to deal with it.

CAPTURING AND CRITIQUING THE CURRENT RESPONSE

Before exploring new and more effective ways of dealing with a substantive problem, it is essential to establish how police currently handle the incidents that together form the problem. It would obviously be presumptuous to assume that whatever is currently being done is ineffective. The opposite may be true. Even if the current response is not effective, documentation of that finding is important in soliciting support for an alternative. But perhaps most important, current responses are likely to consist of a variety of personally crafted practices, and from these one may find a wealth of ideas employed with varied degrees of success to provide a head start in exploring alternatives.

Documenting existing police practices is much more difficult than one might assume. Police tend to respond to inquiries about what they are doing in broad, generic, operational terms. Thus, initially, police are likely to report that they deal with a given problem through preventive patrol, by investigating complaints that are brought to their attention, and by arresting and prosecuting those who violate the law. Investigation, patrol, and prosecution, however, as previously noted, are descriptive of large components of police operations used to deal in a common fashion with a wide range of quite different problems.

When pressed beyond this superficial level, administrators are likely to describe the police response to a given problem in terms that meet public expectations, legal standards, and formal guidelines. But administrators, especially in large police agencies, are far removed from the street and the handling of individual incidents and are, therefore, often ill equipped to describe the current field response accurately. One may obtain quite different pictures of what is happening on the street from different administrators within the same agency.

Individual officers, who are probably in the best position to describe accurately the present response at the incident level, are least inclined to do so. This is due, in part, to their fear of being reprimanded for acknowledging practices that may be in conflict with formal guidance. But even if this barrier is removed, individual officers, as the lowest-level employees, are conditioned to believe that their observations and their insights are not particularly relevant. We know from the various efforts to document police activity in the field that the way in which different officers respond to the same type of incident varies tremendously. There may be as many ways to handle some incidents as there are officers. On the other hand, many responses are highly routinized, reflecting a rather uniform pattern that has emerged on a shift, in a unit (such as a precinct), or in an entire agency. When questions are asked, a practice may be attributed to the orders of a supervisor, the highly publicized comments of a judge, or the informal word passed on by an assistant prosecutor or a veteran officer.

Difficult as it is to capture a comprehensive, accurate picture of current practice, the benefits to be derived from learning about the different ways in which individual officers respond make the effort worthwhile. In handling complicated matters, the need to improvise has prompted some officers to develop unusually effective ways to deal with specific problems. Officers acquire a unique understanding of problems that frequently come to their attention; learn to make important distinctions among different forms of the same problem; and become familiar with the many complicating factors that are often present. And they develop a feel for what, under the circumstances, constitute the most effective responses. After careful evaluation, these types of responses might profitably be adopted as standard for an entire police agency.

AN UNINHIBITED SEARCH FOR A TAILOR-MADE RESPONSE

As long as police viewed themselves as being involved primarily in controlling crime and as having no discretion, it was understandable that—in a formal sense—the only method available to get their job done was to arrest and prosecute persons committing crimes. Yet, because the police have always done so much more than just control crime, they informally used many other means to handle their work load. But absent formal provision of other alternatives, they often ended up adapting the criminal justice system to achieve their objectives. We have long experienced, therefore, the absurdity of police officers arresting people in order to help them (e.g., public inebriates, the mentally ill, and the homeless). And all officers have had some experience in drawing from the "arsenal" of the criminal law and city ordinances a statute or ordinance that, with some stretching, enabled them to take action when action seemed appropriate (e.g., laws relating to vagrancy, trespass, and disorderly conduct).

Increased recognition of the broad nature of the police function and of police discretion, along with judicially imposed curbs on stretching the criminal law, have changed the situation dramatically. In recent years, police have employed many new resources in responding to incidents—such as making referrals to appropriate agencies—and new forms of authority have been made available to the police for caring for some common types of incidents in a more forthright manner (e.g., the authority to detain public inebriates and transport them to a detoxification facility). We are nevertheless periodically reminded of the tendency to resort to traditional law enforcement. As an example, the New York City Police Department was reported as enforcing the mandatory seat-belt law disproportionately against drivers in areas frequented by street prostitutes. "We use whatever tools we can," said the officer in charge (*The New York Times,* Mar. 8, 1985). And we are also seeing some renewed support for truncated use of the criminal justice system (arrest without prosecution) to handle such problems as spousal abuse (*The Wall Street Journal,* May 22, 1984), drug sales, and gangs that engage in violence and intimidate residents of a neighborhood.

An intensified concern with substantive problems builds on recent efforts to develop authority and responses that are more suitable than the criminal law for dealing with some police business. The objective, after identifying problems more specifically, is to develop tailor-made responses: to fashion a response that holds the greatest potential for eliminating or reducing the specific problem. Once police break out of the mold of looking only within the criminal justice system for solutions, large vistas are opened to exploration. Problem-oriented policing includes, as one of its key elements, taking full advantage of this opportunity by encouraging a far-reaching and imaginative search for alternative ways in which to respond to commonly recurring problems, uncurtailed by prior thinking. From the early experiments in problem-oriented policing, it is apparent that the range of possibilities is limited only by the imagination and creativity of individual officers. Physical and technical changes, buoying up old services and creating new ones, and developing sophisticated forms of mediation are but a few of the most common illustrations. Because the range of alternatives that are emerging is such a strong indicator of the richness and excitement associated with problem-oriented policing, a separate chapter (Chapter 8) is devoted to examining them in detail.

It is unlikely that a tailor-made response would consist of a single alternative—though that could be the case. More likely, it would consist of a blend of different alternatives. Thus, for example, an effort to deal with a rash of burglaries in a low-income housing project might, depending on the results of an analysis, consist of any or all of the following:

- Efforts to apprehend those responsible for the burglaries
- Counseling management regarding lighting, lock systems, landscaping that provides hiding places for burglars, fencing, appearance of buildings and grounds, etc.
- Referring uncorrected conditions that are in violation of the law to building inspectors, zoning authorities, or health authorities
- Counseling management regarding contractual arrangements with tenants (e.g., multiple occupancy, short-term leases)
- Working with tenants, informing them of their rights vis-à-vis management, of various government services that are available to them, and of measures that they can take to prevent crimes

• Working with school authorities regarding any problem of truancy that may be related to burglaries, and with recreation and park authorities regarding any problem of idle youth

• Working with various services for the elderly to deal with problems of fear that may exist among tenants

It should be anticipated that an effort to mobilize the community will be among the most common measures included in the development of a tailor-made response. As mentioned earlier, the community is among the major untapped resources available to the police for dealing with problems, and engaging the community holds the potential for invoking informal controls that are more permanent and more effective than any measures the police themselves are in a position to implement.

Although emphasis is placed on developing nontraditional responses, it is recognized that the police will always depend heavily on the legal system in carrying out their function. Problem-oriented policing creates the potential for making much more effective use of various forms of legal controls, including the criminal justice system. In the past, the tendency has been to define criminal conduct in broad terms and then apply the law to a wide range of problems—quite different from each other — creating difficulties both for the police and for the individuals affected. But if a problem is carefully analyzed and some form of legal control is fashioned specifically to deal with it, the police can get at the problem much more directly, and avoid the potential for unfairness and abuse that always exists if the police response is unnecessarily broad and perhaps overly powerful as well. Problem-oriented policing challenges legislatures, city councils, and those who draft the laws to make more discrete use of legal controls—to advance to what might be loosely characterized as equivalent to microsurgery in the medical field (see Chapter 8).

ADOPTING A PROACTIVE STANCE

The police are among the most powerful agencies of government. Individual police officers exercise raw governmental authority. Police authority is not easily controlled. Against a history of considerable abuse, new examples of how that authority can be wrongly used always appear. It is no wonder, therefore, that so large a segment of the public attaches great importance to controlling the police. And it is understandable, too, why both the public and police officials believe that the police, like little children in adult company, are best advised to "listen, but not talk." We do not want the police to be making policy judgments that affect our lives.

It is somewhat heretical, therefore, to suggest that the police be more assertive in making decisions relating to their mission and in deciding how to discharge their responsibilities. Problem-oriented policing nevertheless encourages a more proactive role for the police, subject to appropriate accountability, in the strong belief that greater involvement on the part of the police, based on systematic inquiry, will reduce, rather than increase, the abuse of police authority.

The need for greater initiative takes three forms. The first relates to the initial identification of problems. It should be legitimate for the police to identify emerging problems in the community and, based on much more careful and thoughtful inquiry than has ever been undertaken in the past, offer proposals by which the community might deal more effectively with such problems in the future. Because the police occupy a frontline position vis-à-vis the social ills of the community, they acquire large amounts of data and insights that can be used to clarify community problems. Rather than wait until problems have reached sufficient magnitude to generate community concern and only then react to them (inevitably in an awkward, often defensive fashion), the police should be able to use the data in their possession to identify problems at an earlier stage and to share their knowledge with the community. Although some police were oblivious to the gross inadequacies of past practices in dealing with, for example, chronic alcoholics, the victims of sexual assault, and the victims of spousal abuse (and may even have contributed, through their actions, to compounding these problems), others knew that the problems were serious long before they were widely recognized as such.

One of the best examples of the consequences of "forced silence" on the part of the police is the nationwide problem resulting from the deinstitutionalization of the mentally ill. The potential harm to both the deinstitutionalized and the community when adequate community resources were not available became apparent to the police very soon after these programs were initiated. But the police were not involved in the policy decisions that led to deinstitutionalization, nor was any effort made to equip them to respond to the difficulty created by the presence of the mentally ill in the community. Rarely did a police administrator take the initiative in calling the problem to the attention of the community.

The intelligent management of police resources also requires that the police be more outspoken. It makes no sense for the police to be committed, in an unthinking manner, to devoting the bulk of their resources to simply responding to all citizen demands for service or to engage in a generic form of crime prevention. The ultimate decision on the type of service provided by the police should obviously be made by the community being served, but the police need to be much more active in placing choices before the community. They must demonstrate how specifically targeted responses based on systematic analysis can—in the end—have a greater potential for addressing community problems than current practices.

And finally, at the level of street operations, the police must, if they are to be effective, assume an advocacy role for the community. Admittedly, the role of the police as advocates is fraught with danger. We certainly do not want the police, for example, espousing a political candidate, opposing free speech, or supporting a "lynch-type" hysteria such as occasionally overcomes an area. But given the relationships that have been developed among crime, disorder, and the physical appearances of neighborhoods, we do want an officer to represent community concerns if garbage is uncollected, if fire-gutted buildings are not torn down or replaced, if potholes are not repaired, or if serious crimes are not being fully investigated.

In the range of postures that the police can assume, there is ample room for them to take greater initiative in dealing with community problems. In calling for the police not simply to resign themselves to living with recurring problems, problem-oriented policing urges the police to be more aggressive partners with other public agencies. Greater initiative on the part of the police will not only place the police in a much more positive light in the communities they serve, it will also contribute significantly to improving the working environment within a police agency—an environment, as previously noted, that is often demoralized because so many of the problems left to the police are insolvable or are ignored by others. An improved working environment, in turn, increases the potential to recruit and keep qualified personnel and to bring about needed organizational change.

STRENGTHENING THE DECISION-MAKING PROCESSES AND INCREASING ACCOUNTABILITY

With more widespread recognition of the discretion exercised by the police, much effort over the past several decades has gone into the development of methods for structuring and controlling that discretion (Goldstein, 1967, 1977; Davis, 1969; Walker, 1986). Chief among these have been the increased use of written policies and regulations, increased accountability to elected officials, and resort to a variety of methods for controlling the police, including civilian review boards, judicial review, and increased susceptibility to both criminal and civil liability. Where these controls have been imposed from outside the police agency, they have added to the strain in relationships between the police and the community and have made the police even more defensive.

If the procedures for addressing community problems are widened and given greater visibility, policy decisions will be aired, resulting in greater involvement of the community in these decisions and the articulation of more precise guidance to operating police officers. That would all be for the good, especially as we reflect back on the rather unworkable demands for neighborhood control in the 1970s.

Problem-oriented policing, by virtue of some of the elements already described, encourages and facilitates greater accountability on the part of the police. It pushes the police to think through how they respond to problems and to subject their response to the review of the highest authorities in the department. This reduces the likelihood of individual arbitrariness and value judgments that may be illegal, improper, or simply in conflict with the desires of the community. The bases for police decisions are articulated and supported by relevant facts. If major policy choices must be made, those who represent the community are involved in the ultimate decisions. And once decisions are made and policies are adopted, specific guidance in the form of written policies may be provided to operating personnel.

This process has two side benefits. One is its educational value. Lay members of the community frequently assume that the police have much more authority and capability than they actually have. Exploring problems with the police acquaints the community with the limited alternatives that are available and the restraints under which the police must operate; it relieves some of the pressures on the police. It also makes possible activities that would be rejected out of hand if proposed exclusively by the police. Any proposal, made in the abstract, for police monitoring of citizens is bound to elicit an almost immediate condemnation. But a proposal for legal monitoring is likely to gain widespread support if it is advocated in response to a specific problem that has been carefully documented (if it is demonstrated, for example, that a high percentage of violent sexual offenses are committed by persons on probation or parole for prior sexual crimes, or that a given tavern has consistently served drinks to persons who are already intoxicated).

The second side benefit to be realized from more open decision making is wider recognition that the police must take risks: that they are not infallible. Too much of what the police do is designed not with a primary focus on effectiveness, but rather to justify their actions if called upon to do so. This is accountability run amuck: The desire to be able to justify and provide a legal basis for an action—sometimes even after the action is taken—gets in the way of being effective. In problem-oriented policing, some risk is assumed in developing responses and policies, and an awareness of this risk is shared with the community. It is assumed that it is impossible to be free of risks in handling the incredible array of problems that the police must treat—that, on balance, it is better to acknowledge the risks and accept blame for failure than to operate in a straightjacket, with the lack of candor that must prevail if the police pretend to be omnipotent.

EVALUATING RESULTS OF NEWLY IMPLEMENTED RESPONSES

Concern about effectiveness naturally includes a commitment to evaluation. It is obviously important to guard against replacing one ineffective response with another and to ensure that the claims made for new responses are substantiated. It is also important to periodically reevaluate the effectiveness of a response that has been in place for some time. Without adequate attention, a response may revert to an older, less effective form, or, circumstances having changed, the agreed-upon response may no longer be as effective as when it was first instituted.

The problem-oriented approach calls for developing—preferably within a police agency—the skills, procedures, and research techniques to analyze problems and evaluate police effectiveness as an integral continuing part of management. Given the wide range in the type, level, and size of problems, there will be equal variety in the type of evaluation that is required. It will be relatively easy to measure the effectiveness of new responses to some problems. Others will require more complex procedures. A substantial effort has been made to provide guidance to police personnel in research methodology so that, in modest but sound ways, they can do a better job than they have ever done in the past of measuring the impact of their actions on the problems they handle. (For the best introduction to research for the police, see Eck, 1984.) High-quality evaluations of the effectiveness of major changes are difficult because of the large number of variables that can affect outcomes and because of the enormous effort and cost involved in setting up controlled experiments. For these, the police must develop new and more productive relationships with academics for the skills, time, and independence required. And they must turn to foundations and governmental agencies for the needed financial support. It will take a whole series of developments—staff, specially suited research methods, dissemination, and peer review prior to publication—to enable the police field to establish the arrangements whereby its end products can be evaluated routinely and with confidence. (For further discussion on meeting this need, see Chapter 8.)

CHAPTER 5

THE EARLY EXPERIENCES

Change in policing, as we have noted, occurs unevenly and in small increments. An unpredictable event—a crisis in the community or in the police agency—is often the factor that propels a police agency to adopt new approaches, frequently accompanied by a change in leadership.

Some agencies, once launched in a new direction, make significant, steady progress over a long period of time. Others, after a spurt of progress, sometimes lasting for several years, then suffer serious setbacks. This may be due to a change of priorities, the loss of an especially motivated leader, or a financial crisis. The same type of unpredictable event that sets change in motion can just as easily put an end to a commendable initiative, with a reversion to traditional practices. The police operate in a volatile political environment. Since the benefits of change are not immediately demonstrable, new approaches are vulnerable to attacks arising from ignorance of the complexity of policing, an intolerance of the unfamiliar, and a lack of patience. By comparison, gaining support for a return to old, familiar practices, however ineffective or shortsighted they may be, is easy. These retrogressions are painful to those who have invested their energies and professional careers in bringing about change under difficult circumstances. They leave many individuals disenchanted and cynical. But they must be anticipated.

In the larger picture, new initiatives that do not continue or that do not lead to permanent changes in an organization are not failures if we learn from them. Although it is of little solace to the participants, experiments, however limited, do contribute to the overall advancement of the police field. Support for a broad change in how we conceptualize the police role can develop independent of success in institutionalizing change within a given agency. One agency builds on the efforts of others. The process is greatly facilitated when innovative leaders can move from one agency to another, taking their ideas and styles of policing with them. Unfortunately, such movement is greatly limited—a situation that seriously impedes the development of policing in this country.

One must have this larger picture of change in mind as we describe some of the early experiments in problem-oriented policing. The success of these efforts should not be measured by their life within the agency in which they were initiated but by the contribution that they make to a larger movement in policing.

BRIEF SUMMARIES OF SOME EARLY EXPERIMENTS

Madison, Wisconsin, Police in Collaboration with the University of Wisconsin

As initially conceived (Goldstein, 1979), the objective in problem-oriented policing was to explore how an agency as a whole could analyze a given citywide problem and its response to it. This called for organizing an inquiry at the highest level of the police department. To learn more about what was involved in such an undertaking, the author, with support from the National Institute of Justice (NIJ), entered into a cooperative arrangement with the Madison, Wisconsin, Police Department in 1981 for the study of two community problems: the drinking driver and the violent sexual offender. With the full- or part-time efforts of three persons based at the University of Wisconsin, including two individuals trained in research methodology, and with total access to department records and personnel, the two problems were explored in great detail (Goldstein and Susmilch, 1981, 1982a, 1982b, 1982c). Drawing heavily on the expertise of rank-and-file officers, proposals for significantly altering the department's response were formulated.

The recommendations relating to the drinking driver stimulated much discussion in both the police department and the community, but only small elements of the total proposal were implemented. A new legislative scheme for dealing with drunk drivers was enacted during the study, renewing hopes that increased arrests and stronger sanctions would address the problem. The primary thrust of the recommendations—that more contacts with motorists were preferable to more arrests—gained little support in the department. In contrast, the recommendations relating to serious sexual assaults were implemented in their entirety. The study reached the conclusion that a disproportionate number of convicted sex offenders had chosen to live in Madison upon their release from prison and that the offenses of greatest concern to the community had been committed by ex-offenders. This led to recommendations for daily liaison between the police and corrections personnel and for an intensive program in which both police and corrections personnel monitored selected offenders. The program has since been expanded to include a wide range of other types of offenders. In both studies, much was learned about what is involved in undertaking in-depth inquiries of this kind (Goldstein and Susmilch, 1982c).

Largely independent of these efforts, the Madison Police Department has, as part of its rapid development over the past decade under Chief David Couper, analyzed specific problems in the community and developed more effective responses to them. Among the problems that have received this type of attention have been panhandling, solicitation by street prostitutes, threatening behavior by mentally ill persons, and an annual convention of "hot rodders" who cruise up and down a major thoroughfare.

In an experiment in neighborhood policing, officers have been encouraged to identify problems of concern to their neighborhoods and to find imaginative ways to deal with them. Many interesting examples of innovative problem-solving have emanated from this project. Currently, the department is moving rapidly toward total decentralization to enable officers throughout the city to deal in a proactive way with neighborhood problems. In a district established to experiment with decentralization, officers are urged to engage in problem-solving. Thus, although the Madison Police Department has not made a formal commitment to the full concept of problem-oriented policing, and many of its officers would not recognize that label, the department is incorporating most of the elements identified in Chapter 4 into its changing approach to delivering police services.

Baltimore County, Maryland, Police in Collaboration with the Police Executive Research Forum

Two especially shocking homicides in the summer of 1981 greatly increased the level of fear in Baltimore County and resulted in a decision to hire 45 additional police officers—a substantial number in a department that had 1,400 employees exclusive of civilian support personnel. Rather than absorb these officers into the established organization, which was committed to reactive patrol, Chief Cornelius Behan decided to create a special unit called COPE (Citizen Oriented Police Enforcement), with the mission of reducing fear in the county by intensive patrol and by developing close contacts with citizens. The officers were initially instructed not to engage in traditional policing. (For a full description of the origin and development of the COPE unit, see Taft, 1986. For its evaluation, see Cordner, 1985, 1986. For a discussion of its relationship to community-oriented policing, see Cordner, 1988.)

The unit was divided into three subunits, each under a lieutenant and each assigned to one of the three areas into which the county is divided for police purposes. Given the novelty of dealing directly with fear, some initial uncertainty existed as to what, specifically, the officers were to do. In search of a better-defined framework, those in charge decided to apply problem-oriented policing.

Their application was novel in several respects. No one talked of studying and acting upon countywide behavioral problems. From the outset, the architects of the COPE program focused on local problems: racial conflict at a school; noisy, disruptive bands of teenagers; and fear generated by a series of burglaries and, in a separate incident, by the finding of a body. This led to the need to train the members of the COPE units in the analysis of problems, in looking at them differently from the way they had in the past, and in making use of the freedom they were given to come up with innovative responses. The project quickly confirmed the value of directly involving operating personnel in a process that previously was thought to require specially trained personnel committed to a more rigorous form of research.

The COPE unit has since honed its ability to address substantive problems of a local nature, routinely "diagnosing" problems and developing "action plans" for dealing with them (Higdon and Huber, 1987). Within COPE, adjustments have been made to support the more flexible working environment required by a COPE-type operation. Problem-oriented policing is now synonymous with COPE, but COPE remains a special unit of 45 police officers. Through meetings with all of the command staff and through specially developed training programs, the department has sought to gain acceptance for COPE and, more ambitiously, has succeeded in spreading COPE methods to other units. This process has been aided by the influence of officers who served in COPE and, upon promotion, were placed in charge of regular units of the department.

London Metropolitan Police

Sir Kenneth Newman, who served as commissioner of Scotland Yard from 1982 to 1987, was widely acknowledged as having brought to the job a new intellectual dimension and a willingness to challenge existing practices. From early in his administration, he launched many planning initiatives that, although they had specific goals, were more broadly designed to stimulate creative, critical thinking in the force.

Among these initiatives, he authorized his staff in 1983 "to evaluate the feasibility of adopting the 'Problem Oriented Approach' in the Metropolitan Police," building on the experience that, by that time, had been acquired in conducting the two major studies of sizable problems in Madison. To carry out the evaluation, it was decided "to implement and evaluate four pilot schemes and report on their implications for operations, training, resources, research and management if such an approach was to be adopted Forcewide" (Hoare, Stewart, and Purcell, 1984, sec. 1.1).

The four problems selected for study (one in each of four major areas into which the city was then divided for police services) were Asian gangs, shopper victims in Oxford Street, prostitutes in Bedford Hill, and motor vehicle crime. In a detailed review of the studies, those in overall charge of the project concluded that the problem-oriented approach had the potential to improve police performance, but "its unstructured nature makes it difficult to manage and maintain" (Hoare, Stewart, and Purcell, 1984, Summary).

> The present structure of the Metropolitan Police is probably out of step with the approach, and its adoption would involve risk taking and the abandonment of some of the traditional expectations of line managers. The "Problem Oriented Approach" is more a matter of attitude than skill, and is an idea which would have to be progressively assimilated rather than being imposed (Hoare, Stewart, and Purcell, 1984, Summary).

The individual studies produced many new insights and novel proposals for dealing with long-standing problems. But they also demonstrated that the potential for routinely conducting similar studies and for implementing the results is seriously limited unless greater flexibility is introduced into the organization. This is illustrated by some of the characteristics of the Metropolitan Police cited in the report on the project as making adoption of the problem-oriented approach difficult:

> • The process may be seen as being in opposition to the centralised policy making which is likely to dominate a Force as large as the Metropolitan Police.
>
> • The organisational structure, and its expectations of management may be in conflict with local problem solving.
>
> • A Chief Superintendent's degrees of freedom are likely to be insufficient to support radical initiatives. . . .
>
> • As the result of rapid personnel movements, the divisional management team is so unstable as to defeat long term problem solving.
>
> • Management communications are designed by "line" or "territory"—not by problem . . . (Hoare, Stewart, and Purcell, 1984, sec. 10.3).

The commissioner was well aware of the larger need to create an environment in which greater attention could be given to substantive problems. In a letter to the force in 1984, announcing "the most fundamental changes in 150 years" in the Metropolitan Police, Newman expressed his concern that "the structure of our hierarchy was hindering more than helping the good work done on the ground." He reported that the changes he was making were based on his analysis of what accounted for the difficulties being experienced by the Metropolitan Police (Newman, 1984). He drew four conclusions, two of which paralleled the reasoning behind problem-oriented policing: "too much energy and effort are wasted in keeping the organization going instead of serving the mainline job of policing" and "there is a tendency for our organization to try to cope with problems through superficial changes in the bureaucratic system, rather than looking for real solutions." Thus, Newman sought to reduce the rigidity of the organization to increase the likelihood that projects designed to affect the end product of policing would succeed. The commitment to problem-oriented policing is reflected in Newman's update of the "policing principles" of the Metropolitan Police, published in 1985, in which he writes:

> Many of the isolated incidents to which police are called are symptoms of more general substantive problems with roots in a wide range of social and environmental conditions. The aim of the Metropolitan Police will, therefore, be to work with other agencies to develop what is known as a "situational" or "problem-solving" approach to crime prevention, where, rather than merely dealing with individual acts of law-breaking, careful analysis is made of the total circumstances surrounding the commission of types of crime, taking account of wide-ranging social and environmental factors, in order better to understand—and counter—the causes of those acts (Newman, 1985, p. 12).

Newport News, Virginia, Police in Collaboration with the Police Executive Research Forum

In 1983 the Newport News Police Department entered a period of major transition. A new chief, Darrel Stephens, had been hired from outside the department with a clear mandate to deal with an accumulation of problems that had developed in the management of the department and, especially, to establish more open communication between the department and the community. A number of the standard remedies for modernizing a police agency were implemented almost immediately: improvements in internal communication, accountability, and efficiency; development of written policies; and adjustments in training and salaries. But the chief went further, adopting some practices that were significant departures from the traditional professional model: a style of management that involved operating personnel in the management of the department; an articulated philosophy of service; the setting of objectives for the agency; and a differential-response program, which reduced the amount of time officers spent in responding reactively to calls for police assistance (Eck and Spelman et al., 1987). These latter changes were tied to a commitment of the chief to experiment with the concept of problem-oriented policing. To launch this experiment, he arranged for the technical support of the staff of the Police Executive Research Forum (PERF) and, with the assistance of PERF, he succeeded in acquiring financial support from the National Institute of Justice.

The Newport News project was unique in that, from the outset, the objective was to make ''problem-solving'' an integral part of the daily operation of the entire agency. This meant a commitment to study the department's response to major recurring problems and to alter the response based on these studies. But the department also wanted to encourage officers on the beat to apply the same process to any recurring problems they experienced. More broadly, it sought to inculcate ''problem-solving'' as the way of thinking and doing business within the Newport News Police Department. A task force representative of all ranks within the department was created to direct the project. To spread the concept throughout the department, the task force developed a detailed process that officers could follow in exploring problems. (For a comprehensive description of this set of guidelines, see Eck and Spelman et al., 1987, pp. 41–52.) In the more ambitious inquiries, department personnel had the assistance of PERF staff—as, for example, in the design of a survey instrument to collect data from residents and in the analysis of such data.

Obviously, making problem-solving an integral part of the daily operations of the Newport News department will require a sustained effort over a much longer period of time than has elapsed since the project was initiated. The immediate value of the project is that it tells us what can be accomplished by an agency that sets out with this broad goal in mind. The department studied and acted upon three major neighborhood problems: burglaries in a low-income, government-subsidized housing project; thefts from automobiles parked in downtown parking lots; and robberies related to prostitution in the downtown area. In addition, it dealt with such varied, recurring problems as disturbances at convenience stores, drug dealing at a specific intersection, and robberies in the central business district. Although management most frequently identified a problem in need of attention, survey results at the end of the first formal stage in the project indicated that at least 40 percent of the officers in the department had some exposure to working with the problem-solving process and approximately 20 percent had worked a problem through in its entirety (Eck and Spelman et al., 1987, pp. 97–98). Thus, although problem-oriented policing is far from institutionalized in the Newport News Police Department and further progress depends on a number of local factors, the experience to date demonstrates that problem-oriented policing can be introduced to an *entire* police agency; that personnel at both the management *and operating* levels can be productively engaged in the process; and that the process of identification and analysis can be applied with equal effectiveness to a wide range of substantive problems (citywide or localized, large or small) with impressive results, both in reducing the magnitude of the problems and, as a by-product, in creating a more positive, productive atmosphere in the agency (see Eck and Spelman et al., 1987, pp. 65–96).

PROBLEM-ORIENTED COMPONENTS IN THE COMMUNITY-ORIENTED POLICING PROJECTS OF SEVERAL OTHER CITIES

Systematically addressing substantive community problems is by no means limited to those jurisdictions that have implemented some form of problem-oriented policing. As previously noted (see Chapter 3), community-oriented policing has often led to intensive work on substantive community problems. Although these efforts may be less systematic and more influenced by a desire to improve relations with the community than by a commitment to solve the problems, they are no less relevant to this exploration. Unfortunately, these experiences have not been as fully monitored and documented. There are five notable exceptions in Flint, Michigan; New York City; Los Angeles; Houston; and Edmonton, Alberta.

Flint, Michigan

The Flint Neighborhood Foot Patrol Program began in 1979 and, at its height in 1982, placed a police officer in each of the 64 areas into which the city was divided. It incorporated a number of the basic elements of problem-oriented policing. Initially funded with a grant from the Mott Foundation, the project was eventually supported by a special tax levy approved by the voters. In the larger context of building a partnership between the police and the community, the project dealt with the problems the community identified, and the police officer developed into a neighborhood problem-solver. Officers were relieved of most of the pressures of reactive patrol and were encouraged to work on a given problem from the beginning through to its solution (Trojanowicz, Steele, and Trojanowicz, 1986, pp. 6–7). Both the initiative and the burden for dealing with community problems were left to the officer on the beat. No systematic process for the identification and analysis of problems was used; nor did the department identify and address problems that extended beyond the boundaries of a beat. (For a comprehensive description of the original Flint project, see Trojanowicz, n.d.) Support for the Flint project has wavered since 1987, with changes in mayors and police chiefs, reflecting the fragile nature of such undertakings.

New York City

At the initiative of Commissioner Benjamin Ward and with the technical support of the Vera Institute of Justice, the New York City Police Department launched its Community Patrol Officer Program (CPOP) in 1984. (For a description of the program and a report on its progress, see Ward, 1985; Farrell, 1986; New York City Police Department, 1987a.) The program has since been expanded to cover all of the city's 75 precincts. Under the program, each of 9 or 10 officers in a participating precinct is assigned responsibility for a specific beat. Every community patrol officer (CPO) is expected to provide the full range of police services within his or her beat (though relieved of responding to routine calls). This officer is also expected to work with community residents in identifying local problems and in designing solutions for them. In a critique of the program by the Vera Institute staff, the job of the CPO as a problem-solver was identified as the most distinctive feature of the CPO's role. Urging that attention be given to developing this role, the report asserted: "To the extent that CPOs fail at the planning and problem-solving dimension of the role, their distinctive utility as a police resource is threatened. If that happens, their performance on the street will become much like that of the conventional foot patrol officer" (Vera Institute of Justice, 1987).

Los Angeles

The Los Angeles Police Department has started several programs aimed at achieving some of the goals of community policing, but each has suffered because of the continuing pressures to respond first to calls for police service. In the most recent initiative (1985), however, supported by Chief Daryl F. Gates, the police leadership in the Wilshire area, in establishing its Community Mobilization Project (CMP), vowed to give highest priority to working with the community. In one of the earlier experiments in community policing, the rank of senior lead officer (SLO) had been created to head a team of officers who were given 24-hour responsibility for a given beat, with the understanding that the SLO would devote substantial time to relating to the needs of the community. But the function of the SLO has eroded since the position was first created in 1970, and most SLOs now police in traditional ways. In the Wilshire project, all eight SLOs were taken off routine patrol and assigned to dealing more intensively with recurring incidents by viewing them as related and giving sustained attention to the underlying problems. As a result of these efforts, the officers are credited with totally eliminating troublesome conditions that had long plagued the areas to which they are assigned. (For a detailed description of CMP and prior developments in the Los Angeles Department, see Kennedy, 1986.)

Houston

The Houston Police Department has been undergoing rapid change since the appointment of Lee P. Brown as chief of police in 1982. The introduction of a wide range of innovations, reflecting extraordinary sensitivity to all of the new insights and research findings in policing, has contributed significantly to developments on the national scene (see Skolnick and Bayley, 1986, pp. 81–116; Tumin, 1986). Not surprisingly, a common characteristic in these innovations has been the commitment to fashioning a partnership with each neighborhood. In implementing a concept of neighborhood-oriented policing, Houston officers will continue to respond to calls for service, but they will also be expected to initiate "self-directed activities"—defined as actions taken by officers, in collaboration with their neighborhoods, to identify and address community problems. Management is urged to encourage officers to think about their work in more abstract ways and to examine conditions that cause and perpetuate problems. Community policing, as adopted in Houston, is defined as an interactive process in which the police and the community jointly define problems, determine the best ways of addressing them, and combine their resources for solving them. Numerous steps have been taken to create a working environment that supports individual officers in broadening their role (Brown, 1985; Brown and Wycoff, 1987). In addition, Houston has undertaken to study a number of substantive problems that cut across many neighborhoods, for example, in its comprehensive study of "crack houses" established for the sole purpose of selling the drug (Brown, 1988b).

Edmonton, Alberta

Chris Braiden, a superintendent in the Edmonton, Alberta, police, has been recognized in both Canada and the United States as an unusually articulate advocate among practitioners committed to major change in policing (see Braiden, 1986). With the strong support of his chief, Leroy Chahley, Braiden designed a pilot program for Edmonton that incorporates many of the elements commonly associated with community policing but places special emphasis on proactively solving problems. From among the 561 grids into which the city is divided by the police for administrative purposes, only 36 are included in the project. But the selected areas accounted for 28 percent of all of the calls received for police service in the previous year. These grids were assigned to 21 beats. Upon implementation of the project in 1988, a constable was permanently assigned to each of the beats, operating on foot out of a storefront office manned by citizen volunteers. Each officer is systematically provided with data that aid the officer in identifying problems. In one grid, it was found that 58 percent of all calls generated from the approximately 1,000 addresses in the grid came from only 21 locations. The constables are freed from many of the usual organizational constraints and are encouraged to make maximum use of their knowledge, skills, and creativity in solving problems within their beat. If the results of the ongoing evaluation are positive, it is planned to expand the program to other areas of the city.

These are only five examples. Other cities that have adopted various forms of community policing with a strong, identifiable problem-solving component include Oxnard, California; Savannah, Georgia; Evanston, Illinois; Tulsa, Oklahoma; and Beloit, Wisconsin. Also of special interest are the changes introduced in the Halton Regional Police Force in Canada (Loree, 1988).

It is encouraging that projects initially conceived as community-oriented are tending to focus on community problems, but the fact that they are doing so does not, by itself, mean that these projects have become problem-oriented policing. The programs described—in Flint, New York City, and Los Angeles—incorporate a number of the basic elements of problem-oriented policing spelled out in Chapter 4. They reflect a commitment to probing into those situations that give rise to large numbers of incidents; to giving officers time to work on such situations in a proactive way; and to encouraging officers to use nontraditional responses. But the programs do not require the type of systematic analysis built into the Baltimore County and Newport News projects. And they do not apply the same pressure on officers to use resources beyond those already available. Absent systematic analysis and constant pressure to use nontraditional methods, there is always a risk that some of these units may deteriorate into special squads (referred to in the past as tactical units or "clean-up squads"), which are viewed as having the time to handle problems that cannot be handled by officers assigned to regular patrol and which deal with these problems in the most traditional, expeditious manner.

COMMON THEMES IN THE EXPERIMENTAL PROJECTS

In the chapters that follow, I draw heavily from each of the experiments described here, citing ways in which they have contributed to developing the concept of problem-oriented policing. Both the benefits and the difficulties will be covered. It is important to note here, however, that these diverse efforts have some common themes that bear directly on subsequent explorations.

It is striking that the catalyst for experimentation in Baltimore County was the addition of new personnel. The availability of additional personnel was what led the Kansas City Police Department to test the value of preventive patrol as far back as 1972. And the promise that increases in personnel would be used in new rather than traditional ways gained the needed support of both citizens and elected officials for added police in Flint, Michigan, and in New York City. To what extent does this reflect a growing resistance on the part of both police professionals and the public to hiring more personnel to carry out traditional, reactive policing? The opportunity to direct new resources to deal with community problems in nontraditional ways is apparently an attractive alternative.

In initially urging police agencies to look critically at how they handle substantive problems throughout a city or other area, it was assumed that the managerial level was the appropriate point at which to start analysis. Management's efforts were expected to lead to a greater concern for substantive problems throughout a department. It was contemplated from the outset that much greater use would be made of the expertise of rank-and-file officers, but that their contribution would be elicited as part of a study of problems at a higher level in the organization. But the projects in Baltimore County and Newport News were much more ambitious, persuasively demonstrating that one need not wait for the concept to "trickle down" from on high—that much is to be gained from reorienting the way in which *all* police officers approach their job. Broadening the concept in this fashion not only makes good sense; it increases the potential for more immediate application and, therefore, for more quickly realizing beneficial results. At the managerial level, long periods may elapse between analysis and a decision to take any action, if in fact any action is taken. At the operating level, by contrast, the time between analysis of a problem and acting upon that analysis is much shorter, and the impediments are fewer.

Welcome as this added dimension is to the overall concept of problem-oriented policing, it is important to recognize that engaging rank-and-file officers more directly in a street-level analysis of problems adds to the complexity of the concept. There is a world of difference between what is involved in critically examining, at the highest levels of the organization, problems of a citywide nature (e.g., spousal abuse) and in examining specific problems of a more local character at the operating level (problems relating, e.g., to an individual or an intersection). The first requires a major research effort, the second, a high-quality investigation but without the usual focus on establishing criminal intent. Yet these radically different undertakings mirror each other in that they reflect a common commitment to encouraging critical, creative thinking throughout the police agency—at the bottom as well as the top. Making effective use of these analyses requires developing a sense for the varying levels at which problems can be most effectively addressed and learning how inquiries initiated at different levels in the organization interrelate.

Incorporating street-level analysis of local problems into problem-oriented policing increases the importance of controlling the quality of whatever inquiries are made. Introducing more rigor into the collection of data and their analysis, to avoid various biases and errors, is difficult enough at the highest levels of the organization. The skills in research methodology required for such analysis are not often found in a police agency. The Madison project made use of trained researchers from outside the department. The London Metropolitan Police, with personnel trained in research methods in their employ, were able to meet their needs from within the agency, augmented by one outside consultant. The Newport News project, in examining some of its problems, used the research skills of the PERF staff.

When we speak of analysis of a problem by operating personnel, as occurs in Baltimore County and Newport News, we assume a much looser form of analysis in which a higher value is placed on initiative and persistence and less on the standards for ensuring the validity and reliability of data. This less formal analysis may be appropriate for problems defined and dealt with at the operating level. And it may be, over time, that officers can be trained in techniques that will increase the objectivity and validity of their inquiries. As a minimum, officers must be taught to recognize those situations in which more rigorous inquiry is required so that they can obtain needed assistance before any judgments are made.

It does not follow, from this discussion, that studies conducted by a research and planning unit or by a staff person in a chief's office will always be more rigorous than those conducted at the street level. One would expect that these units would be more likely to have the time, skills, and breadth of perspective to conduct a more rigorous study. But they may be pressured by other business or simply not have the commitment. I have seen the results of studies by street officers that were conducted with a much higher regard for sound research methodology than studies conducted by the planning and research units of large city departments.

To the credit of both the Baltimore County and Newport News programs, mechanisms have been introduced to control to some degree the quality of inquiries. In Baltimore County, officers are required to submit reports summarizing their analysis and plan for action, which are reviewed by higher-ranking officers with greater experience in the analysis of problems. Concern about this review raises the quality of the initial inquiry. The critique that is provided is helpful in maintaining high standards. In Newport News, officers are expected to present their analysis of a problem on which they are working to the Problem Analysis Advisory Committee. The need to do so and the helpful, supportive discussion that takes place are raising the quality of street analysis.

From among all of the experiments described, the Newport News project is the only one in which the officers addressing community problems are not set apart from the rest of the organization. It is understandable why police administrators create separate units or designate special personnel when they want to experiment with new styles of policing. It is much easier to manage the project, to shape it as it develops, and to protect it from the contaminating forces of the larger organization. But there are serious costs in creating separate units. Both the benefits and the costs are examined in detail in Chapter 9, and some thought is given to how they might be reconciled.

CONTINUING EXPERIMENTATION

Like change within the police bureaucracy, the spread of an idea in policing is not a neat process that can be tracked easily. The results of the early experiments were disseminated in a manner designed to encourage other agencies to experiment with the concept (Behan, 1986; Taft, 1986; Eck and Spelman, 1987; Eck and Spelman et al., 1987; Higdon and Huber, 1987; Spelman and Eck, 1987a, 1987b). Additional police agencies made a formal commitment to experiment with problem-oriented policing with support from NIJ and PERF (St. Petersburg, Tampa, and Clearwater in Florida). Others have been urged to adopt the concept by citizens' groups that have studied their operations (e.g., Philadelphia). And under a grant from the Bureau of Justice Assistance, PERF is assisting five large urban police departments (in Atlanta, Philadelphia, San Diego, Tampa, and Tulsa) to experiment with the problem-oriented approach as applied to drug-related community problems. Each of the agencies selected a target zone of activity and then carefully documented the nature of the drug-related problems within that zone. These drug inventories help the police officers focus on specific, manageable problems rather than the more amorphous and overwhelming "drug problem." In four of the cities, the target zones include large public housing complexes, and in all the cities officers have been working closely and for the most part successfully with public housing officials to address the problems. The project is ongoing and thus has not yet been formally evaluated, but the progress is encouraging. (For an interim report, see Police Executive Research Forum, 1989.) In several of the police agencies, officers working outside the project's target area have begun to adopt problem-oriented approaches to other problems. Some of the departments are considering formally implementing the problem-oriented approach throughout the department, even before evaluation of the project is completed.

The most visible indications of adoption and experimentation, however, are not always the most significant. Police officers who thoroughly understand the concept and incorporate it into their approach to their job, though currently working in an environment that is hostile to change, may be in a position to contribute much more to advancing the concept at some future time in their career. Thus, although continued experimentation and implementation are obviously of the utmost importance, so too are the further development and sharing of the idea.

CHAPTER **6**

IDENTIFYING PROBLEMS

Chapter 4 provided a description of the basic components of problem-oriented policing. But that description, at best, is the skeleton of the concept. Considerable work remains to be done to equip police to identify problems clearly and to develop a process for analyzing and solving them.

The COPE project in Baltimore County met this need for their department by intensive training in which officers explored the concept in detail and worked through case studies. The process was further developed through the close supervision that was possible in a relatively small, specialized unit. Out of these efforts, a standardized procedure gradually emerged, which was documented and has since been made available to other police agencies (Higdon and Huber, 1987).

In Newport News, where the objective was to introduce the concept to an entire department, it was clear from the outset that more specific guidance would be required. A department task force met the need by creating a four-step process that officers were subsequently trained to use: (1) scanning, which was designed to identify the problem; (2) analysis, which called for learning about the causes, scope, and effects of the problem; (3) response, which encompassed actions taken to alleviate the problem; and (4) assessment, which reminded officers of the need to determine if the response worked (Eck and Spelman et al., 1987, pp. 103–133).

Although some cringe at the "cookbook" character of such instruction, a realistic assessment of the task of introducing a new way of thinking into a police agency supports the effort. It is preferable, on balance, that officers be given a map and be alerted to the lack of detail, alternate routes, and the possibility that they will occasionally have to take detours, than that they be given no map at all out of fear that it will be taken too literally. The principal danger in providing a detailed procedure is that it will be used to oversimplify the concept: that more effort will be invested in moving mechanically through the recommended steps than in the explorations and thinking that the steps are encouraged to stimulate.

In this and the next two chapters, I elaborate on the major steps in implementing problem-oriented policing. Although I draw heavily on the experiences of both Baltimore County and Newport News in developing a specific process for solving problems, my objective is broader than was theirs. Recognizing that the concept is still in a formative stage and that one of the primary purposes of this book is to stimulate further development, I explore implementation at a more general level, offering some concrete suggestions and examples, but also flagging important issues as I move along. This chapter focuses on identifying problems, Chapter 7 on analyzing them, and Chapter 8 on developing new and more effective responses.

WHAT IS THE MEANING OF "PROBLEM"?

The identification of problems requires, first, greater clarity of what we mean by "problem." A start was made in Chapter 4 toward giving more specific meaning to the term as it is used in this book:

- A cluster of similar, related, or recurring incidents rather than a single incident
- A substantive community concern
- A unit of police business

By attributing these meanings to "problem," the several agencies that have experimented with problem-oriented policing and the personnel within the agencies have achieved a fairly consistent understanding of what it is on which they are focusing. Within these definitions, there has been no pressure to standardize the way in which problems are defined. That has been fortunate, allowing a natural process of definition to occur from which we have learned a good deal. The following list of problems that have received attention illustrates the variety of ways in which incidents have been clustered:

- Motorists who drive away from self-service gas stations without paying (citywide)

- Disorderly youth who regularly congregate in the parking area of a specific convenience store
- Street prostitutes and the associated robbery of their patrons in a specific neighborhood
- The drinking driver (citywide)
- Larcenies from vehicles parked in a largely abandoned downtown area by workers at an adjacent shipbuilding facility
- An apartment complex with a high rate of burglaries and a high level of fear among its residents
- Spousal abuse (citywide)
- Panhandling in a business area that created fear among those using the area
- Elderly people living alone who, stricken with illness or experiencing injury, may be unable to summon help, resulting in prolonged suffering or death (countywide)
- A specific individual who persistently harasses residents in a neighborhood, provoking residents to threaten retaliation
- An annual ethnic carnival with a high incidence of disorderliness, racial conflict, and street robberies
- The enticement of children into situations in which they are subject to sexual assault (citywide)
- Robberies of commercial establishments at major intersections of a main thoroughfare of a suburban area that is a corridor leading out of a large central city.

This list—and the larger experience from which it is drawn—reflects the tendency of the police, left to define problems, to do so in a somewhat eclectic fashion. They are inclined to use one of the characteristics of a problem to influence the way in which incidents are clustered and the problem is thereby identified. Among the most common characteristics are the following.

1 *Behavior* Behavior is probably the most frequently used organizing theme for clustering incidents, especially when the focus is on a citywide problem: e.g., noise, theft of vehicles, sale of drugs, sexual assault, drinking drivers, spousal abuse, runaways.

2 *Territory* A collection of different behavioral problems, concentrated in a given area, will typically result in the problem being identified by the place name of the area: e.g., Crown Heights neighborhood, Bryant Park, the intersection of Main Street and 2nd Avenue, Garden Village Apartments, Joe's Tavern, the residence at 2458 23rd Street. The problem at the intersection may involve merchants and pedestrians who are bothered by alcoholics, panhandlers, prostitutes, or individuals who are mentally ill and/or homeless. The most frequent problem identified in

territorial terms is the low-income housing project, for the obvious reason that it is a convenient, umbrellalike way of describing collectively the wide range of interrelated behavioral problems (burglary, theft, vandalism, arson, truancy, child neglect, assault, liquor violations, drug use and sale) commonly found in such housing complexes. When asked to identify some problems on which they have focused, the officers engaged in experimental policing in such varied places as Houston, New York City, Baltimore County, and Newport News each included, among the major problems on which they were working, several housing complexes.

3 *Persons* A problem may be identified in terms of offenders, complainants, or victims (e.g., the elderly); in terms of a large class of people (e.g., shoppers), a group (e.g., a gang), a family or an individual (e.g., an identified repeat offender or the person who persistently harasses a neighborhood); or based on a condition that distinguishes the individuals, as would be true in describing a problem as the alcoholics, the homeless, the mentally ill, or the developmentally disabled.

4 *Time* Both the public and the police tend to define some regularly recurring, predictable problems primarily in terms of an event or by the season, the day of the week, or the hour of the day in which they most often occur: e.g., an annual rock concert, Halloween party, or ethnic festival (any one of which may involve a subset of problems such as assaults, injuries, traffic congestion, sexual harassment, excessive consumption of alcohol or drugs, or potential racial conflict); thefts from parking areas in shopping malls prior to Christmas; burglaries in student housing when unattended in vacation periods; drunk driving in the period immediately after the closing of bars on weekends.

The typologies that emerge are not mutually exclusive or even tidy. A problem defined primarily in terms of territory could often just as easily be defined in behavioral terms. It is not yet clear what significance, if any, there may be to the way in which problems are naturally defined. Nor is it clear if, for purposes of analysis, one way of defining problems is preferable to another. It may be that none of this matters: that the primary concern ought to be to define the problem in terms that have meaning to both the community and the police.

The desire to move simultaneously to encourage increased concern with substantive problems at all levels in the police organization requires superimposing another perspective in defining problems—influenced by anticipating the scope of the analysis. This leads to a distinction between problems requiring "top-level analysis," "street-level analysis," or analysis at some intermediate level in the pyramidal structure of a police agency. If the condition of concern exists with some uniformity throughout a city or, by its very nature, is not localized (e.g., drunk driving), it is likely, from the outset, that one would be inclined to define the problem as citywide, requiring analysis at the top level of the agency or by a unit with citywide responsibility. This would also be the case if the department were pressured to respond to a communitywide interest, as police have done in examining and revising their response to the problems of missing children, child abuse, and abuse of the elderly.

If, on the other hand, a problem exists in only one area of a city or is of much greater concern in one area than in another, it makes sense for the inquiry to be limited to that area. Thus, the London Metropolitan Police focused on street prostitution in Bedford Hill, motor vehicle crime in West Ham, Asian gangs in Southall, and shoppers as victims on Oxford Street.

As problem-oriented policing is pushed further down to the operating level of an agency and officers are encouraged to engage in "street-level" analysis, problems are likely to be defined in much narrower terms. In Baltimore County and, even more so, in Newport News, officers understandably tended to define problems in terms of a specific housing complex, street, dwelling, business establishment, or even individual.

Given an option, is it preferable to examine a behavioral problem citywide or as it occurs in a more limited area? What is the interrelationship between inquiries initiated at different levels in the organization? Ideally, in an agency fully committed to problem-oriented policing, the inquiries would support each other. Intensive explorations of citywide problems that lead to the design of new responses should benefit all members of a department if the results are communicated effectively. At the other end of the spectrum, a police officer who confronts a problem on his or her beat may be able to deal effectively with the problem—especially if it has a unique local quality—without involving anyone at a higher level. But since the results may be of value to officers in other areas who experience similar problems, one may hope that procedures would be established to share whatever is learned. If the problem is common to many other beats, the officer may properly conclude, depending on the nature of the problem, that any exploration—to be profitable—will require time and resources far beyond those available to the officer. Procedures must be developed to enable officers to nominate such problems for analysis at a higher level in the organization.

Based on experiences to date, one is led to conclude that, if an option exists, problems ought to be explored as close to the operating level as possible, with the results made available to others who experience the same problem. The broader the inquiry, the more it is removed from the context in which the problem exists, the more it appears to be drained of much of the richness and creativity reflected in localized inquiries. If this conclusion holds up, a large police agency would benefit more from sharing the results of three separate inquiries into a common problem than from a citywide inquiry. But realizing such a benefit would depend heavily on correcting the enormous—even embarrassing—gaps that currently exist in the exchange of the most basic information about how the same problems are handled in different units of a large police agency.

WHO IDENTIFIES PROBLEMS?

Although the objective in problem-oriented policing is to focus on problems of concern to the community, it does not follow that one can simply look to the community to somehow send the police a clear message that defines the police agenda. The task of identifying community problems is a tricky business, requiring a careful blend of community initiatives, the willingness and ability of the police to listen, and responsible use of the knowledge and expertise that the police develop.

The Community

Quite naturally, one turns initially to community members. But, as Murphy and Muir note in their study of community-based policing for Canada, several difficulties quickly surface:

> Though various problems may be identified through individual citizen complaints or police committees, etc., these may not represent the most important policing problems in the community, nor be widely shared. Communities often lack the kinds of information necessary to make informed decisions in regards to policing priorities. Perceptions of policing problems tend to reflect personal experience and this may or may not be a reliable indicator of general community concerns (Murphy and Muir, 1984, p. 160).

Murphy and Muir's observations were confirmed in my own observations of community meetings organized by the police for the purpose of identifying community problems (as distinct from meetings called because of intensified concern about a specific, major problem, such as robberies, burglaries, or racial tensions). One is left wondering how much significance can be attached to the concerns expressed, given the factors that influence who attends such meetings. It is not surprising that participants are likely to identify "quality-of-life offenses" as their greatest concerns: streets that are difficult to cross; disorderly youth; disreputable-looking individuals; cars illegally parked in front of their homes; abandoned cars; speeding cars and screeching tires. A commander of one of the most crime-ridden precincts in New York City reported to me that the most common concern of those attending police-initiated meetings with the community was noise. These concerns may accurately reflect the interests of a neighborhood. But they may also reflect a lack of awareness of other things that may be going on. Participants will often ask the police—whom they picture as possessing all kinds of information on their neighborhood—to tell them what the police know and what should be of concern to them. One leaves such meetings with a new awareness that the police benefit by learning that behavior to which they may give a low priority is of much greater concern to the community than they had assumed; that without such meetings, police suffer from a biased view of community concerns because their interactions with the total community are limited. But one also becomes acutely aware that, absent overt indications of a serious crime problem, the responsibility for articulating the need to deal with more serious problems will often fall to the police, since they have the fullest understanding of the magnitude and consequences of such conduct.

However clear members of a community may be in setting out their problems, the police cannot agree in advance that they will focus on the community's choices. Some communities will pressure the police to define as problems conditions or behaviors that are not illegal, with the implication that the police, for example, ought to remove obnoxious individuals from a neighborhood, stop the curb sale of books, or chase street entertainers or gatherings of teenagers. The behavior may well constitute a problem for the community, but the obligation of the police to protect Constitutional rights requires them to make an independent judgment regarding the problem and what can be done about it.

With varied awareness of these pitfalls, police agencies have set out to try to define community concerns. Murphy and Muir describe a rather elaborate process that was used in an experiment by the Royal Canadian Mounted Police in 1983 in which, after an exchange of information and a citizen survey, a dialogue was generated between the police and the community (Murphy and Muir, 1984, p. 162). A less formal method to identify community concerns, depending heavily on door-to-door surveys, has been used as part of the experiments in Baltimore County, New York City, and Houston, with the results subsequently considered along with data collected from other sources.

The most important point that emerges from these efforts is the need for openness. Police must, in the first instance, extend themselves in order to learn about the concerns of the community. (This contact and the expression of interest have benefits far beyond what may be contributed to defining problems.) Their findings must be combined with information from other sources and subjected to careful analysis, but in the process the police must guard against common biases that can result in dismissing or "defining away" matters that are of real concern to the community and appropriately the business of the police.

Police Management

Police management has a larger role in identifying community problems than may be assumed, given the emphasis on the need to listen to the community. The large volume of incidents called to police attention and dutifully recorded enables the police to identify problems long before they become apparent to the community. How the community ranks these problems, of course, is another matter, but one cannot expect them to get any attention if they are not identified in the first instance.

Police management is equipped to summarize the number of crimes occurring in a given area and will often feed this information back to community groups. But because of the dominant orientation toward the handling of incidents, little tradition exists for the police to take the initiative in identifying long-standing and recurring problems. That is why such old problems as spousal abuse, sexual assault, child abuse, and missing children—long known to the police—have only recently been studied, and new responses to them developed. It took groups outside the police to draw attention to them. And except for what is done in the context of traditional crime analysis, police management does not have a system in place whereby, based on continuing analysis of the data it routinely processes, it can flag newly developing problems—whether a common form of behavior, an individual, or a specific location. This explains why, when a particular case gets a great deal of attention, the police often seem somewhat surprised themselves by the results of a media investigation that reveals an extensive prior record of similar behavior attached to the offender or the location. With the benefit of hindsight, one often has the uncomfortable feeling that the incident (e.g., a homicide) that received the publicity was predictable, had some system of monitoring been in effect.

This failure of police management has been highlighted in recent studies that draw attention to the small percentage of all the addresses to which the police are summoned that account for a high percentage of all calls for police assistance. Sherman found that 48.8 percent of all of the calls made to the Minneapolis Police Department in a year were generated from just 5 percent of the locations from which all calls were received (Sherman, 1987; see also Pierce, Spaar, and Briggs, 1984). Computers now commonly used for processing such data make scanning for potential problems of this sort a simple procedure.

Eck and Spelman identified 16 potential sources to which both police management and rank and file can turn for information in identifying problems (Eck and Spelman, 1987, p. 46). Among them, in addition to the data on calls for service, are crime analysis, letters of complaint, elected officials, business groups, neighborhood organizations, and the various units within the police department that have specialized responsibilities. After police acquire more experience in identifying problems, less obvious sources probably will emerge as important, such as claims filed with insurance companies, fluctuations in the market value of property, cases treated in emergency rooms, experience in the supervision of individuals on probation and parole, and the insights of social and other agencies (e.g., the schools) having responsibility for problems that are also of concern to the police (such as runaways, the homeless, sexual assault, the mentally ill, the poor, and truancy).

If a police department's management were strongly committed to reducing the problems it must handle, it might operate like an insurance company that, for monetary reasons, is constantly working to reduce its losses. It would have the equivalent of the researchers who study the conditions that contribute to insurance claims and the underwriters who constantly review clients. The underwriter located at the headquarters of an automobile insurance company, with access to several sources of data about accidents and traffic convictions, initiates warnings to clients and may even cancel an insurance policy. Although police managers do not have equivalent power, they must nevertheless develop methods whereby, using data readily available to them, they can alert operating personnel or the community or both, depending on the nature of the problem, to situations that should be evaluated. Such evaluation may eliminate cause for concern, or it may lead to the identification of a problem that begs for attention.

Rank-and-File Officers

As mentioned earlier, police officers on the beat—especially if they are permanently assigned to an area—are in the best position to identify problems from the bottom up. They rarely do so because the system simply does not expect it of them. That is what makes some of the community-oriented policing programs unique. Officers operating in this mode are expected, as an integral part of their function, to be alert to recurring problems and to attempt to deal with them. In New York City, the community patrol officer (CPO) is

> expected to be the Police Department's planner and problem-solver on the beat level. Theoretically, this is the most distinctive feature of the role because it is through this planning and problem-solving behavior of the CPO that the Department will develop effective strategies for ameliorating the community's most pressing problems, and will coordinate the police, citizen and other public and private resources directed at those problems (Vera Institute of Justice, 1987, p. 4).

The potential role of the rank-and-file officer in identifying problems, and how this relates to focusing on the concerns of the community, is illustrated in these quotations from a lead officer in the Community Mobilization Project in Los Angeles:

> People were not necessarily concerned with what our department's mainly concerned about, robberies, burglaries, theft of motor vehicles. . . . What they were concerned about was a group of winos that they'd been calling about for years and years that are loitering on this corner down here, the prostitutes along Washington Boulevard, the graffiti on the walls that's getting worse and worse, day after day after day, that no one is doing anything about. . . . Before a radio car would pass by, yell "Hey guys, get out of here," two minutes worth of work and they're on their way to the next five calls they're holding (Kennedy, 1986, p. 16).

The Newport News experiment made effective use of its project task force, consisting of officers drawn from the field as well as managers of different ranks, to identify the first two major problems that were studied. Subsequently, the responsibility for identifying problems was assigned to all members of the department, consistent with the primary objective of the effort, which was to spread problem-oriented policing throughout the department. Officers varied in their willingness to assume the responsibility. (For a description of some of the factors that influenced the officers' responses, see Eck and Spelman et al., 1987, pp. 43–47.) Those who became involved indicated that their personal experience was the most common source for identifying problems. In the New York City project, success in identifying and dealing with problems was found to be more a result of the officer's personal ability than the training that was provided. Recognizing the radical nature of the change in orientation required for a police officer to focus on problems, the project monitors sought to strengthen the capacity of *all* community patrol officers to identify and subsequently deal with problems (Vera Institute of Justice, 1987).

The potential benefit to be realized if rank-and-file officers are oriented not only to identify problems, but to take the first steps to see that something is done about them, is enormous. Consider, for example, this illustration involving a relatively traditional crime problem that should have been picked up by procedures already in place for identifying crime patterns as part of routine crime analysis:

> A neighborhood patrol officer responded to a call from a citizen who reported that thieves had just removed a hot water heater from a vacant single-residence home across the street. A sign on the home indicated that it was owned by HUD (Housing and Urban Development)—a federal agency that makes low-cost mortgages available to certain eligible citizens. The citizen

who summoned the police, having an interest in the neighborhood, told the officer that the home had just been listed for sale in the newspaper that morning for the first time. The citizen wondered if the thieves were simply using new listings of HUD-owned homes, all of which would be vacant after they were repossessed because of default on mortgage payments, as targets for their thefts. The officer, at this point, had two options. He could simply report, in the required manner, still another theft from a vacant home—not an unusual occurrence in that community—and end his handling of the case. That was all that was expected of him. Or he could alert someone at a higher level in the organization to the need to review theft-from-residence reports and to contact HUD representatives to determine if theft from vacant homes in their custody was a problem. And if so, he could suggest that, among other things, they carefully review the manner in which homes in their possession are advertised for sale, and what relationship this might have to the incidence of theft. The officer followed the second alternative, but did so by including the recommendation in his report on the case—a method of communicating a message in a police agency that is not likely to bring results.

Clearly, from the limited observations that have been recorded or actually made in the field, whether officers identify a problem for attention will depend not only on whether they have developed "antennae" for doing so, but also on whether their actions will be viewed positively by their peers and supervisor. It follows that increasing their involvement in identifying problems hinges on creating an environment within the organization that is supportive of problem-oriented policing. With such support, the process can work in reverse as well; i.e., the identification of a problem by a central unit may lead to development of a new response by the operating unit.

In Baltimore County, the COPE unit was alerted by traditional crime analysis to a change in the pattern of auto theft. After years in which theft of vehicles for sale and for their parts had eclipsed joyriding by teenagers (entailing the theft, use, and eventual abandonment of the car), the crime analysis unit noted a new pattern in which youths as young as 12 years of age played a game in which they set out to see who could steal the best car. Upon locating a vehicle, they popped the door open with a "slim jim" or a "dent puller." Already conditioned to think in terms of nontraditional responses, the COPE unit established that the two tools could be purchased at any auto-parts or hardware store for as low as $6.48. Only one store—other than locksmiths—limited sales to those over 21. Convinced that the easy accessibility of the tools facilitated the activity among these particular youths, COPE initiated a study to determine the feasibility of restricting the sale of the tools to persons over 21 or to those engaged in auto repair, and to determine the feasibility of including the tools among those classified as burglary tools under Maryland statutes.

REDEFINING PROBLEMS AFTER PRELIMINARY INQUIRY

It is inherent in the nature of the inquiry process—actually one of its major values—that analysis of a problem often leads to redefinition of the problem. This is illustrated in two ambitious, top-level studies conducted in Madison, Wisconsin.

> The first problem was initially defined broadly in behavioral terms as sexual assault. And the initial commitment was to examining the problem as it existed in the city as a whole. It was expected that, as the study proceeded, the different forms of sexual assault would be separated out for analysis. But early investigation revealed that the primary reason for the problem being selected for analysis—widespread fear—stemmed from the most violent assaults that had been committed. These were few in number. It was also learned at an early stage that the offenders in these cases had previously been convicted of sexual assaults and were on probation or parole at the time they committed their latest offense. The number of convicted sexual offenders under supervision in the county was found to be five times greater than the number convicted in the county. This revealed that ex-offenders from outside the city had been attracted to living in the city for a variety of reasons. The analysis thus led gradually to redefining the problem in terms of the class of individuals involved—sexual offenders under supervision in the community. At that point, attention was shifted to examining the total community's response to these offenders and the dangers they pose.

> Initially, the second problem was defined as shoplifting. Those making the inquiry had what they thought was a clear notion of the type of behavior that was of concern—the removal of merchandise from stores without paying for it. But early data revealed that a large percentage of the individuals who had been categorized as shoplifters were taking items into their possession within the store, removing price tags, and then, without leaving the store, presenting the items to a clerk as if they were returning purchased merchandise, requesting a refund. In some stores, attempts to defraud the merchant in this fashion outnumbered the instances of actual shoplifting. Thus an entirely different problem, which called for a separate analysis, surfaced alongside the study of shoplifting. Inquiry thus led eventually to explorations of new types of responses that had no relation to the more narrowly defined shoplifting problem.

Although their inquiries must, of necessity, be much less penetrating, officers assigned to exploring problems at the operating level similarly find that their early inquiries frequently lead to redefinition of the problem. When first selected for attention in Newport News, the New Briarfield problem was described as residential burglary—namely, theft of television sets and food stamps from residents of a low-income housing project. That is the way it had been perceived by the police for years. A few weeks into the inquiry, the real problem was seen as the exploitation of the rental units by absentee owners, resulting in intolerable conditions that constituted violations of law of a far more serious nature than the petty thefts that had previously drawn police attention to the apartment complex. Likewise, in Baltimore County, threshold inquiry into a complaint of a burglary problem in a well-maintained housing project made it clear that the real problem was that the elderly, long-established residents feared the teenagers who had moved into the complex. Based on stereotypes, the elderly expected the youths to be noisy, larcenous, and violent. The number of burglaries was insignificant.

The likelihood that a problem would be redefined after a preliminary inquiry became so common in the COPE project in Baltimore County that the project managers incorporated a formal step into their procedures so that officers are now required, after initial inquiry, to "rediagnose" the problem on which they are working. Thus, for example, a problem initially defined in terms of an intersection at which loud, disorderly youngsters were perceived by the elderly residents as using drugs and alcohol was redefined as a conflict in the use of public space. Unusual as such language is in the world of policing, the more precise description of the problem reflected a more accurate understanding and was therefore important as a basis for constructing an effective solution.

SELECTING FROM AMONG PROBLEMS

Given the lack of systematic attention to substantive problems over the years, the most likely situation—whether at the top of a police organization or on the beat—is that far more problems will be identified than can be explored adequately.

At the highest levels in an organization, where the larger, citywide problems are most likely to be examined, some setting of priorities will be required because staffing, under the best of circumstances, is bound to be limited. Moreover, the broader the inquiry, the greater the need to allow time for the careful collection and analysis of data. A single study might require six months or a year, depending on the size of the jurisdiction and the level of staffing. What should get highest priority?

At the other extreme, on the beat, officers may be presented with a wide range of problems that vary in both magnitude and complexity. Officers have fewer resources, and implementation of a new response may place new demands on them. How do they decide what should get their attention? Some general factors are beginning to emerge as important considerations in making such judgments:

- The impact of the problem on the community—its size and costs
- The presence of any life-threatening conditions
- Community interest and the degree of support likely to exist for both the inquiry and subsequent recommendations

• The potential threat to Constitutional rights—as may occur, for example, when citizens take steps to limit the use of the public way, limit access to public facilities, or curtail freedom of speech and assembly

• The degree to which the problem adversely affects relationships between the police and the community

• The interest of rank-and-file officers in the problem and the degree of support for addressing it

• The concreteness of the problem, given the frustration associated with exploring vague, amorphous complaints

• The potential that exploration is likely to lead to some progress in dealing with the problem.

The appropriateness of several of the latter considerations, because they appear to be rather pragmatic, may be questionable. But so long as the police do not limit themselves to dealing with easily solvable problems, it is reasonable, for example, to consider the likelihood of improving a situation as a factor in favor of getting involved. That is not only natural, it also can increase the number of problems that are handled—and handled effectively. Likewise, as long as one does not lose sight of the commitment to dealing with the problems of the community rather than those of the police, considering police interest in the problem is appropriate, since it usually stems from a frustrated need to handle a recurring situation. Thus, for example, a department-wide exploration of the problem of noise gained momentum because rank-and-file officers were frustrated by their inability to deal with the problem, by the extraordinarily high volume of complaints about noise that they received during their busiest periods, and by the amount of paperwork the calls required.

How does one square the importance attached here to preexistence of public interest in a problem and previous urging that police take the initiative in bringing otherwise dormant or hidden problems to public attention? Much depends on the nature of the specific problem. It was the police in Newport News who focused public attention on the problems created by absentee ownership of the New Briarfield housing complex. Happily, their initiative was well received by city government officials and by the community. But the police may not always be successful in engaging the interest of either their own personnel or the community, in which case the potential for implementing a new response—if it requires efforts outside the police department—may be severely limited. That does not mean that the effort was wasted. The time simply may not be ripe. Overall change in policing, as noted previously, is often possible only if linked to a crisis. This applies in the handling of specific problems as well. A critical incident related to the problem may be the catalyst that creates needed support.

In the Madison project, for example, the recommendations that emanated from the study of sexual assault were hurriedly implemented because, near the end of the study, a 10-year-old girl was sexually assaulted and murdered by a man who fit the pattern of offenders on whom the study had focused, i.e., persons previously convicted of sexual assault who were on probation or parole in the community. In Newport News, a study initiated by a police officer of the problems associated with abandoned structures led to a series of recommendations that were shelved until a newly elected official gave high priority to the problem. A police request to solve a serious traffic hazard by changing the location of a school bus stop was ignored until a local television station publicized the hazard.

If forced to choose from among equally serious problems that warrant attention, it is appropriate to consider the "ripeness" of the problem. Clearly, the greater the degree of concern, the more likely will be support for the results of the inquiry. Pragmatic as this is, however, giving priority to problems of more current and intense concern should be balanced with the previously mentioned need to address less visible problems of equal magnitude and seriousness, lest the process deteriorate so that the police are once again assuming a reactive stance.

CHAPTER 7

ANALYZING PROBLEMS

Gainesville, Florida, experienced a sudden increase in convenience store robberies in the spring of 1985. In a project that was independent of any commitment to problem-oriented policing, the Gainesville police, going far beyond traditional crime analysis, conducted an in-depth study of the problem as it had developed in Gainesville and searched the country for knowledge about the problem and strategies for dealing with it. Their detailed analysis of the robberies in Gainesville focused their attention on the different experiences of the stores, depending on whether they had one or two clerks on duty. It was concluded that stores staffed with only one clerk during the night hours were unusually vulnerable to robbery. Confronted with different conclusions by the management of one of the major chains, the department arranged for an independent study by a university-based psychologist that called for interviews with 65 persons serving time in state institutions for having robbed convenience stores; interviews with 24 individuals who had been the victims in convenience store robberies; and an evaluation of the layout and structure of the stores. The independent study confirmed the police conclusion that the presence of two clerks was the primary factor in deterring convenience store robberies in Gainesville. The nationwide inquiries about the problem and strategies for dealing with it had led the police to several communities that had enacted ordinances designed to reduce robberies in convenience stores. With these precedents and their local data, the

Gainesville police proposed a local regulation to their city council, including a requirement that two clerks be on duty during specified periods of time. The council approved the police proposal. The minimum staffing requirement was challenged in the courts but upheld as an appropriate exercise of local government authority to increase public safety, in large measure because of the persuasive data the police had carefully collected and analyzed. In the period immediately following adoption of the ordinance, convenience store robberies are reported to have dropped by 65 percent (Clifton, 1987). Predictably, the long-range impact has been challenged by various interest groups, and efforts to respond definitively to the challenges reflect the difficulty in isolating the effect of any single change.

In a contrasting example, a sergeant in Philadelphia was introduced to the concept of problem-oriented policing. Shortly after being reassigned to a new district, he became aware that officers were being dispatched to a bar several times a day to answer a complaint of loud noise. Responding together with his officers, he found that there was no loud music and no disorderliness. It was a relatively quiet neighborhood bar, whose owner was anxious to cooperate with the police. The complaint was always categorized as unfounded. Upon inquiry, the sergeant established that police had been dispatched to the address 505 times in six months. Asked for the source of the complaints, the sergeant was told by central communications that this was not the type of call on which the name of the complainant was routinely recorded. Upon request, call-takers subsequently identified the complainant who apparently was responsible for all of the calls that had been made. The sergeant then approached the complainant with an offer to help deal with her concerns. Studies with a decibel meter established that the level of noise was not a violation of the noise control ordinance. Apparently it was not just the noise, but the vibrations created by the jukebox speakers, which were attached to a common wall, that was the source of her irritation. Arrangements were made to move the speakers to an inside wall and for the parties to communicate with each other directly. The complainant is pleased, and the calls to the police have stopped (Bugg, 1988).

These two cases are classic examples of what is involved in problem-oriented policing: in the identification of problems, their analysis, and the development of an effective response. They are described here because they illustrate so well, in sharply different circumstances, the importance of in-depth inquiry before deciding on a course of action. The first case is an excellent example of "top-level" analysis of a citywide problem. The second is an equally good example of "street-level" analysis of a local problem, involving just two addresses and two citizens. Yet despite the enormous difference in the nature of the problems, the process for solving them reflects some common steps. This chapter explores these steps—the various ways in which problems (both big and small) can be analyzed—and examines some of the issues and difficulties that arise in such analysis.

TYPES OF INFORMATION TO BE ACQUIRED

Once a problem has been defined in a tentative way, the obvious first step in analysis is to determine what information is needed. This should be a broad inquiry, uninhibited by past perspectives; questions should be asked whether or not answers can be obtained. The openness and persistent probing associated with such an inquiry are not unlike the approach that a seasoned and highly regarded detective would take to solve a puzzling crime: reaching out in all directions, digging deeply, asking the right questions.

Invited to participate in such an exercise, groups of experienced police personnel will pose a wide range of appropriate questions. They will also quickly acknowledge that, except for some hunches, they usually do not have the answers to the questions they pose. Here, by way of example, is a list of some of the questions that the police in one jurisdiction asked in order to examine critically their citywide response to theft from vehicles left in parking facilities.

- What was the reported incidence of such thefts?
- What is the total magnitude of the problem? Do such thefts often go unreported? Are there factors that encourage reporting (e.g., a police report is needed for an insurance claim) or that discourage reporting (e.g., losses are immediately reimbursed by employers without filing a police report)? What can be done to obtain a full picture of the problem?
- What is known, based on traditional crime analysis, about the reported offenses (i.e., location, time, type of vehicle [make, model, year], registration, form of entry, items stolen [car parts, such as radio, or contents])?
- What is the correlation between incidence of reported thefts and specific circumstances in the parking facility (i.e., lighting, paving, fencing, access, attendants, visibility from the street)?
- What are the contractual arrangements for parking? Who owns the parking facilities? Does the experience in public and private facilities differ significantly? What are the responsibilities of management relating to thefts?
- What happens to the stolen items?
- What are the characteristics of those who have been apprehended for theft from vehicles (i.e., age, other criminal involvement, past record, residence)?

• What has been the experience in prosecuting those who have been arrested and charged?

• How are parking facilities affected by zoning or building-code requirements? Are these enforced? Are the facilities regulated in other ways?

• Do parking facilities create problems that are called to the attention of other city departments?

• To what degree are losses compensated through insurance? Is proof of the value of loss required? Is there any concern about fraudulent claims? Do claimants have different experiences with different insurance companies?

• How do insurance companies view the theft problem? What data do they have that might supplement the material in police files?

• What interest, if any, do nearby merchants, residents, or employers have in the theft problem?

• What steps, if any, have parking facility owners and car owners taken to deter theft (e.g., cameras, private security patrols)? What have been the results? Are car owners alerted to the theft problem?

• How do those who commit thefts choose their targets? What factors do they consider in selecting facilities and cars?

• What responsibility, if any, do the police have to patrol private parking facilities? What is the perceived value of patrol?

• What is the extent of the typical investigation when a report of a theft from a vehicle is received?

• What use, if any, has been made of special surveillance in attempting to apprehend offenders? With what effect?

• To what degree is car theft associated with drug use or sale?

• What arrangements do probation and parole agents have for monitoring the activities of individuals currently under their supervision who were convicted of theft from vehicles?

• How does the problem of theft from vehicles in this city compare with the problem elsewhere? What has been discovered in studies that have been made of the problem elsewhere? How have other police agencies responded to the problem?

The range of questions that an operating unit or a beat officer would raise in analyzing a more narrowly defined problem, such as misconduct in a specific park, would obviously be more limited, but would nevertheless reflect the type of queries in the broader inquiry.

Faced with the need to guide a large number of operating personnel through this questioning process, the Newport News project gave some structure to it by developing a comprehensive "problem analysis guide" (Eck and Spelman et al., 1987, pp. 53–64; for the guide itself, see pp. 115–122). Drawing on prior work in Kansas City (Kansas City, Missouri,

Police Department, 1974) and in England (Ramsay, 1982; Clarke, 1983; and especially Poyner, 1980, 1983), the guide listed all possible avenues of inquiry—many more than any officer or group of officers would find relevant to a specific problem. It organized the possible lines of inquiry under three major categories: (1) queries about the actors involved in the problem, which include victims, offenders, and "third parties," such as witnesses; (2) queries about the incidents that compose the problem, including questions about the sequence of events, the social and physical context of the events, and the immediate effect of the incidents; and (3) queries about the responses to the problem by the community and its institutions. The guide not only provided officers the means to ensure that their own inquiries were sufficiently broad, it also communicated the problem-oriented concept, and it shared with all officers the collective experience of the first officers involved in the experiment.

SOURCES OF INFORMATION

Where does one turn for the desired information? This stage is well served by a healthy curiosity, a high level of creativity and imagination, and a broad, open perspective. It requires a readiness to reach well beyond traditional sources. Enterprising officers and researchers have uncovered extraordinarily rich sources of very relevant information. Yet, as anyone who has taken the most elementary course in research methods knows, the collection and use of data can be a tricky business. Without appropriate checks for validity and reliability, one can easily be misled. That is why this section on identifying sources of information is followed immediately by a discussion of the cautions that must be exercised.

Academics usually start a research project with a search of the *relevant literature*. Police consider this an odd starting point, because few of the problems on which the police are likely to focus have been researched in ways that are useful to the police. This is especially true regarding the concerns of officers on the street. But skipping over this step may result in duplicating work that has already been done elsewhere. If relevant studies are available, they may provide a quick way to acquire needed background and ideas on how best to analyze a problem. Some studies (such as Reppetto's study of residential crime [1974], Cohen's study of prostitution [1980], Scarr's study of patterns of burglary [1973], and Humphreys's study of solicitation by homosexuals in public places [1975]) would be extraordinarily helpful to those setting out to examine these problems locally for the first time. As we note in Chapter 9, a new generation of studies that explore problems with a specific concern for the police role in dealing with them is becoming available (e.g., Loving on spousal abuse [1980]; Murphy on the mentally disabled [1986]; Karchmer on arson [1985]; and Finn and Sullivan on special populations [1987]). The English police, especially, seem to have an increasing number of "problem-specific" publications available to them, usually the result of research sponsored by the Home Office (e.g., Zeisel [1976] and Stone and Taylor [1977] on vandalism in schools; Clarke on vandalism [1980b]; and Maguire [1982] and Winchester and Jackson [1982] on burglary of dwellings).

The study of the drinking driver in Madison drew heavily on the massive literature on that problem. More localized information also may turn up in a literature search. The study of Asian gangs in London, for example, was greatly advanced by the discovery of a publication on the Asian school population in Southall (Hoare, Stewart, and Purcell, 1984, sec. 5.3). Limited time should be invested in searching the literature, however, since much of it is not relevant, and many of the inquiries on which reports have been published are based on data less valid than the data that can be acquired through a local inquiry.

Most police agencies do not have easy access to whatever literature is available on substantive problems. The most valuable publications are often not widely distributed; local libraries rarely have them. Police agencies have access to the large collection of the National Criminal Justice Reference Service, operated by the U.S. Department of Justice, but the value of this service is heavily dependent on the preciseness of the inquiry and the capacity of its computerized systems to select the literature that is most directly responsive. Despite the lack of easy access, enterprising officers who get involved in the study of a problem do a surprisingly good job of acquiring key studies; and these, in turn, through their references and citations, lead to other relevant works and informed individuals. Ways in which these resources can be made more readily available, especially through newly established computer information networks, are described in Chapter 9.

A vast amount of data about the incidents that the police handle are stored in *police files,* but these data are rarely tapped for the insights they might provide. Acquired as a result of the reporting requirements imposed on all officers, these reports currently are used for a variety of purposes: to maintain a record of a continuing investigation; to provide a basis for a prosecution; to communicate information from one unit of a department to another; to record the police action should subsequent questions arise; and to account for the way officers spend their time. Because the purposes for which the reports are prepared determine the way in which the data are collected and stored, they may be of limited value for research about some substantive problems, and the reports themselves may be difficult to use. Nevertheless, reviewing a mass of reports on, for example, sexual assault, theft from autos, or noise has proved to be an effective way to quickly acquire a feel for the similarities among cases, the range of complex circumstances that distinguish them, and the difficulties the police face in handling them. Such a review also alerts the researcher to the limitations of the reports.

Tapping police files is also a logical starting point in analysis of a street-level problem, for example, a problem defined in terms of a specific address. Whether a comprehensive picture of the problem can be obtained from this one source will depend on the nature of the incidents contributing to the problem. Continuing use of police data for analysis of substantive problems ultimately should change the way in which such data are collected and stored so that the information needs of officers on the street are better served (see Spelman, 1987 and Chapter 9).

Like a review of police reports, tapping the knowledge of *rank-and-file police officers* is an excellent way to begin to explore a problem. Asked to reflect on the hundreds of cases they handle, they will typically pour out a mix of hard facts, rich insights, and strong opinion. Given the biases that develop in routinely handling similar incidents and the absence of any expectation that police will acquire a full picture of a problem, their views require careful follow-up and independent verification, as discussed later in this chapter. But this need for follow-up does not diminish the enormity of their contribution.

Victims are among the major "consumers" of police service. They have a special kind of knowledge about the problem that made them victims. Reinterviews of those who suffered losses while shopping on Oxford Street in London was the principal means by which a comprehensive understanding of this problem was acquired by the Metropolitan Police. (Significantly, this reinterviewing was done after it was concluded that "the whole system for recording crime is not geared to revealing information to penetrate what is really going on" [Metropolitan Police, 1984, p. 7].) Since much of policing is aimed at minimizing the suffering of victims, the police can use this source not only to further their inquiry, but also to gain a better understanding of the needs of victims. Such understanding is vital to formulating a police response to them and should also help reach victims who currently do not turn to the police. Feedback from victims about the way in which they were treated by the police can alert officers to relatively simple ways in which they can improve the quality of their service. Had this been done some time ago for victims of sexual assault, the police would have learned to handle such cases with the sensitivity they require and thereby avoided the strong criticism of recent years.

The larger *community,* so important in the initial identification of problems, is obviously a rich source of further information. Door-to-door surveys have been used to learn about the specific nature of a problem from those citizens who are directly affected. These responses are helpful in better focusing an inquiry, and they provide leads that can be pursued through other ministudies. If citizens are merely passing on rumors, dealing with these misunderstandings may be the most effective way in which the police can respond to the perceived problem.

In exploring a problem, we tend to examine it from numerous perspectives before even considering—if ever we do—making direct inquiries of *those who appear to be causing the problem.* The adversarial relationship obviously gets in the way, as does police skepticism about any contribution that the alleged wrongdoers can make. Yet convicted offenders and others who appear to be contributing most directly to a problem are potentially the best source of information about that problem—just as a person involved in crime may be a valuable informant. A relaxed approach, outside an adversarial context (e.g., after conviction) and with assurances that there will be no negative consequences, has demonstrated that such individuals can often provide unique insights to the police. The Newport News study gained valuable information from prostitutes and those who had been convicted of theft from automobiles. The Madison study learned much from a questionnaire administered to those who had been convicted of drunk driving and were attending, as part of their sentence, an educational program. And the Gainesville (Florida) study used interviews with convicted robbers of convenience stores to rank the factors they considered in selecting their targets.

Information that will enable the police to better understand a problem is often readily available, merely for the asking, from *other agencies.* These agencies may be dealing with the same problem, or it may be part of their regular function to record the relevant data. Often the desired information is collected, but not compiled in ways that are useful to the police. If the data are stored in computer files, it may be relatively easy to extract the desired information. Thus, in the Madison study of drinking drivers, arrangements were made for the state agency that maintains records on all traffic accidents to write a computer program that extracted needed data, and similar arrangements were made with the courts for information on what happened to cases that went to trial. Obviously not all records are open to the police. Where analysis of a problem would be greatly aided by data that are confidential, however, it may be possible to use aggregated data, not traceable to individuals.

Other agencies have been very helpful to the police. Inquiring officers are often amazed at how easy it is to obtain specific, reliable information that sheds much light on a problem (e.g., demographic data about a specific neighborhood; detailed information from the records of prosecutors, the courts, and corrections officials on the processing of criminal cases;

data on ownership and sale of buildings, building-code violations, and claims for losses made to insurance companies). In the Community Patrol Officer Program (CPOP) in New York City, officers find that a good initial source is the staff of the Community Planning Boards—created to facilitate citizen participation in government and to monitor and coordinate city services in each of the 59 areas into which the city has been divided for these purposes.

While it is, of course, important to study a problem in the local context, it would be foolish to ignore what has been learned about the same general problem in *other communities*. The problem may be so common that many communities have addressed it. Such an inquiry was of great benefit to the Gainesville study cited earlier. When the problem stems from some peculiar characteristic of the community, the potential value of such inquiries can be increased by directing them to communities with a similar characteristic (whether a port city, a college community, an airline hub, or a city having similar industries or demographics).

Information is often collected within a police agency about a particular problem, but it is not shared or stored in a way that facilitates retrieval. With rapid changes in key personnel and the absence of an "institutional memory," such material is lost. This is especially true in large city police agencies, where work done in one unit or area is not known in another. Some studies have benefited from an intense effort to search *department archives* to locate ad hoc studies of this nature, or even by retrieving a personal copy of a study from an individual identified by word of mouth as having been primarily responsible for it.

RIGOR OF THE INQUIRY

Given the need to interest police in acquiring information, one risks dampening their enthusiasm by lengthy cautions about the need to evaluate the information they obtain. But information is of little value unless it is collected objectively, with a strong commitment to preciseness and accuracy so that the validity of the facts is ensured. (For an especially helpful discussion of research methods as applied in policing, see Eck, 1984.) The requirements of rigorous inquiry may seem burdensome, but should not be foreign to the police, for when the police bring criminal prosecutions, they are held to a standard of proof that is arguably higher than that used in social science research—proof beyond a reasonable doubt. They know, in that context, what is required to establish "the facts." And they know, too, how a lack of preciseness and accuracy can mislead an investigation. Drawing on this analogy, many police officers will view the task as a challenge, like "getting the facts" in a difficult criminal investigation.

Several factors account for the importance of assessing the quality of the information that is acquired. All in-house research—in every organization—is suspect as self-serving. An understandable pressure exists to use inquiries to confirm preconceived notions and to gloss over findings that raise questions about the credibility and competence of key personnel. Furthermore, police are reluctant to acknowledge that their capacity to deal with a problem is more limited than is generally assumed (Weatheritt, 1986, p. 123). In the Madison study, for example, there was some reluctance to accept the finding that the police were severely limited in their capacity to arrest drunk drivers. The finding contradicted the message that the police had sought to reinforce over the years: "Drunk drivers go to jail" (Goldstein and Susmilch, 1982a, pp. 138–141).

Police, moreover, are generally assumed not to have the skills required to research a problem carefully and objectively. Weatheritt, in her study of police innovations in England, comments on the difficulty of conducting research on substantive problems within a police agency:

> One obstacle is the lack of analytical skills within forces and the low status that such skills often have. If this lack is to be remedied, forces will have to attract or identify the right people, train them properly, and provide them with the organizational backing they need. Even apparently simple problems can pose considerable analytical difficulties; indeed, identifying the precise nature of the problem—an essential first step—may itself be half the battle (Weatheritt, 1986, p. 122).

Distorted, unschooled use of data by police administrators in the past has led to a widespread tendency to dismiss facts presented by the police as potentially biased and intended to support some deeply embedded police "value." Too often their use leads to the comment, "What else would you expect from the police?"

Greater care in conducting research on substantive problems—at whatever level inquiry is made in the police organization—does not mean that the studies will become overly complex. Several "top-level analyses" of large problems, conducted with varying degrees of outside involvement, concluded that sound, defensible results could be obtained using relatively simple research designs (Metropolitan Police, 1984, p. 8; Goldstein and Susmilch, 1982c, pp. 14–54). A Home Office study of drinking and disorder in the center of a city in northeast England included this comment:

> One of the purposes of this study was to illustrate a method of inquiry which could be adopted relatively easily by people at the local level. The data used . . . are fairly easy to assemble, and no particularly complex analyses have been employed in looking at patterns. . . . The other main methods of data collection—observation and informal interviews—are even simpler. There are, of

> course, many pitfalls to trap the unwary in the conduct of social research, but the sources of data and methods of presentation do not require resources which are beyond the police or local authority departments, who will often have staff with at least elementary research and statistical skills (Hope, 1985, p. 58).

Several specific considerations will affect the choice of research methods:

- Severe constraints on time and cost. Police agencies do not have the resources to conduct lengthy studies. Furthermore, problems and the environment affecting them (e.g., the law) can change rapidly, with the potential that prolonged inquiries may become irrelevant.
- Uncertainties at the outset about the kind of data and knowledge required to formulate effective strategies. One starts with questions and seeks data to answer them (as distinct from starting with a set of data and answering questions put to the data). Sufficient flexibility must be maintained to develop the study as it moves along.
- The emphasis on gaining insights that will contribute to improving the quality of police service. This requires resisting the temptation to explore intriguing and perhaps intellectually stimulating issues of a more theoretical nature.
- The aversion of the police—like most others—to long reports and to quantitative data. If the results of the effort are to be useful, they must be communicated clearly and concisely.

Meeting these needs requires modifications in accepted social science methods, with some possible sacrifice in the rigor of the research. The Madison studies experimented with an "eclectic approach," adapting a variety of different methods to explore diverse lines of inquiry. In each inquiry, it was uncertain whether an accurate picture could be captured, given the time and resources available. To discover a new pocket of data, a new twist in understanding the problem, or a conflict with an earlier finding was unnerving. But when the findings were put together and the conflicts were resolved, the conclusions could be reported with a high degree of confidence (Goldstein and Susmilch, 1982c, p. 49).

The difficulties in ensuring quality research are increased greatly at the operating level in a police agency. No one really expects an officer exploring a problem on his or her beat to use research methodology. But one can hope that the officer will be sensitive to the need to guard against the distortions, biases, and prejudices that research methods are designed to avoid. The monitoring systems established in Newport News and in Baltimore County, which subjected the inquiries of officers to review by supervisors and by panels of peers, some of whom had training in research, helped in this quest for objectivity.

CAUTIONS IN THE USE OF DATA FROM POLICE FILES

The police will naturally tend to turn first to the information filed within their agency. Rank-and-file officers are accustomed to using department record systems in an unquestioning manner for information needed in the daily operations of a police agency (e.g., Does this person have a record of convictions? Is this car stolen? What property was taken in this burglary?).

Use of these same files to research problems has several limitations. The data in them cover only that portion of the problem that comes to police attention. The files do not describe a total problem as it exists in the community. Of perhaps even greater importance, the description of the problem that can be developed from police files may be seriously distorted because of the factors that lead to police involvement.

- A study of domestic violence based on calls made to the police may make it appear that domestic violence is a problem of the poor, ignoring the fact that many such calls come from neighbors who are disturbed because they live in close proximity to the dispute. Domestic violence occurring in detached dwellings, common to more affluent areas, is not as likely to involve the police.
- An analysis of the victims of sexual assault is likely to show a high incidence of young victims, because younger women are under greater pressure from parents and other guardians to report such offenses.
- An analysis of persons arrested for drunk driving does not describe the drunk driver in the community. It says more about the criteria employed by the police in deciding who should be arrested.
- Any study of the characteristics of offenders is obviously of limited value—based as it must be on those reported crimes in which the offender was identified. Were knowledge available about the unreported offender and the unidentified offender, an entirely different view of the problem might emerge.

One has to look to other sources for supplementary data to obtain a more comprehensive picture of the problem. Thus, for example, a much more accurate picture has been acquired of the drinking-driver problem (both the incidence and the characteristics of offenders) through testing of drivers stopped at roadblocks than through analysis of arrests.

Essential parts of a problem may be lost because of the traditional ways in which information is stored by the police. The most severe cases of sexual assault, for example, may not show up in the files of sexual assaults because they involved more serious offenses as well and are therefore classified as homicide or attempted homicide. Any attempt to examine the past behavior of an individual by tracing his or her criminal history may be thwarted because the record contains only the criminal charge on which the individual was convicted, which is often a reduced charge resulting from a plea bargain. A study of sexual offenders in some jurisdictions could lead the unaware to the conclusion that sexual crimes are preceded by a pattern of trespassing, when in fact the charges of trespassing may be indicative of prior sexual assaults that could not be easily proved.

Police reports—and the data they record—are understandably greatly influenced by the use that is normally made of them. When an arrest is made, the police want their reports to include all the information that will support the arrest. They also want their reports to convince the reader that they acted reasonably and within their legal authority. This may result in a rational format being imposed on a less than rational event. Description of a problem based on such reports could be distorted.

Despite their limitations, police reports are vital—and often very helpful—to an inquiry. A well-prepared police report gives the reader a good sense of the many dimensions of a problem—the character of the people involved, the atmosphere in which it occurred, the motivations of the actors, and the intensity of the interactions. These extremely important factors do not easily fit into forced coding schemes. Thus, for defining the nature of problems, there is no substitute for a careful reading of the reports. Computer-generated data are of limited value for this purpose.

Valuable as police reports are, they are not enough. In the report on the study of thefts from shoppers in London, the authors note: "Clearly much crime sheet data and property lost reports are useful, but a research method is required which leads to a more open method of recording in order to more accurately represent the events surrounding the theft or loss" (Metropolitan Police, 1984, p. 7). A high-ranking officer in the Metropolitan Police, after completing a study of street mugging in his area, reported with a sense of disbelief that the information most crucial to his study was simply not recorded in the voluminous reports that the police routinely file and habitually criticize as unnecessarily burdensome.

Needed data may be recorded but may not be easily retrievable. Although major advances have been made in the use of computers in police work, they have been designed primarily to feed the traditional interests of managers. Thus, they provide details about calls handled per shift or citations issued per officer and about the average time taken on a call. In contrast, officers working in relatively "modern" police agencies who recently studied two common problems—noise and thefts from vehicles—had to scan the daily logs of their respective departments to locate the incidents included in the scope of their studies, and hand-tally the data they needed. This is all the more remarkable, given the ultimate finding by the officer who studied the noise problem that 6 percent of *all* calls made to the police were complaints about noise and that they accounted for as much as 22 percent of all calls during the early morning hours (Balles, 1986).

These various gaps in needed data can often be filled by a special computer program or—when the data have not been collected—by a carefully planned one-time collection effort. One can arrange to collect specific data, either by having officers supplement the information they usually record or through a door-to-door survey. But to get the cooperation of officers, they must be assured that each such request will not become a permanent addition to the agency's reporting requirements and that the results of the effort are likely to help address the problem being researched.

DIFFICULTIES IN TAPPING THE KNOWLEDGE OF RANK-AND-FILE POLICE OFFICERS

Although much of the important information on the substantive problems of policing is stored in the minds of rank-and-file police officers rather than in books, in reports, and on computer tapes, tapping that information and processing it in ways that make it useful are not easy. The challenge is in capturing the rich insights gained from experience and from thoughtful consideration of problems while avoiding prejudice and mere opinion. The views of some officers are heavily influenced by the nature of their assignments, by their personal values, and often by the cynicism they have developed on the job. Generalizations and stereotypes they develop can get in the way of effective policing.

Other officers are surprisingly clinical in their ability to describe the problems with which they deal. They pride themselves on getting beyond existing stereotypes and the sweeping generalizations of their co-workers. This attitude is often a product of their style of policing. The more they invest in getting to know the people whose problems they handle, the more they recognize that some of the oft-repeated generalizations about these problems are not accurate.

It follows that some types of inquiries can benefit most from the observations of officers who, through initial screening, are judged to have acquired valuable insights into the problem being explored. If opinions of a cross section of officers are desired, interviews must be structured in ways that penetrate beyond superficial impressions of the problem. Specific questions grounded in knowledge about the problem will be helpful. Although many initially find it awkward to respond when asked to think about their work from a radically different perspective, once engaged, they extend themselves to be responsive and objective. Information acquired from officers in this manner can usually be verified from some other source.

A more worrisome situation arises in street-level analysis of problems when discretion in studying a problem is delegated to the officer, and the officer is empowered to act based on the study. Unmonitored, an officer in such a situation could take off in the wrong direction. When this appeared to be the case in a few incidents in Newport News, the need for a more penetrating inquiry was recognized by the supervisor or by the task force reviewing the officer's analysis, and the officer was required to conduct a more comprehensive inquiry. As more and more police problems are subjected to analysis, it is predictable that some will not be adequately researched. A heavy responsibility falls on both training and supervision to impress officers with the importance of objectivity in their assessment of problems.

OBTAINING AN ACCURATE PICTURE OF THE CURRENT RESPONSE

As first noted in Chapter 4, a critical review of the way in which the police have responded to a problem in the past is an integral step in a fresh analysis of the problem. But the natural inclination, upon acquiring new knowledge about a problem, is to make light of this step—moving rapidly on to developing new strategies. Several factors account for this tendency. Because the problem has persisted, the police may dismiss whatever has been done in the past as ineffective and therefore of no relevance. They may fear as well that the past response was so poor that documenting it could be embarrassing to the department—that by characterizing it as the "current response," they create the impression that it has been officially endorsed.

In all probability, a uniform, coordinated response is not in fact in place; the number of different responses may be as great as the number of officers. Beyond that, individual officers may employ different responses to similar incidents. The initial task, therefore, is to collect these varied responses and to obtain some impression of the frequency with which they are used. One can then relate them to the problem to which they are applied. In this inventory and analysis, one is likely to find some responses that are far more effective than others, which should, therefore, be advocated for widespread adoption; some that are ineffective, which should be supplanted; some that are illegal, which should be banned; and some that have substantial merit but require the working through of complex issues before they can be adopted.

Good ideas for handling problems, which may have been among the repertoire of informal practices in the past, have often emerged from the early experiments in problem-oriented policing in a roundabout way. When individual police officers were given license to use their imagination and discretion in developing alternatives for solving problems, they frequently implemented informal common-sense responses that worked. When these responses are described, other officers often rush to claim (perhaps out of a natural tendency for veterans to challenge what is characterized as "novel") that they have done the same thing in the past. And they are probably right. The *difference* is that the officers now are free to describe the response without concern that it violates department policies or reflects an undue amount of discretion.

Such was the case, for example, in one of the beats policed by a CPOP officer in New York City. The officer found that none of the traditional responses curtailed the offensive behavior of several street people who spent their days on a relatively short stretch of street lined with small, independent stores. The officers arranged for the storekeepers to employ these individuals to perform a variety of tasks, such as keeping the sidewalks clean, thereby contributing to solving the problem of which they were previously a part. Upon retelling, this example was often recognized by other officers as a response they had used but not reported, because it was not in keeping with what was formally expected of them.

Thus, the nontraditional, widely admired ways in which veteran officers solve community problems, assuming they meet several other tests, can become the accepted, endorsed way of carrying out the police job. As Egon Bittner has said of problem-oriented policing, it makes explicit what was implicit and unrecognized in the past; it has the potential for making routine what was exceptional (Taft, 1986, p. 30).

But in a systematic effort to identify current responses, one may find that the most common, current response to a problem reflects an unarticulated policy decision to ignore it—to do nothing. Whole categories of responses may best be characterized as "generic sluff-offs." These include the common instructions to patrol officers in briefing sessions to "keep-a-check," "chase'm," "see-a-man," or "give some extra patrol." These are not responses to a problem; they are merely a way of placating a complainant. In the context of problem-oriented policing, frequent resort to them should be taken as a sure sign of the need to address the underlying problem more adequately.

If the effort to inventory current practices is successful, it is bound to identify some that are questionable or even illegal. Suits filed against police agencies and media investigations periodically document the worst of police responses to a problem. Popular accounts of the inside operations of police forces, written more to entertain than to inform, offer many examples of police practices in which vulnerable individuals—who the officers have concluded are the prime source of a given problem—are threatened, coerced, muscled, or tricked into stopping whatever it is that they are doing (see, e.g., McClure, 1986). In a given department, the underground will know well if these practices exist, what they are, and who engage in them. Retired officers, with no fear of the consequences, will regale a willing listener with endless tales of this old-fashioned type of "problem solving"—usually characterized as both clever and effective. Major progress will be realized if an effort to analyze current responses to a problem results in police agencies uncovering these practices on their own and taking the initiative to stop them.

More perplexing are the questions raised by the identification of practices that are borderline: practices that make sense, given the conditions under which police operate, but that have no legal underpinning so that, if called to account, the officer may be "out on a limb." In the Madison study of drunk driving, for example, some officers acknowledged candidly their informal alternatives to making an arrest, given that the number of drunk drivers far exceeds the capacity of the police to arrest all of them. Among the alternatives:

- Make the driver walk home.
- Have one of the other individuals in the stopped vehicle take over the driving, provided that he or she is not also impaired.
- Call a cab for the driver and secure the vehicle.
- Escort the driver home with his or her car.
- Insist that the driver take time out to eat.
- Remove the ignition key and either hide it in the vehicle where it is not easily accessible (e.g., in the trunk), or deposit it at some point (e.g., the police station) with information left with the driver as to where it can be picked up (Goldstein and Susmilch, 1982a, p. 118).

Acknowledging these alternatives was a healthy exercise. It demonstrated that even if the police cannot possibly arrest all intoxicated drivers, they can reduce the likelihood of an accident. In open discussion of the relative value of the alternatives, guidelines were proposed for maximizing effectiveness and minimizing unfairness in how a driver is treated. Discussion with police officers in other jurisdictions confirms that the practices are quite common. But lurking behind this acknowledgment of existing practices is the worry that the police do not have any discretion in deciding what to do if a driver has been drinking. They worry that if a released driver is involved in an accident, the municipality may be held liable for death, injury, or damages. Acknowledgment of the alternative practices also opens the police to charges of less-than-objective enforcement of the law. Furthermore, it detracts from the deterrent effect of the illusion that all drunk drivers are certain to be arrested. A penetrating exploration of the problem of the drinking driver and how the police might best respond to it requires openly confronting these concerns.

The reasoning behind current practices of individual officers can be instructive. In the study of the drinking driver, it was found, for example, that some officers give high priority to making arrests; others give it a low priority. Some ignore the intoxicated driver because they dislike dealing with frequently obnoxious and combative offenders, or simply do not view their conduct as serious, or have an alcohol problem of their own that makes them sympathetic to the drinking driver. Many factors influenced officers in deciding whether to stop a suspect vehicle: the volume of other police business, the seriousness of the driver's traffic violations and driving behavior, and the nearness to the end of a shift (Goldstein and Susmilch, 1982a, p. 117). When these considerations surface, it is an indication that the inquiry has penetrated the facade that blocks the full understanding required if problems are to be addressed more effectively.

What does it take to acquire an accurate picture of current responses? A rank-and-file officer who has responded to a series of related incidents (and therefore may have an interest in defending these responses) may be unable to describe that response objectively. But the reverse may be true. Officers who understand and are committed to the concept of problem-oriented policing feel that they have a license to be critical of past practice and therefore may err by being overly critical. This is especially true if an officer is newly assigned to a problem, with no reason to defend past actions.

The task is more complicated when the objective is to summarize how an entire police department responds to a large substantive problem, such as the handling of runaways, street robberies, or landlord–tenant conflicts. The rich descriptions of police operations in the leading ethnographic studies of the police (Skolnick, 1966; Rubinstein, 1973; Manning, 1977; Reuss-Ianni and Ianni, 1983) are a strong argument in favor of depending heavily on field observations and interviews of rank-and-file officers. One cannot easily quantify such data, though some efforts have been made (e.g., Sykes and Brent, 1983). Direct observation opens an otherwise locked box, revealing the range of responses, the extent to which field practices differ from policies and administrative perceptions, and the complicated forms in which problems are presented to the police.

One can efficiently schedule observations to coincide with the self-initiated operations of the police (e.g., enforcement of speeding through the use of radar). But the study of most problems will require the investment of a great deal of time, since incidents are not concentrated in either time or location. The cost may be prohibitive. It can be reduced somewhat by carefully targeting field observations, accompanying police officers identified by department records as more frequently handling the particular type of incident, and making productive use of time between incidents by interviewing officers.

The value of interviews will vary depending on the rapport established. Some officers, given the opportunity, will be very forthcoming. Others will not speak candidly until they learn the purpose of the inquiry and the effect that their candor might have on them. Interviewers must be prepared to invest time to get beyond superficial responses.

All of these observations argue in favor of a limited number of high-quality contacts with operating personnel rather than a more comprehensive approach. But if the objective is to describe the total department response, an in-depth inquiry employing a smaller number of officers obviously calls for a representative sample. For obvious reasons, surveys in which officers are asked to respond in writing to queries about current responses are not likely to be a viable substitute for either field observations or in-depth interviews. They may be useful, however, at the outset of an inquiry to identify roughly the range of responses and, at the conclusion, to determine the frequency with which different responses are utilized.

As for some problems, it may be feasible to collect an officer's responses to one or more scenarios of incidents. (See, e.g., Krantz et al., 1979.) An incident can be presented in a written narrative or in a film, or it may be acted out. This technique has the potential for controlling some of the variables that influence officers in real-world situations. The drawback, of course, is that the officer's response to a hypothetical situation in a laboratorylike setting may differ from his or her actual response on the street.

ENSURING ADEQUATE DEPTH

Although one assumes a questioning attitude from the outset in analyzing a problem, it is essential, after getting this far, to ask if the inquiry has been comprehensive and has been conducted in sufficient depth. Traditional ways of viewing a problem often creep back in to limit the analysis.

A study of the problem of theft from merchants by shoppers illustrates the need. It is easy, accepting how we have commonly responded to shoplifting, to become enmeshed in exploring ways in which to increase the number of arrests—including more efficient processing by the police. If one digs deeper, however, it becomes apparent that shoplifting is heavily influenced by how the merchandise is displayed and the means used to safeguard it (see, e.g., Poyner and Woodall, 1987). The police often accept these merchandising decisions as givens and are resigned to processing as many shoplifters as a store chooses to apprehend and deliver into their hands. More in-depth probing raises questions about the effectiveness of arrests as the primary means to reduce shoplifting and the propriety of delegating to private interests the judgment of who is to be arrested. The police may then focus on ways to curtail theft and on the use to be made of arrest, including the criteria to be employed in deciding whom to arrest. If the analysis of the problem of shoplifting had been superficial, limited to exploring ways to increase the number of arrests, the whole purpose of the exercise would have been lost.

Although one can aid police officers—especially at the street level—in identifying information they should consider, as was done with a checklist in Newport News, it is harder to provide assistance in measuring the adequacy of an analysis. Not all problems can be examined in the same way. A question that can furnish new insights into one problem will have no relevance for another. There may be no way of predicting what avenue of inquiry to take. But here are some probing questions that may gauge whether a problem has been analyzed in sufficient depth.

What is the community or governmental interest in the problem? Traditional policing responds to the most visible and vociferous interests. Has the analysis of the problem uncovered other interests as well? Identified as an essential element in problem-oriented policing in Chapter 4, this question has served to "smoke out," for critical examination, important interests that might otherwise be hidden by traditional perspectives. As illustrated there, street prostitution, for example, will evoke expressions of moral concern in the larger community, but other groups are also affected, including the neighborhoods and the prostitutes themselves. In the study of the problems associated with the New Briarfield housing complex in Newport News, the initial concern was to protect occupants from petty offenses. The more probing inquiry quickly identified a broader range of interests: providing residents with a greater sense of security, ensuring that housing meets minimum standards, and protecting renters from exploitation by their landlord. By responding to this broader range of interests—and thereby going far beyond traditional concerns—the police gained new credibility with the citizens who were affected, and the petty offenses to which the police previously limited themselves were dramatically and permanently reduced.

Multiple interests often compete for scarce police resources. Should efforts devoted to missing children address concerns about the harm that might befall a child who may be lost or kidnapped, or the interests of children in avoiding parents who are abusive, or the interests of a parent in a disputed custody? And what consideration, if any, should be given simply to the interest of the parents in exerting control over the child? Multiple interests may even be in direct conflict. In Oakland's central business district, the dominant goal of merchants was to control the behavior of street people (i.e., prostitutes, panhandlers, the homeless or mentally ill, and alcoholics), which detracted from the enormous investment made in upgrading the area (Reiss, 1985). Yet the street people also had an interest in being left alone, provided they were not violating the law. What weight should be given that interest? How should it be accommodated?

Have institutional interests, over time, been substituted for broader community and governmental interests in dealing with the problem? A penetrating analysis of the interests being served in responding to a problem may reveal that, over time, current practices have become more heavily influenced by the personal and institutional needs of the police than by the larger interests of the community. For example, given the frustrations experienced in dealing with problems such as the homeless, the down-and-out drunk, or the drinking driver, and the frequently unpleasant nature of the contacts, it is understandable that police may slip into a position in which the desire to avoid such contacts becomes their dominant consideration. An officer who sets out idealistically to solve a neighborhood dispute may, after being totally frustrated in the effort, attempt merely to prevent the conflicting parties from calling again until his or her shift is over. To free a precinct of a problem, officers may chase it to another precinct. And in responding to some common calls, such as complaints about noise, the dominant interest may be to handle them in the most expeditious manner possible so that officers remain free to assist others, should they be endangered. Personal and institutional interests in dealing with a problem cannot be ignored. But something is drastically wrong if they so strongly influence the way in which the police respond to a given problem that the community's interests are no longer served.

What factual basis is there for the claimed interest? Are frequently identified problems really problems? The reasons for police (and government) involvement in some problems are restated with such frequency and certainty that they are never challenged: e.g., shoplifting increases the costs of goods for all consumers; marijuana use leads to addiction to other, more dangerous drugs; petty gambling feeds organized crime; truancy contributes to burglaries; runaways become prostitutes; and missing children are brutalized or murdered. In a fresh analysis of a given problem, we should ask how often these consequences actually occur. What facts are available to support the oft-repeated claims?

The factual basis to support a specific interest in a problem not only may differ from what is commonly assumed to be true, it may vary from time to time, based on changed circumstances. For a long time, for example, police involvement in dealing with street prostitution was justified as a control on the spread of venereal disease. But with changes in medical treatment and in sexual mores, the spread of venereal disease was no longer attributable primarily to prostitutes. Thus, whatever other factual basis there may have been for dealing with prostitution, such as the involvement of juveniles or assaults on prostitutes and their patrons, there was little support for dealing with prostitution as a health hazard. But now, as knowledge is acquired about AIDS and the manner in which it is transmitted, new grounds may exist for highlighting concern about the spread of disease in shaping the police response to prostitution.

When the evidence supports police involvement, what priority should be given to each interest in shaping the police response? Identifying and assessing the importance of often competing interests give the police a basis for deciding how influential a specific goal ought to be in shaping their response.

Exhibitionists, for example, are of concern to the police because they are viewed as sex offenders who may commit serious sexual assaults; because their behavior is offensive; and because they engender widespread fear. The expectation that they will commit more serious offenses tends to have the strongest influence upon the police response. But is this expectation justified? If not, higher priority could be given to reducing the nuisance factor and reducing fear.

The same type of analysis has proved useful in examining such street-level problems as the announcement by a large group of protesters that they intend to demonstrate against another group of citizens in a congested area of a large city. The police have a responsibility to prevent conflict between the opposing factions, protect First Amendment rights, protect property from damage and vandalism, and maintain the free movement of traffic. Without further analysis, the goal of expediting traffic may take precedence over the freedom of the demonstrators to protest. More careful analysis, however, may lead to the conclusion that the inconvenience to motorists of a temporary detour may be justified to facilitate peaceful protest.

These are difficult value-laden questions for which there are no clear answers. One can persuasively argue that they ought not to be decided by the police, but by the community or, more appropriately, by elected officials responsive through the political process to the community. But focusing on who should ultimately make the choice misses the major point being made here. In the absence of sufficient in-depth analysis of what the police are expected to do, the questions—important as they are—are not being raised in the first instance. The police are in an excellent position to do so.

CHAPTER 8

THE SEARCH FOR ALTERNATIVES: DEVELOPING TAILOR-MADE RESPONSES

After a problem has been clearly defined and analyzed, one confronts the ultimate challenge in problem-oriented policing: the search for the most effective way of dealing with it. This requires a process both broad and uninhibited—broad in that it breaks out of the rigid mindset of the past, and uninhibited in that it explores sensible responses without regard, at least initially, to potential impediments to adopting them. After all possible alternatives have been set out, new ideas must be analyzed with concern for obvious factors, such as their legality and the values of the community, and with appropriate consideration of their potential effectiveness, cost, and practicality.

From the outset, one is constantly battling a natural tendency to revert to traditional responses. Indeed, the tendency is so strong that the Baltimore County Police Department, to force open consideration of alternatives, initially prohibited the officers engaged in problem-oriented policing from employing traditional practices—even though, in some instances, after exhaustive analysis, these practices clearly emerged as the most logical, effective response to a given problem (Behan, 1986; Cordner, 1986; Taft, 1986).

Because of the freedom associated with the process and the potential for new discovery, the search for new alternatives can be an exciting exercise. It is a fresh and often stimulating activity in a working environment that, in the past, has been confining, frustrating, and, for some, debilitating. The early experiences in problem-oriented policing, moreover, indicate that the search can be productive—that many opportunities for improving the quality of policing can be found. Harvesting this potential and actually implementing new ideas bring rewards and satisfaction—both for the police and for the community affected. The enthusiasm generated encourages additional efforts, thereby creating the potential for compounding the value of the process.

MAKING THE SEARCH FOR ALTERNATIVES AN INTEGRAL PART OF POLICING

Under the umbrella of crime prevention, practitioners have long advocated and sometimes succeeded in implementing a variety of programs—apart from enforcing the law—that were intended to reduce problems: e.g., improved street lighting, the marking of property, better locks, and organizing neighborhoods. (Some programs, such as police athletic leagues, in which police arrange for athletic activities for otherwise idle youths, have a long history.) Many police agencies have a special unit whose personnel devote all of their time to crime prevention activities.

In recent years, numerous efforts have been made, both in this country and elsewhere, to revitalize and expand these programs (see, e.g., Whittaker, 1986). Among these efforts, the work sponsored by Britain's Home Office has special significance. Drawing on the research of Jacobs (1962) and Newman (1972), they introduced the "situational approach"—a concept that emphasizes changing the environment (rather than trying to change people) and the need to concentrate on *specific* types of offenses or locales. Thus, in attempting to deal with a specific problem, they looked first to approaches such as hardening or removing the target of the offense, reducing the payoff, and surveillance (Clarke, 1980a; Clarke and Mayhew, 1980; Poyner, 1980, 1983; Hough, 1980–1981).

These crime prevention efforts, from ad hoc improvisations (by officers on the beat) to highly developed concepts (the "situational approach"), have produced alternative responses of the type that problem-oriented policing is designed to produce. But problem-oriented policing requires incorporating these efforts into the mainstream of policing: making them an integral, institutionalized part of police management and operations. To do this requires at least five major adjustments in current thinking:

1 Recognition that the search for alternatives is a legitimate, fully endorsed, and appropriately rewarded enterprise, central to carrying out the police function; that it reflects a consistent, agency-wide commitment to improving the quality of police service. Feelings of working on the periphery of policing, or of acting wisely but surreptitiously, are eliminated.

2 Acknowledgment that the search for alternatives extends to methods for dealing with the full range of problems the police are expected to handle; that it is not limited to just those measures that have a potential for reducing "crime."

3 Acceptance that the search goes beyond ways in which to affect the environment or "situational" factors; that it includes, more broadly, *anything* that might be done to deal with the problems the community looks to the police to handle.

4 Agreement that the search for alternatives will be preceded by a careful analysis of the specific problem of concern. Striking out in a new direction without first thinking about a problem is discouraged.

5 Commitment to developing a specific response that can be applied to a specific problem in a specific place under specific conditions, and usually in combination with other responses to the problem. This is intended to dissuade the police from applying a generic response to a generic problem, or to applying a single response haphazardly to a wide range of different types of problems.

THE RANGE OF POSSIBLE ALTERNATIVES

The categories under which possible alternatives are examined have been chosen simply because they provide a convenient framework in which to explore their potential and the issues raised. They are not intended to be fixed, exhaustive, or exclusive of one another.

Concentrating Attention on Those Individuals Who Account for a Disproportionate Share of a Problem

A relatively small number of individuals usually account for a disproportionate share of practically any problem the police handle. Police have long been alert to the phenomenon of the "one-man crime-wave." Increased awareness of the percentage of serious crimes committed by repeaters has led to the adoption of repeat offender projects (ROP). These concentrate police resources on acquiring the evidence to support the arrest and conviction of "career criminals." A report on one of the most ambitious projects, launched in the District of Columbia, is cautiously positive, reflecting both the difficulty of evaluating such a program and the complex legal, ethical, and policy issues that it raises (Martin and Sherman, 1986). The literature on efforts to deal with the repeat offender has increased dramatically in recent years. (For an overview of the repeater phenomenon and the policy issues raised in dealing with it, see Moore et al., 1984; for an overview of police programs for dealing with the repeater, see Gay and Bowers, 1985.)

Against this background, it is not surprising that problem analysis, which routinely includes an in-depth inquiry about the individuals involved in a problem, frequently reveals the repeater phenomenon in new contexts—especially with regard to problems of public order, which have not received as much attention as serious crime problems. And this, in turn, has led to the realization that one of the most effective ways to reduce the magnitude of a much wider range of problems is to design programs specifically to deal with those who account for a disproportionate share of them.

> In Madison, for example, the bizarre and sometimes offensive conduct of mentally ill persons on the streets led to citywide concern about the problem of the deinstitutionalized. Their number was repeatedly estimated in news accounts as being in excess of 1,000. But when the problem was studied, it was determined that no more than 20 individuals accounted for most of the incidents and that their behavior often resulted from failure to take prescribed medications. The local mental health service established a program of special, intensive care for these individuals, monitoring them through a variety of arrangements, including, when deemed necessary, obtaining court approval for a limited guardianship. The program has continued, with newly identified patients being added to the monitored group. The original problem—both the fear and the actual incidents—has been greatly reduced, and it appears that the mentally ill in the program have also benefited.
>
> A similar problem that invites this type of response is that of the public inebriate. A relatively small number usually account for the vast majority of incidents requiring attention and for the bulk of police transports to either a detoxification center or a jail. The Madison police and the local detoxification center established a joint program to monitor 30 of their most frequent clients. A field team of ex-alcoholics sought out these individuals and, if they were found to be drinking, attempted to divert them to other activities. Arrangements were made to transport them to the detoxification center if they were incapacitated. If they refused repeatedly to enter a treatment program, an intensive effort was made to initiate a commitment proceeding, which could result in detention of up to 14 days and, if committed, a treatment program (in the community) of at least 90 days. The number of incapacitated alcoholics on the streets of the city has greatly diminished.

In the development of such programs, great care obviously must be exercised in selecting the target group or individual, in choosing methods for acquiring evidence (when the behavior constitutes a criminal offense), and in applying tighter restrictions, as needed, on the individual. In the programs described, the potential for abuse is minimized because initial selection for inclusion in a targeted group is based on a documented record of prior interventions that met established legal standards. The behavior that brings individuals back into the system when they are targeted is usually self-initiated, highly visible, and easy to verify. And the programs for more intensive treatment are authorized by existing law; further curtailment of freedom (guardianship, commitment, or revocation of probation) requires prior judicial approval.

But the need to control especially troublesome individuals currently outstrips our ability to do so in ways that are effective and also meet standards of fairness and due process. Common sense tells us, for example, that the problem of the drinking driver would be greatly reduced if we could identify and curb those who most frequently drive after drinking. Yet in each state, a significant percentage of people who have been convicted of drunk driving, paid high fines, served time in jail, and lost their licenses, continue to drive—unlicensed and uninsured. Short of prolonged periods of incarceration, what does one do about such offenders?

Connecting with Other Government and Private Services

The police officer is to government as the general practitioner is to the entire medical establishment. Officers can recognize needs, diagnose problems, and handle some of them directly, but they do not have the time, training, or resources to handle all of the problems that come their way in their entirety. In-depth exploration of the problems that police commonly confront frequently leads to a recognition of the need for (1) more effective referrals to existing government and private services; (2) improved coordination with agencies that exert control over some of the problems or individuals for which the police are held responsible; and (3) police initiative in pressing for correction of inadequacies in municipal services and for development of new services.

Referral to Another Agency Police agencies now commonly encourage their officers to provide information to citizens in need of help about various services available in the community. Officers are provided with lists, telephone numbers, and descriptions of the services provided. But the practice is by no means universal. Some police agencies make no effort to dispense such information. And even if information is placed in the hands of officers, little may be done to ensure that it is conveyed and that the other agency becomes involved.

More effective procedures must be established for referring individuals to services that will help them deal with problems that otherwise continue to require police attention. Police officers should be given some incentive to make referrals, and they should become sufficiently familiar with the services available to determine when referral is appropriate.

This can be achieved through cross-training, with officers spending time in the agencies and agency personnel spending time in the field with the police. Direct contacts between counterparts at the lowest levels should be encouraged, in contrast to traditional procedures, which frequently require that any contact between a police officer and another agency be made through a memorandum or report sent up through the hierarchy of the police agency, across the desks of the department heads, and then down through the levels of supervision of the other agency. Most important, effective use of referrals requires that the police receive assurance that the referred party will get the services promised: e.g., counseling and shelter for victims of spousal abuse; support services for victims of sexual assault; dispute resolution for landlord–tenant conflicts; and counseling and shelter for runaways.

Numerous questions arise about referrals. Should the police limit themselves to simply providing information about the service? Should they offer to make appointments? Should the police contact the other agency, rather than leave the initiative to the citizen? Should referrals be followed up to ensure that contact has been made? Should the police coerce (probably through threat of more punitive action) an individual to make the connection?

In the absence of advance agreement, police are often disappointed by the failure of other agencies to respond to their referrals, even when the agencies have an obligation to act. Residents in Flint, Michigan, for example, told the officer permanently assigned to their neighborhood that their primary concern was a burned-out dwelling that was an eyesore. They wanted it demolished. The officer established that city ordinances required its demolition and filed a report with the city's building inspection department requesting that the ordinance be enforced. Apparently, however, the number of partially destroyed structures was so large and the enforcement staff so small that nothing was done. As a result, the officer felt that his credibility with the community had been compromised.

Even when they are worked out in advance, arrangements can be very fragile and often deteriorate over time—especially where there are frequent changes in personnel and leadership. Agencies may not be able to deliver on their commitment—either because of lack of interest or too heavy a workload. The most dramatic example relates to child abuse. Given the numerous appeals that have been made to report alleged child abuse, police find that the social agencies responsible for making the initial investigations are overwhelmed; those reporting a case may actually have difficulty contacting the agency.

Successful programs in which police make extensive use of referrals include several common characteristics: a strong working relationship between the police administrator and the head of the agency to which referrals are made; strong support for cooperative efforts from the municipal or county executive, with some pressure on the agency to give high priority to police referrals; an arrangement for troubleshooting when a report is received that a case is not being handled according to prior agreements; and constant monitoring to identify ways to handle the problem more effectively.

Coordinating Police Responses with Other Agencies Coordination implies a much stronger relationship with another agency than referrals. It applies to those situations in which the other agency shares some direct responsibility for controlling the particular conduct.

The study of repeat sexual offenders in Madison uncovered a serious communication and policy gap between the police and the Wisconsin Division of Corrections. Though employees of the two agencies often had telephone contact, they did not know each other. The police had stereotyped the probation and parole officers as "soft" social workers; and the probation and parole officers had stereotyped the police as "hard-nosed" and insensitive to the needs of ex-offenders attempting to reintegrate themselves into the community. There was little trust and little sharing of information. Yet both agencies recognized the need to provide more intensive monitoring of sexual offenders under supervision in the community. Based on their many common objectives, the agencies established a new, trusting relationship. They now work together much more closely to monitor repeat sexual offenders and also many other probationers and parolees.

Existing relationships between the police and the agencies that have a special responsibility for a problem should be reassessed regularly and strengthened. Some police agencies have increased their capacity to deal with youth-related offenses, especially truancy, by developing a much closer relationship with school officials (Reiss, 1985; Pate et al., 1986). Concern about the drinking driver should include a reexamination of the day-to-day working relationship with the agency that licenses motorists, and exploration of alcohol-related problems would benefit from a review of the ongoing relationship with the agency that regulates the sale of alcoholic beverages.

Conflicts of interest are assumed to stand in the way of efforts to coordinate governmental programs to control a common problem. It is widely assumed, for example, that a program for joint monitoring of ex-offenders cannot be implemented in many jurisdictions because the police do not sympathize with the role of corrections and the rights of ex-offenders. It is feared that information provided about ex-offenders will be used by the police to subject them to frequent investigation as suspects in unsolved cases and, more generally, to harass them and thereby make more difficult their adjustment in the community. Likewise, some school officials restrict contact with police, convinced that the faculty's relationship with students in a learning environment is threatened if teachers and principals are seen as communicating with the police about students. The Madison case study suggests that these perceptions of conflicting interests are often overstated. Communication between agencies can lead to recognition of common goals, development of mutual respect, and establishment of a working relationship that benefits the agencies, the community, and, most important, the individuals who are subject to some form of control.

Correcting Inadequacies in Municipal Services and Pressing for New Services Because police officers work around the clock, on the streets and in people's homes, they are among the first to see evidence of inadequacies in government service and the need for new services. They are also in a position to see the effects—both good and bad—of policies implemented by other agencies. Some city administrations expect the police to report specific inadequacies (e.g., potholes, street lights that are out, missing signs); others have no such expectation. But rarely are the police encouraged to offer criticism of overall operating practices or policies that result in poor service or gaps in needed services.

Police did become more involved in critiquing other municipal services in the 1960s, when racial tensions in large urban areas sometimes erupted into violence. For pragmatic reasons, the police pressed other municipal agencies to correct conditions that contributed directly to a heightening of tensions: e.g., the failure to collect rubbish on a street inhabited by blacks; the closing of swimming pools and parks at times when the demand for their use was greatest.

Police involvement in systematically analyzing problems of concern to the community places them much more fully and directly in the business of observing, critiquing, and working to improve municipal services. Unlike the administrators and budget analysts at city hall, the police in the field not only see direct evidence of inadequate services and needs that are unmet, they see the connection between these conditions and the problems for which they are held responsible. Given license to act on their assessment of needs, police agencies have pressed other agencies to correct conditions that caused specific problems and, more broadly, to review policies and practices that create problems of continuing concern.

Some of the best examples emerge when the police take on, as a problem, a specific housing complex—usually because of an initial concern about assaults, robberies, burglaries, and the fear that these offenses generate. Officers then may initiate requests to other city agencies to enforce building codes; eliminate zoning violations; remove accumulated rubbish and debris; improve adjacent streets and lighting; control rats and other health hazards; and remove overgrowth on adjacent city property. In Baltimore County, in-depth inquiry led police to pressure the county's development agency to initiate legal proceedings against a landlord who was in arrears on a loan that had been obtained to correct building and zoning violations that remained uncorrected.

If it has become apparent in the analysis of a problem that an entirely new service is required, the police have pressed for the service or, in some cases, initiated it on their own. Here are some examples:

- A center to help refugees new to a large city, including distributing clothing and assisting in finding employment (Cowart, 1986)
- A program to coordinate the removal of graffiti
- A detoxification program for alcoholics where none had existed
- Instruction in word processing for a group of unemployed single women, and arrangements for day and respite care for their dependents
- Establishment of a dance hall free of alcohol, drugs, and smoke in an area in which youths aimlessly congregated with a high potential for conflict
- Construction of new basketball courts in an area in which idle youngsters were creating a number of problems
- Establishment of a system staffed by volunteers for daily checks on the welfare of elderly persons living alone

The agencies that have taken these initiatives, both in correcting inadequacies in municipal services and in pressing for new services, are convinced of their value. The programs are far more effective in eliminating problems or reducing their magnitude than whatever was done in the past.

Traditionally oriented police officers, nevertheless, are very reluctant to fill gaps in municipal services and to provide new programs. They are understandably concerned that they may be committing themselves to a constantly increasing, ill-defined work load and to inevitable conflict with other agencies. The police have suffered over the years because of public expectations that are far in excess of what they can possibly fulfill. Their agencies have been saddled with miscellaneous tasks unrelated to even the broadest concept of the police function, acquired merely because of their mobility, their capacity to respond around the clock, and the widespread impression that police have plenty of time to spare.

Consider, for example, the initiative of the New York City police in providing transportation to the elderly so that they can shop safely. It clearly makes the elderly less vulnerable to crime and generates enormous goodwill for the police department, with the result that the elderly assist the department in a variety of ways. But does it relieve other agencies of this responsibility? Are the police forever committed to providing this service? And if so, how will the priority currently assigned to this initiative compare with that of other initiatives the police may come up with to solve other problems in the future?

To meet these legitimate concerns and still achieve some of the objectives of problem-oriented policing requires setting some realistic boundaries. These are beginning to emerge as a result of recent experiences. Police are limiting their concern with the operations of other municipal agencies to those matters that, if unattended, become knotty problems for the police. And when the police initiate a new program, they often do so as catalysts, expecting what emerges to sustain itself or be adopted by another agency. The police themselves cannot possibly continue all the new programs that they initiate.

The situation, of course, is most acute in economically depressed areas where municipal services have been severely reduced. In dealing with street robbery, a police chief may agree to press those responsible for the care of trees on city property to trim trees so that street lighting will be more effective or, in desperation, may even approve of his officers, together with local citizens, doing the job. But the chief worries that the police will then become the agency to which citizens turn for this service.

Working through these issues requires more involvement by the chief executives of municipalities. They must recognize that the police, as the "foot soldiers" of city hall, are in a unique position to draw attention to community needs and failures in service and thereby contribute to improving the overall quality of municipal government. They also must recognize that some of the proposals emanating from problem-oriented policing will be much more cost-effective if handled by other agencies than if left to the police. Convincing another city agency to incur the one-time cost of moving a bus stop may save the police countless hours ineffectively handling the dangerous situation resulting from its present location. In the example relating to tree trimming, the police could take the initiative in the annual budget process to demonstrate the relationship between untrimmed trees, serious crime, and levels of fear. They could argue that what may be viewed as a dispensable luxury in municipal services is, in fact, a necessity for security. Support of this nature by the police for programs in other municipal agencies is one way to avoid assuming the task and to maintain good relations with these agencies while pressing for better services.

Using Mediation and Negotiation Skills

Police are expected to handle many types of conflicts. These may involve a few people, as in disputes between persons living together, tenants and landlords, customers and merchants, and neighbors. Or they may involve hundreds, as in political protests, civil rights demonstrations, labor–management strife, and urban rioting. Conflict may be at the heart of many problems initially defined differently. The conflict often relates to the use of public space. Thus, for example, keeping order on a busy street lined with stores may mean minimizing conflicts in the varied use of the street by customers, delivery people, those passing through the area, peddlers, alcoholics, the homeless, and the mentally ill. The problem of noise is essentially a problem of conflict. Drug peddling, which is a major problem in its own right, also becomes a problem of conflict when the peddling offends neighbors and regular users of the parks and streets where it is concentrated. Analysis of these problems, whether collectively (e.g., all landlord–tenant disputes or labor–management strife) or individually (e.g., a frequently recurring dispute between two neighbors), leads to exploring the use that police should make of mediation skills to resolve conflicts.

Like other alternatives, this one has a long history. Romantic accounts of the beat officer of the past describe him as an artist at settling disputes. A classic study of the police officer as "street-corner politician" describes informal practices dominated by a desire to work out solutions to various conflicts (Muir, 1977). Kelling's description of Officer Kelley's methods for managing his foot beat provides an excellent example of how a particular officer, in an informal manner, negotiated a set of rules to minimize conflict among those (including drunks, addicts, beggars, and vagrants) who use the streets he is assigned to policing (Police Foundation, 1981, pp. 118–119).

One version of the professional model of policing limited the police role vis-à-vis some types of conflict to making an arrest when a law was violated, thereby avoiding involvement in frustrating problems for which the police had no ready solution. But attitudes have changed in the past several decades. Few police continue to view their role in conflicts in this limited way. A positive value is now attached to preventing conflict and to deescalating a situation without making an arrest. Officers have been trained to intervene in conflicts: to defuse volatile situations. In the 1960s and 1970s, when the police were called on to handle large disturbances, agencies acknowledged that more was involved than enforcing the law when they developed "conflict-management" programs. Especially significant in popularizing the concept of mediation in policing was the work of Morton Bard (1970) on domestic disturbances, though the emphasis given to mediation over arrest, especially if there is any indication of violence, has since been strongly criticized.

The experiments in problem-oriented policing have demonstrated that conflict resolution is often the most sensible response to a problem. In the COPE project, for example, police involvement in attempting to solve a long-standing feud within a neighborhood organization resulted in a decision to train an officer in the mediation and arbitration skills used in labor–management relations. His successful handling of the dispute and his certification as a professional arbitrator led to his handling other problems requiring such skills. One of the most common uses of negotiation by problem-oriented officers has been in attempting to eliminate conditions in housing complexes that invite criminal conduct and generate fear. Officers in both Newport News and Baltimore County have frequently negotiated agreements between managers and residents. And on the beat as well, officers work out mutually acceptable solutions to problems. A simple example is the officer who, finding that a noisy assemblage in front of a tavern had been a source of neighborhood complaints for years, convinced the owner to make an area in the rear yard of the tavern usable and convinced the revelers to gather there. Careful analysis of situations in which a particular police officer has a long-established relationship with a given area will often reveal that the officer, without full awareness of what he or she has done, has negotiated an elaborate set of miscellaneous rules to avoid conflict that are well understood by the potentially conflicting parties and that, if violated, will result in some form of police action.

Yet despite the progress of the past several decades and the common resort to some form of mediation in problem-oriented policing, the commitment to mediation in response to specific problems is limited (Palenski, 1984). Against a background of major work in the development of mediation and other dispute-resolution techniques in both the public and private sectors, relatively little systematic attention has been given to perfecting the methods of responding to disputes by the governmental agency that probably handles the greatest number of them.

Promoting mediation requires that we examine some of the difficult issues that arise when the police use this technique. In the first instance, we must be clearer on what we mean by mediation in policing. The term conjures up a rather elaborate process, like that used, for example, in labor–management relations. How much of this has relevance to policing? How deeply should police become involved in resolving conflicts? Is the objective simply to separate warring parties, or is it to work out lasting settlements?

Do the police have the neutrality required of mediators? It is widely assumed that the police would be biased in addressing a problem or handling an incident—as agents of the state, as reflective of the majority culture, and as imposing a set of values associated with controlling human behavior. The development of policing in this country has been shaped (and limited) by worry over the ability of the police to act in a neutral manner—an anxiety justified by numerous examples of flagrant alignment with one side in handling a confrontation. Although police are still frequently accused of bias, especially in the treatment of minorities, enormous strides have been made in handling persons and problems impartially. In numerous disputes that police are called on to handle, the parties now accept the police as a neutral party. An assessment of their ability to behave impartially should be a major factor in considering the feasibility of encouraging police to use mediation.

But even if the police can serve as neutral referees in some types of disputes, do they elicit voluntary agreement to settlements of conflicts? Or are agreements entered into because the parties feel coerced by an unspoken threat of what might happen if they are uncooperative or fail to agree? Are the police prepared to walk away from a situation if their efforts at mediation fail? Is the police role in resolving disputes more accurately described as arbitration rather than mediation?

Finally, can a police agency commit itself to resolving disputes without conveying a signal that this downgrades the seriousness with which they view the problem? This question has been raised most sharply with regard to spousal abuse. Police in many jurisdictions have not taken spousal abuse seriously in the past. The use of mediation has been seen as further evidence that police are not prepared to treat violence within the family as a crime. This has led to legislation in some states to mandate arrest if evidence exists that a crime has occurred. As a result, police are denied the opportunity to use an alternative such as mediation when circumstances (e.g., the age, physical infirmity, or mental condition of one or both parties) may make mediation the more appropriate response.

Although the issues posed by police use of mediation are complex, they are not so complex as to constitute a barrier to the increased use of this response. The arguments in favor of equipping the police to be more effective peacemakers are strong, but the effort will be more productive if it reflects greater sensitivity to the questions raised here.

Conveying Information

Conveying sound, accurate information is currently one of the least used, but potentially most effective, means the police have for responding to a wide range of problems. Several factors contribute to this situation. The police have a monopoly on some information in which the community has an intense interest. They are experienced in dealing with situations that the average citizen only rarely encounters. They are assumed to have access to facts and to know the law, which gives them a special credibility. They are authority figures; citizens listen to them. The public, on the other hand, is hungry for solid information bearing on the problems of concern to them. They routinely turn to the police as a trusted source of some types of information and also when they simply do not know whom to contact. They turn to the police in highly specific situations, when, for example, they experience a personal crisis, and also when they want general information about something that has gone wrong in the community (e.g., a television station that suddenly goes off the air). They expect the police to know what is going on.

Problem-oriented policing draws attention in two ways to the use of information as a response to community problems. First, the commitment to systematic inquiry into community problems will result in police acquiring even more information than they now possess. If a problem has been analyzed properly, this information will be more precise and reliable than that previously available and will enhance the capacity and credibility of the police. Second, systematic inquiry often leads to the conclusion that a problem should be addressed by conveying information to the public. The potential uses of information as a response to a problem are so varied that each is examined separately.

To reduce anxiety and fear. A problem may be perceived by the community as larger and more aggravated than it actually is. Candid sharing with the public of information about the problem may substantially reduce—or perhaps even eliminate—it. Examples: (1) In recent years, concern about sexual assault has resulted in broadening the definition of what constitutes sexual assault to include offenses in addition to rape, and it has led to programs that encourage victims to report offenses. As a result, sexual assaults, as counted by the police and reported by the media, have increased dramatically. This, in turn, has often generated widespread fear. A careful breakdown of the offenses reported can be used to reduce fear without diminishing the significance of the problem. (2) In the Baltimore County COPE program, which focuses on fear, officers responded to some problems by simply telling the community what had been done: the responsible party had been taken into custody, or a mentally retarded young man was shown not to be the child molester he was rumored to be. (3) Persons experiencing a crisis for the first time (an automobile accident, a lost child, or a home burglary) may be much more anxious than is justified by the incident. Sharing solid information on what happens in such situations, based on the experience of the police in handling many of them, can be an effective way to reduce anxiety and fear.

To enable citizens to solve their own problems. Earlier we described the role of the police as go-betweens in arranging for the delivery of municipal services to which citizens are entitled (e.g., the correction of a building code violation). In some situations a call from the police will bring results when a citizen's call may be ignored. But the police are finding that arranging for a service does not always require their intervention, but sometimes simply an explanation of how the service can be obtained. Thus a community police officer in New York City discovered that, with new procedures in place, it was not difficult for a citizen to arrange for the removal of an abandoned car. From then on, the officer simply provided instructions on how to do so. Those who receive citizen calls to the police can identify a large number of common problems for which solutions are sought. Through a mailing or a carefully prepared tape-recorded message, the police can instruct the callers on how best to solve these recurrent problems.

To elicit conformity with laws and regulations that are not known or understood. The effectiveness of existing legal controls often is limited by lack of knowledge of them. Examples: (1) Bar owners often do not understand their criminal liability for serving additional drinks to persons who are already intoxicated. (2) Many cities have parking restrictions for snow removal or street cleaning that make parking extremely difficult even for those who want to comply with the law, and are particularly troublesome to newcomers. An intensive effort to educate citizens about regulations, special permits, and alternative places to park can increase compliance. (3) New immigrant groups may be oblivious to the norms of our society. A neighborhood police officer instructed the local Hmong population regarding those laws that conflicted with their own norms; another persuaded immigrants not to fire their weapons in the air as a form of celebration.

To warn potential victims about their vulnerability and advise them of ways to protect themselves. Police have long sought to educate vulnerable groups: school children about molestation, sexual assault, and drugs; Christmas shoppers regarding thefts from their unattended vehicles; the elderly regarding swindlers; bargain hunters regarding fake jewelry sold by street peddlers; and car owners regarding the theft of unlocked cars. Intensive study of a behavioral problem will almost inevitably disclose the need to reach potential victims, but will have the added value of enabling the police to target the vulnerable population group with much greater specificity. Thus a study of residential burglaries concentrated in a small neighborhood revealed that almost all entries were through a sliding-glass patio-type door. This led the police to distribute pamphlets in the area with specific instructions on how to secure such doors. A study of problems associated with college football games found that most burglarized cars belonged to fans of the visiting team. This led to a recommendation that tickets sold to visiting fans be accompanied by a warning not to leave valuables in their cars. And a study of thefts from automobiles led to a recommendation that those registering in specific hotels be notified, when registering, of the need to remove certain types of valuables from their cars.

To demonstrate to individuals how they unwittingly contribute to problems. Citizens often do not realize how their own actions contribute to problems. The police can demonstrate this relationship and hope that their appeal for cooperation will be heeded and that the problem of concern will thereby be reduced. The fear generated by panhandling, for example, can be eliminated quickly if the activity is made unprofitable—if people do not respond to a panhandler's requests for money. The police appeal may be strengthened if it can be demonstrated that the funds collected by panhandlers are often used to support a self-destructive lifestyle of chronic alcoholism and if assurances can be made that panhandlers will not go without food and shelter.

To develop support for addressing a problem. As was previously noted, police, by the very nature of their function, learn about growing community problems (e.g., a new drug being used by children, a violent gang, an increase in child abuse) to which the vast majority of the community may be oblivious. Winning support for a new response to a problem is difficult if those being asked for such support have no knowledge of the problem and are not affected by it. This is especially so if the community is ambivalent about giving police attention to a problem identified generically as, for example, prostitution or gambling.

Problem-oriented policing better equips the police to deal with these situations because it requires that the police first obtain hard facts and document the specific consequences for the community. As an example, the Madison police were aware that small-stakes gambling, which had been going on for several years in a particular park, was causing some wider problems. Participants were getting into fights; weapons were sometimes used. Neighbors were complaining about the noise, the litter, and the rowdiness of the gamblers and were afraid to use the park. Most citizens, however, were unaware of the problem. For many years the police had not made gambling a high-priority concern. Officers responsible for dealing with the problem knew that if they simply went into the park and arrested the gamblers, they would look petty and capricious and would lose a degree of respect from city residents. The officers chose, therefore, first to publicize the problem by relating the details of the situation to the media and to other city officials. This generated the support the police needed to use their authority to investigate, arrest, and prosecute the offenders. In similar fashion, conveying information about some of the more harmful effects of street prostitution enables a police agency to take more aggressive action against street prostitution than may otherwise seem justified.

To acquaint the community with the limitations on the police and to define realistically what can be expected of the police. The exploration of some problems will inevitably lead to the conclusion that the community has unrealistic expectations of what the police can do or does not understand the limitations on police authority. A common example occurs in those cities in which streets in downtown shopping areas have been converted to malls. The outdoor furnishings often attract derelicts, drunks, the mentally ill, addicts, and the homeless. Merchants, who may have paid for the improvements and whose business prospects depend on giving the area a new image, often blame the police for allowing the situation to "deteriorate." They will insist that unsavory individuals be arrested or chased from the area. The police must inform the merchants that derelicts and others who do not conform to prevailing standards of dress and behavior also have rights and, absent the commission of a crime, cannot be arrested. Only after this basic message has been communicated will there be any possibility of gaining support for alternative means to deal with the problem.

New awareness of the importance of conveying information as a principal method for addressing community problems requires careful consideration of the means by which information is passed on. The police already have a major vehicle available to them: the daily contacts they have—over the telephone and in person—with citizens requesting assistance. But police employees are rarely equipped to make full use of these contacts to provide information. Citizens are often left unsatisfied because the employee—whether an officer or a dispatcher—does not realize that conveying solid, accurate information is an integral part of a satisfactory police response. Beyond this established opportunity for exchange, police are experimenting with new ways to get information to the community. Meetings with community groups have long been recognized as an occasion for conveying information, but relatively little consideration has been given to both the type of information that is best conveyed in these settings and the most effective way to present it. Too often there is simply an accounting of reported crime and police activity. Some departments prepare newsletters for specific neighborhoods, but so far with uneven and generally disappointing results (Lavrakas, 1986; Pate et al., 1985). Most exciting is the potential for the useful exchange of information when police survey a neighborhood. COPE officers, who initiated their surveys in an effort to measure the level of fear, found that the occasion it provided to talk with citizens was of great benefit to both the police and the citizens—not just to cultivate the relationship, but to pass on information. This unanticipated benefit should stimulate new interest in the long-established practice of the neighborhood-centered Japanese police units—kobans—in using residential surveys for "extending the koban's knowledge of its community, for demonstrating the availability of police service, and for developing personal relations between police officer and citizen (Bayley 1976, pp. 84–87). The recent American experience, related to the Japanese experience, leads to speculation about what the full potential might be if, as part of the current move toward community policing, more emphasis is placed on one-to-one contact with citizens with the primary objective of conveying vital information regarding particular problems of direct concern to them.

Mobilizing the Community

As explained in Chapter 3, greater community involvement is an underlying premise—of central importance—in problem-oriented policing. Greater community involvement is therefore reflected in most of the alternatives examined here. But in addition to being a built-in component, "organizing the community" is a distinct alternative that can be employed by itself or along with other alternatives in responding to a problem. Within the context of problem-oriented policing, it usually means mobilizing a specific segment of the community to help implement a specific response to a specific problem for as long as it takes to deal with the problem. For a recurring problem such as residential burglary, "organizing the community" may mean organizing a neighborhood crime watch with the hope that it will become a permanent organization. As noted in Chapter 3, this type of response differs significantly from the organizing efforts now commonly associated with community policing, in which the police set out to create more permanent community organizations for more general purposes: to improve communications with the police and to deal with a broad range of problems that might be of concern to the police or the community.

Here are some examples of problems that were attacked in the context of problem-oriented policing by organizing some segments of the community and a description of what, specifically, community members were encouraged to do:

Abandoned cars In the area in which this was a problem, arrangements were made for one citizen on each block to inventory all cars parked on the block each week. Cars that were found to be parked in the same location for a designated period were assumed to be abandoned. The responsible citizen was schooled in how to request that the vehicle be removed.

Fear among the elderly in a housing complex Inquiry revealed that the source of the fear stemmed from lack of familiarity with and understanding of younger families of mixed racial composition moving into the complex. Police, with the help of a county program for the elderly that promoted interaction with youths, involved the residents in a plan designed to enable the seniors to relate to the younger people as individuals rather than as intruders and troublemakers.

A series of rapes and a homicide-rape, with resulting fear Police worked with the neighborhood to create a telephone network that reached 124 homes in 11 minutes, enabling the police to elicit citizen help in locating and identifying the offenders. The system failed several times, but in three months, after corrections were made, it was used to solve several serious crimes, and these arrests, in turn, led to identifying those responsible for the crimes that led to establishing the network.

Tensions in a housing complex stemming from racial conflict Claiming that their employees were assaulted and robbed, a local pizzeria adopted a policy of not delivering within the housing complex. Residents were angered by the decision, attributing it, in part, to the racist attitude of the management of the pizza establishment. Police were working on a range of problems, including assaults and robberies, in the complex and, in doing so, coordinated their efforts with an established neighborhood association. Those meetings were used to air the conflict with the pizza establishment. A proposal emerged that management employ residents from within the complex as a first step toward healing the conflict and restoring service.

The form of community organizing will vary, reflecting different levels of involvement by the community. In some circumstances, with short-term needs, the police may be very pragmatic, limiting their objective to eliciting the help of the community in implementing a police-designed response. In other situations, the police may engage the community in the design of a response. Ideally, consistent with the emerging definition of the police role as facilitators helping the community to police itself, the police involvement will take the form of teaching members of the community to identify problems and teaching them how to mitigate or solve them on their own.

Organizing targeted groups of citizens for a limited purpose does not negate the value of a police agency working to organize larger groups and total neighborhoods to establish more permanent relationships. A strong network of community organizations obviously can be of great value to the police—to assist in acquiring information regarding serious crime, to ensure open channels of communication with the police to avoid misunderstandings and a potential buildup of tensions, and to make use of the sense of community to reduce dependence on the police. But efforts by the police to create such organizations where none has previously existed often are extremely difficult in the absence of a specific problem of common concern on which the police and the public can focus. (For an exploration of the effectiveness—and limitations—of efforts to mobilize communities with a general commitment to crime prevention, see Feins, 1983; Kelling, 1985a; Wycoff et al., 1985; Farrell, 1986; Kennedy, 1986;

Rosenbaum, Lewis, and Grant, 1986; Rosenbaum, 1987; and Skogan, 1988.) The problem of fear, by itself, obviously is not sufficiently specific.

Organizing the community to deal with a given problem does not require assembling a representative cross section of the community, as is usually the case when police try to create larger, more permanent community organizations. Rather, the type of community involvement that is sought will stem from the analysis of the specific problem and a tentative judgment about what should be done about it. Thus, for example, in attempting to deal with a continuing conflict between youngsters and elderly residents, police may initiate separate efforts to organize the two groups—with the eventual objective of bringing them together.

It follows from this discussion that any effort to mobilize the community, especially when the objective is to empower the community to do things for itself, requires more than sending out a call for people to come together. It is a complex, delicate task that requires careful prior analysis of the demographic makeup of the population that is affected by the problem. As one should expect, the potential to engage the community is often least where the problems are most acute, since the problems themselves may be a product of the absence of any sense of community. Community organizing of all types—especially of hard-to-organize groups—requires special skill. If police come to depend more heavily on community organization, the officers involved ought to have the benefit of the experience and relevant training developed in other areas in which community organization has been important.

Making Use of Existing Forms of Social Control in Addition to the Community

In addition to turning, in a general sense, to the community, the police have always sought to solve some problems by mobilizing specific forms of social control inherent in existing relationships—e.g., the influence of a parent over a child, a teacher over a student, or an employer over an employee. Numerous new examples have emerged in the problem-oriented projects of situations in which the police have more aggressively sought the help of those who, because they have some power over an individual, may be able to influence his or her behavior:

- Parents, in controlling the reckless driving or vandalism of their children
- Apartment managers, in exercising control over disruptive tenants (Engstad and Evans, 1980; Kelling, 1985a; Asbury, 1988)
- Contractors, in controlling the disorderly behavior of their workers (Kelling, 1985a)

- University officials and alumni, in controlling members of fraternities and sororities
- Friends, in controlling the driving of those who are intoxicated

In these situations, there is no formal basis for intervention either by the police or by another agency, such as will exist, for example, if a person is on probation or parole, is truant from school, or appears to be in violation of the conditions of holding a license. The person or group to which an appeal is made to exercise control does not have a legal obligation to do so, or that obligation is unclear.

Several arguments can be made for maximum use of informal controls that are already available in the community. First, invoking informal nongovernmental control may truly be the most effective means for dealing with the problem. Second, doing so reinforces the concept of the police as facilitators in getting the community to control itself rather than depending on the police and the criminal justice system for control. Third, it supports the strong preference, when an option exists, for using the least restrictive, least intrusive method of dealing with a problem. The potential in making greater use of already existing social control systems is enormous. And because the approach makes such good common sense and is so often effective, the incentive is strong to attempt to realize its full potential.

But to do so requires recognizing and protecting against the "down side." The police initiative in invoking social controls is an extraordinarily delicate undertaking that, if misused, can produce negative consequences for both citizens and the police. Whenever the police urge someone to do something, their request (simply because of who the police are) carries considerable weight. When appeals are made to third parties to exercise control over a situation, several things can go wrong. The police have no control over how judicious the third party will be in restraining the conduct of concern to the police. The consequences of sharing information to which only the police have access may be unduly damaging. In the worst scenario, the police may intentionally advance a judgment as to how a problem should be solved—using third parties to exercise the control—that is in conflict with basic principles of free speech, other Constitutional guarantees, or simply the sense of propriety that governs the relationship between the police and the citizenry. Because there have been some gross examples of such abuses at both the federal and local levels (especially in dealing with political dissent), an unqualified appeal that the police make use of existing social mechanisms to assist them in carrying out their job raises, in the minds of some, the fear of tactics commonly associated with a "police state."

The effect that the negative experiences have had on public attitudes toward the police poses a classic example of the common dilemma in working through solutions to frequent problems that arise in the community. In their day-to-day operations, police make—and probably always will make—some use of this type of response. They must do so. They simply do not have enough resources and formal methods of dealing with the range of behavioral problems they must handle. Legal controls are often inadequate: The penalty may no longer seem punitive, the standards of proof may be too high, and the prospect of arrest and incarceration may be too remote. Should we shy away from more fully realizing the benefits of careful use of the alternative, out of fear of the potential for abuse, knowing well that it will continue to be used? I argue the opposite: We ought to take on the work (and the risk) that is necessary to realize the maximum benefits in police mobilization of other social control mechanisms, while working to reduce to a minimum the potential for abuse—by openly acknowledging the response, by setting forth the circumstances under which it is used, and by subjecting its use to tight review and control.

Progress along these lines, although difficult, is facilitated within the framework developed in problem-oriented policing because the competing interests (i.e., effectiveness in dealing with the problem versus potential interference with privacy and the rights of an individual or group) can be weighed as they relate to dealing with a specific problem. A justified response to one problem may be ill-advised or too risky for another. Thus, as an example, to control violence, it would seem fairly obvious that police are warranted in making full use of whatever legal authority a school administrator exercises over students, but if the problem of concern is the use of alcohol or marijuana, many more questions would be raised. We need to invest more effort in working through these questions.

Here are four examples of practices that should stimulate thinking among those concerned with both the effectiveness and the fairness of the police. Are these practices desirable or undesirable? Should they be encouraged or discouraged? What are some of the factors that lead to different conclusions?

- A police officer was assigned to work with high school officials regarding the usual range of problems that arise in a high school setting, but with special emphasis on controlling student use of alcohol. If she found a student athlete to be using alcohol, she reported the incident to the student's coach. By informal agreement, the student would be required to run extra laps in practice or might be forced to sit out the next game. Both the officer and the coach contended that the arrangement was effective, especially since the punishment was meted out by someone the student usually respected; and they contended that the arrangement was preferable to formal processing, assuming that adequate grounds existed, with the consequences of a juvenile record.

• A neighborhood police officer knew of several "drug houses"—the homes of women who sought to supplement their income through the sale of marijuana to young children after school. The problem of drugs was so severe in this area that these situations were not considered of sufficiently high priority to warrant the attention of the specialized drug unit of the police department. Moreover, it was extremely difficult to acquire needed evidence when the only persons to whom sales were made were youngsters. Satisfied that the women made such sales regularly, the officer informed all of their neighbors of the situation. The officer reported that the pressures applied by the neighbors resulted in an end to the sales or in the women moving out of the area. From the officer's perspective, the problem had been solved; the access of the especially young children to drugs was greatly reduced.

• Officers concerned about a problem of robbery of convenience stores concluded, based on their investigations, that a substantial percentage of the robberies were falsely reported by employees to cover their theft of receipts. A check of police files indicated that some of the employees had previously been convicted of theft. Without naming specific individuals, the police conveyed this finding and their conclusion to management and urged that steps be taken to review the backgrounds of their employees and to institute measures to prevent internal theft.

• In an investigation of drug sales, police learned that drugs were being routinely peddled, during lunch break, to employees of a firm producing sensitive biomedical equipment that, if it malfunctioned, could be life-threatening. Police alerted management to their observations (without naming specific individuals) in the hope that management would take measures to dry up the demand of their employees.

Several factors emerge as important in weighing the propriety of enlisting third parties to assert control over a problem: the seriousness of the conduct; the certainty with which responsibility can be established; the confidence one has in the ability of the third party to handle the matter fairly; the availability of alternatives and their relative effectiveness; and, as an overall consideration, the risks that may be involved.

Altering the Physical Environment to Reduce Opportunities for Problems to Recur

A vast amount of work has been done in exploring ways to reduce crime by making changes in the physical environment—in the design of buildings, parks, streets, and lighting (see, e.g., Jacobs, 1962; Newman, 1972; Jeffrey, 1977; Clarke and Mayhew, 1980; Hough, 1980–1981; and Fowler and Mangione, 1986). In a response to the "broken window" syndrome described by Wilson and Kelling (1982), several experiments have been conducted to determine if intensive efforts to clean up a neighborhood affect the level of crime, disorder, and fear (Pate et al., 1986). And the Oasis projects provide an accumulation of experience on the effect of a grass-roots program of improvement in specific neighborhoods and housing projects, undertaken with the cooperation of housing officials and the police, on the quality of life in an otherwise deteriorating neighborhood (for a convenient summary, see Lindsey et al., 1985).

Much of the early work in altering the physical environment was undertaken without regard to a specific problem, but in the belief that it would have a generally positive impact. In the context of problem-oriented policing, the need for physical changes grows out of the analysis of a specific problem. The search is more focused and therefore more likely to produce an alternative that is directly applicable to the problem of concern.

Poyner's work in England, undertaken independently, is especially significant in the support it lends to problem-oriented policing in that he has meticulously taken apart larger problems (e.g., street attacks) and analyzed specific portions in great depth with the objective of attempting to reduce or eliminate the specific problem through environmental change (Poyner, 1980, 1983; Poyner and Woodall, 1987). As a result of his study of pickpocketing in Birmingham, for example, he recommended that barriers be installed at bus stops to protect bus riders from the pickpockets who enter the waiting crowd to steal wallets. His study of theft from bags carried by shoppers in crowded marketplaces led to exploration of the possibility of redesigning the spacing between stalls. Following the pattern set in Poyner's work, a Home Office study of shoplifting in a specific record store recommended elevating the checkout stands, relocating merchandise, making merchandise less concealable, and installing theft-warning devices (Ekblom, 1987).

Much of the attention in exploring environmental changes to date has been on reducing serious crime, with frequent reminders that the opportunities for doing so are still numerous. The problem-oriented policing projects have expanded the use of environmental change to frequently recurring public order problems, often through the initiative of individual officers. (The description at the beginning of Chapter 7 of the Philadelphia police sergeant's response to the long history of noise complaints about a neighborhood bar is an excellent example.) Here are some others:

- To deter drunken festival goers from climbing street poles and performing dangerous acrobatics, officers arranged to have the poles greased just before the festival
- To avoid daily conflict between two groups of students on their way home from school, arrangements were made to relocate a bus stop

• To meet the complaints of neighbors about a resident who undertook major car repairs in front of their apartments, arrangements were made with management to set aside a special site for car repairs

• To deal with two quite different problems, the dumping of garbage and the racing of dirt bikes, ditches were dug and landscaped, creating barriers to the intruders

• To deal with the vandalism to property and other disruptions caused by commuting students who parked in a quiet residential neighborhood, arrangements were made to increase the number of permits issued to students for the under-used school parking area and to limit parking on neighboring streets on school days

The big frustration in using this alternative is that, although many changes in physical environment can be carried out easily and with little if any cost, on a larger scale, the cost of making changes in permanent physical structures becomes a major impediment. This, however, is all relative. The problems associated with high-rise public housing in St. Louis were considered of such magnitude that they resulted in a decision to level these enormous structures. Though such action may not appear feasible initially, because of cost, the police could make a strong case for the expenditure of substantial sums to correct many of the conditions that give rise to seemingly insolvable problems for which they are then held responsible.

A classic example is the problem of graffiti in the New York City subway system—a phenomenon that, although admired as pop art by some, was generally viewed as the ultimate symbol of urban decay (and a situation out of control) in that city. Almost every inch of every subway car, both inside and out, was covered by the distinctive markings of the youthful artists. Massive resources were invested in attempting to reduce the problem through intensive police patrols of the cars when in use and the surveillance of the yards in which the cars were stored when not in use—all with the objective of arresting and prosecuting the offenders. Little was accomplished. A change in the administration of the New York City Transit Authority in 1984 led to an in-depth inquiry, which, in turn, led to the conclusion—for which there was some precedent in previous studies of vandalism—that the satisfaction of placing distinctive signatures and other markings on the trains came from viewing the markings on future trips. If the markings were removed immediately, the incentive for making them would be eliminated. With the delivery of new subway cars from which graffiti could be more easily removed and a program of repainting older cars, the new administration initiated a policy to make one line of the system at a time graffiti-free. Once cleaned, any subway car on the line found to have graffiti at the end of an operating day was taken out of service until the graffiti was removed. (In addition, the sale of spray-paint cans to minors was restricted, and theft of them was deterred by a city ordinance requiring merchants to secure them prior to sale.) Aside from the high cost of the program, some initial inconvenience was caused riders because of the large number of cars that had to be taken out of service. But this number was gradually reduced, and as of May 1988, 86 percent of the 5,956 cars in the system were graffiti-free (*The New York Times,* May 6, 1988). It would be very difficult to compute with any precision the relative cost of the two approaches to dealing with the problem. It is, however, abundantly clear that not only is the newest approach successful; it has replaced a sense of futility, resignation, and despair (especially on the part of the police) with a sense of accomplishment, hope, and optimism that other seemingly intractable problems in a large, complex urban area can also be solved.

The police have learned through these experiences the importance of being more involved in the planning of new facilities and municipal services. One of the results of the study of theft from vehicles in Newport News was to arrange police representation on the committee planning the construction of a new parking garage. Although architects appear to have become much more sensitive to matters of security (as, for example, in the construction of new subway systems), a police agency that is on top of the major problems for which it is responsible could contribute further, through early involvement, to preventing problems of both crime and disorder through the design of new construction.

Increased Regulation, through Statutes or Ordinances, of Conditions That Contribute to Problems

If a municipal or state health department concluded, for example, that salad bars created the potential for the spread of disease, it would regulate the way in which restaurants operate their salad bars. If a fire department concluded that a certain material was combustible, it would move to prohibit its use in construction. In the past, police have not had as strong a tradition of initiating proposals for regulations to prevent some of the problems they must handle. One notable exception, in recent years, has been the adoption of burglary-prevention ordinances, which, for example, may include minimum standards for lighting and lock systems. (See, for example, the Oakland provisions described in Engstad and Evans, 1980, p. 152. See also Blanchard, 1973.) The Portland, Oregon, Police Bureau has been among the most active agencies recently pressing for such regulations. Another exception is the effort to control false burglar alarms.

Studies of a specific problem will often draw attention to factors contributing to the problem that can be controlled by regulation. That was the result of the Gainesville, Florida, study of convenience store robberies described in Chapter 7, where the city council, through an ordinance, required the stores to adopt practices designed to reduce robberies (Clifton, 1987).

In examining the problem of noise, for example, it is obvious that the number of complaints would be greatly reduced if minimum soundproofing were required in the construction of apartment houses. In studying the overall problem of theft from merchants, it is clear that such theft could be substantially reduced if store owners are prohibited from displaying merchandise unattended and unsecured outside their buildings—especially when the business is closed. It is also clear that the practice of defrauding merchants by requesting refunds on merchandise stolen but not removed from a store could be greatly reduced by requiring a receipt for the exchange. In responding to the problem of graffiti in New York City, controls were established by ordinance over the sale of spray paint, especially to minors.

What are the pros and cons in moving in this direction? Our society quite properly resists overregulation, especially as it affects individual rights and free competition. Except for the Gainesville example, none of these problems is life-threatening, as might be the case if disease were spread or a fire broke out. That probably accounts for the lack of strong support for regulation. The cost is limited to the police time involved and the effect on the quality of life of those adversely affected, as in the case of noise. Each community might arrive at a different judgment in balancing these factors. As a middle ground, a community as a matter of policy might opt against regulation, but—with regard to the merchandising practices, for example—instruct the police to assign low priority to investigating offenses that could so easily be prevented. Are the police sufficiently assertive in identifying such conditions and practices and in encouraging communities to choose, through their governing bodies, from among the alternatives they have for dealing with them?

Developing New Forms of Limited Authority to Intervene and Detain

Analysis of specific problems often leads to the conclusion that satisfactory resolution requires some limited authority (e.g., to order a person to leave) but does not require labeling the conduct criminal so that it can be dealt with through a citation or a physical arrest followed by a criminal prosecution. The best response to a dispute in a bar or on the street may be simply to separate the combatants and send them on their way.

Should the police be required to take formal action against one or both of them in order to separate them? In like fashion, the best response to demonstrators who have blocked access to a building may be to remove them and, in the case of disorderly street gatherings, to order individuals to "move on." If that is all that is needed, should the police be required to cite or arrest the protesters or to identify and arrest those responsible for the disorder?

New pressures on the police make them cling even more tightly to use of the criminal justice system in such situations. The public, in the past two decades, has expressed great concern about the use of authority by the police, and the police have developed much greater sensitivity to this concern. If officers are perceived as functioning primarily within the criminal justice system, it is widely assumed that authority is spelled out clearly, standards for taking action are firmly established, and elaborate controls exist that reduce to a minimum the likelihood that authority will be abused. It is also widely assumed that when the police function outside the criminal justice system, much less formal guidance exists for judging both the legality and the propriety of what they do.

This tendency to take comfort in police operating within the criminal justice system has been reinforced by two highly publicized court decisions (*Irwin* v. *Ware,* 1984; *Thurman* v. *City of Torrington,* 1984) and a series of more recent cases that have followed their lead. In the two cases, the police were found liable for deaths and injuries that occurred because they had evidence that a crime had occurred, but chose not to make an arrest. The decisions properly stimulated police to think about the serious consequences of failing to act when the need for some form of action was patently clear. But they are unfortunately being cited widely to give new life to what was a gradually fading notion—that the police are compelled to enforce the law all of the time: that they have no discretion. If potential liability, rather than effectiveness, becomes the dominant concern in deciding what a police officer should do, officers will make an arrest even though some other form of action is preferable.

In reality, neither the guidance provided by the criminal law nor the controls asserted within the criminal justice system are as effective as they are often thought to be (LaFave, 1965; Skolnick, 1966; Davis, 1969, 1975; Bittner, 1970; Force, 1972; Rubinstein, 1973). The damages awarded for failure of the police to arrest underlines the need for the police to correct their practices so that arrests are made when clearly warranted. But the awards also underline the need for legislative clarification of both the authority of the police to exercise discretion and the liability of the police for not making an arrest when grounds for an arrest exist (see, e.g., American Bar Association, 1973; Goldstein, 1977). Providing new forms of limited authority responsive to specific problems, subject to appropriate review, may in fact be a more effective way of meeting some of the concerns about potential abuse (American Bar Association, 1973).

Two methods are available for crafting a more effective response. One is to define the conduct of concern more specifically as a criminal or ordinance violation and create a procedure for dealing with it *within* the systems for processing crimes or ordinance violations that does not invoke the full panoply of steps in these systems (i.e., physical arrest or citation, prosecution, and trial). This possibility is explored in the next section, which discusses the potential for making more discriminate use of the criminal justice system. The other method also requires defining the conduct of concern more specifically, but then establishes a procedure for dealing with it *outside* the criminal justice system.

The best example we now have of the second procedure is the system in place in approximately two-thirds of the states for responding to the problem of public inebriates. Police are authorized to take incapacitated individuals into custody for transportation to a detoxification facility where they may be held for a period of time, usually 72 hours. Those who are intoxicated but not incapacitated may choose between being transported home or to the detoxification center. Taking an incapacitated person into custody is not considered an arrest, and police are freed of liability in taking a person into custody without making an arrest. Where adequate facilities for detoxification have been provided, this system has proved to be eminently more sensible than arrest followed by detention in a drunk tank until sober, at which time the individual is often released.

Somewhat analogous authority has been given to the police to arrange for the temporary detention of the mentally ill—an improvement over an older practice in which there was no alternative to arresting them in order to care for them. (Those who attempted suicide were arrested and charged with that as the offense!) But this new authority is much more restrictive than the authority relating to the alcoholic, and the standard for establishing the need for intervention is more rigid, with the result that many mentally ill persons are taken into the criminal justice system—often with the encouragement of mental health professionals who feel that their adjustment to community living requires adherence to community standards and sanctions for failure to conform. The complexities that arise from jailing and prosecuting mentally ill persons raise many issues that are ripe for further exploration.

Currently begging for attention is the difficulty created by the absence of appropriate authority to deal with the homeless when their lives are endangered. At one point, several cities improvised by simply proclaiming that the homeless would be taken into custody and transported to a shelter, for their own protection, when the temperature dropped to 5°F or below (*The New York Times,* Jan. 23, 1985). Related is the need for some authority to intervene when the conduct of homeless persons goes well beyond being unsightly or constituting a nuisance and actually prevents others from making use of public facilities. The police need limited authority, when specifically defined conditions exist, to order homeless people to desist or to move, or to take them to a shelter for a period of time. Without such authority, the police are forced to use vague criminal charges and act on their authority to arrest—a process that is unkind to the homeless, distasteful to the police, and inappropriate for the criminal justice system. As the courts increasingly challenge this use of the criminal law (see, e.g., *People* v. *Bright,* 1988, which struck down the 23-year-old state loitering law used by New York City transit police to arrest homeless people in public areas of train stations and bus terminals), the need for some specifically drawn authority that results in action other than a criminal prosecution becomes even more apparent.

Drafting and gaining approval for new forms of authority is an ambitious undertaking—requiring far more than the efforts of a police officer, police administrator, or even a single police agency. But a clear definition of the need and some of the initial impetus must come from them. The distrust stemming from an awareness of past abuses and the illusion that the criminal justice system ensures protections must both be overcome. The work of Robert Force (1972) still provides the best exploration of the complexities in moving in this direction, and his recommendations are even more persuasive today, given the increase in street-order problems. By analyzing problems first and only then exploring the need for governmental authority, problem-oriented policing lends renewed support to the approach that Force so clearly outlined.

More Discriminate Use of the Criminal Justice System

Despite the heavy emphasis on developing alternatives to the criminal justice system, problem-oriented policing does not preclude its use. For many problems, the most desirable response may be to make full or partial use of the system. But this use should be much more discreet than in the past, reserved for those problems for which the system seems especially appropriate, and employed with much greater precision. A response employing the criminal justice system can take several different forms.

Straightforward Investigation, Arrest, and Prosecution The most direct and effective way to deal with certain problems remains identifying, arresting, and prosecuting the perpetrators. In the simplest scenario, a community may be plagued by a series of murders or sexual assaults that appear to be the work of a single person. Nothing short of the identification, apprehension, and prosecution of the offender will solve the problem, though the effort may well tax the resources of an entire department. Why state so obvious a point? To emphasize that, in the context of problem-oriented policing, the straightforward arrest and prosecution of the person who commits a serious crime—whatever one may have done to try to prevent such crimes—continues to be the preferred way to deal with the problem. This places a high value on the hard work associated with criminal investigations. The folklore associated with police work has always emphasized the challenge involved in identifying the responsible party and obtaining the evidence. Less glorified but equally challenging is the need to probe into complex problems, such as, for example, youth gang activity, to identify precisely those responsible for planning and carrying out indiscriminate assaults that result in serious injury or death (as distinct from using large numbers of arrests for relatively minor offenses in an effort to control the gangs).

With increased recognition of the limited capacity of the police to deal with crime by simply reacting when a crime occurs, much experimentation has occurred within the past decade with more proactive forms of investigation, such as decoys to apprehend street robbers and sting operations to apprehend burglars, organized groups of auto thieves, and drug sellers. These developments are compatible with the overall concept of problem-oriented policing when analysis indicates that arrest and prosecution have the greatest potential for dealing effectively with the problem. A proactive strategy designed to impact on a particular aspect of the problem increases that potential.

Selective Enforcement with Articulated Criteria The police always have available to them the option of increasing their enforcement of laws that might bear on a specific problem, although they may not routinely enforce them because they lack the resources, the problem has low priority, or enforcement is judged to be ineffective.

When the police step up enforcement of a seldom-used law, their actions are often characterized by the media as a "crackdown." Crackdowns are not new in police work. Too often they constitute the only response that the police make to a worsening situation—reflecting a narrowly limited concept of what the police can do and, more generally, a lack of imagination and initiative. They are easy to carry out and they cater to mass media coverage and public expectations. But those that are made with an accompanying message that the police intend to "get tough" on a continuing basis will usually fail. The police seldom have enough resources to sustain the operation and make their threats credible.

In contrast, a police agency may wisely conclude, after analyzing a specific problem, that one element of their total response ought to be a carefully planned, creative program of strict enforcement of laws that previously were seldom or never enforced. To succeed, the effort must be targeted to have a maximum impact on the specific problem of concern, and it must be sustained over a prolonged period.

Selective enforcement is always vulnerable to criticism as being arbitrary and capricious—and ample evidence exists that laws that are not enforced uniformly have been used to harass specific groups. To avoid such allegations, it is incumbent on the police, if they decide to make use of selective enforcement, to articulate the necessity for selectively enforcing the law, the impact enforcement will have on controlling the larger problem, and the criteria they will employ in deciding who is subject to arrest and prosecution (Davis, 1969, 1974, 1975; Goldstein, 1963, 1977).

The most extensive experience that the police have had in selective enforcement, too often ignored, has been in the control of motorists. Police have become quite adept at making discreet use of limited resources to achieve a relatively high level of conformity by motorists with the rules of the road—depending heavily on selective enforcement. Guidelines have evolved, often based on an analysis of accidents, to determine times, days, and areas in which enforcement should be concentrated; violations that should receive priority; and accepted tolerances beyond legislated standards. Much in the accumulated experience of the police in using selective enforcement to control traffic has application to other problems that police handle.

Enforcing Criminal Laws That, by Tradition, Are Enforced by Another Agency State statutes define a broad range of conduct as criminal, including the violation of numerous regulations governing business, the professions, and the environment. Police officers are sworn to enforce all the criminal laws. But by tradition they limit themselves to what is referred to commonly as the criminal code of the state. Practice varies, however, even in the use of the criminal code. Officers in some jurisdictions automatically refer some categories of cases to the district attorney or some other agency.

One of the consequences of urging police officers, in the context of problem-oriented policing, to explore all possible alternatives to dealing with a problem has been to open the eyes of officers to other types of violations that may be involved in creating the problems (e.g., the defrauding of customers by merchants; the violation of building codes by landlords; the disregard of environmental regulations; a variety of illegal business schemes for maximizing profits and avoiding taxes). If dealing with these violations appears the most effective way to solve the problem, all that may be required is to call the violations to the attention of the agency that normally has responsibility for enforcement. But if the agency is not responsive, the police may have to take the initiative, conducting an investigation in an area in which they are not experienced and doing so at the risk of offending the other agency. Yet documentation of violations—even short of what may be required for a prosecution—may be just what is needed to mobilize another agency to act. Such was the case, for example, when the Newport News police conducted their inquiry of the range of problems in the New Briarfield housing complex (Eck and Spelman et al., 1987, pp. 66–72).

One of the side benefits of this option is the increased credibility that the police may realize in the community. Citizens who view the police as biased in favor of protecting the "establishment" get a different perspective if they see a police readiness to enforce laws applicable to a broader range of interests and offenses that may be more serious than relatively petty offenses against which the police will unquestioningly take action.

Defining with Greater Specificity That Behavior Which Should Be Subject to Criminal Prosecution or to Control through City Ordinances Study of a problem may conclude that the behavior is of sufficient concern to warrant intervention, and that the best response is to subject those responsible to some form of sanction, but the behavior is not specifically prohibited. This situation arises most clearly with regard to street-order problems. In the past the police depended on generally worded statutes or ordinances, such as those defining disorderly conduct, trespass, and vagrancy, as the basis for making arrests in many ambiguous situations. But as we have noted, this stretched use led to court challenges, which, in turn, led to the statutes being declared overly broad and therefore unconstitutional. As a result, police authority to maintain order is much less clear than the average citizen assumes it to be. The move to authorize the police to intervene and detain for purposes other than a prosecution (for example, to provide treatment or shelter as previously described) has met some of these needs. But many patterns of behavior remain that deeply offend a community, with a strong consensus that the police should have some authority to intervene. A common example is harassment and intimidation by youth gangs. In the absence of a basis for arrest or citation, support has been expressed for dealing with some problems through the use of informal authority, candidly referred to as "kicking ass and taking names." (First articulated in Wilson and Kelling, 1982, the pros and cons are interestingly debated in Kelling, 1985b, and Klockars, 1985. See also Sykes, 1986, and Klockars, 1986.)

Problem-oriented policing leads to one possible way out of this dilemma. The courts have repeatedly expressed a willingness to uphold legislation dealing with recurring problems if the legislation is narrowly drawn and describes exactly the behavior that is prohibited (see, e.g., *Gregory* v. *City of Chicago,* 1969). Local analysis of problems makes it possible to meet these criteria—to describe precisely the offensive conduct that the police desire to control. Thus the need for the authority grows out of a systematic analysis of the problem, which is quite different from proposals for new authority that are drawn in a vacuum.

The Madison police, for example, found in their inquiry into panhandling that they could not make use of what remained of the vagrancy statutes because the district attorney felt that the statute would be successfully challenged as unconstitutional. Their study resulted in a recognition that the community was not concerned about all forms of panhandling. The community wanted to preserve the opportunity for street performers to solicit funds but wanted to prohibit panhandling that constituted harassment. And so, with the help of the city attorney, an ordinance was drafted to define harassing panhandling. It was quickly enacted by the city council.

In Baltimore County, police became concerned about neighborhood disputes in which one party would be harassed repeatedly, though the behavior was not illegal. In an especially tragic case, a frail, aged man shot two teenagers who had taunted him repeatedly. This led the department to join with others in support of a state statute defining a new offense of harassment. In like manner, police efforts to deal with specific problems have led to ordinances being enacted in Oakland to prohibit loitering by prostitutes and in Madison to prohibit gambling in public parks.

Some react negatively to the police initiating requests for legislation. One can understand that reaction if the police seem to be merely lashing out at a problem. It is quite different, however, if the request is a carefully honed proposal that grows out of thoughtful study. In Madison, for example, officers who studied the problem of enticement of children into vehicles supported a statute redefining enticement, since the legal definition left them powerless to act if they could not prove that the enticement was for immoral purposes. Their testimony was persuasive.

Intervention without Making an Arrest Suppose it is concluded that stopping, educating, and warning individuals that they have violated a law is judged the most effective way of reducing the magnitude of a problem, and that a commitment to arrest in all cases would be unrealistic because of the large number of violations, the time required in processing an arrest, and the potential for overloading the criminal justice system. And even if arrests could be made, warnings may be as effective—or perhaps even more effective—in controlling the problem. If the police have the clear authority to arrest, can they intervene without going that far?

This alternative is controversial and lends itself to abuse, but it is considered and used with sufficient frequency to warrant exploration. It is, for example, built into the response of most police agencies to motor vehicle violations. Many more drivers who violate the rules of the road are stopped and warned than are cited or arrested.

The Home Office Prevention Unit in Great Britain recommended just such a response to store detectives trying to curb shoplifting. They reasoned that since many youngsters were stealing trivial amounts of goods at the risk of serious punishment, they apparently did not expect to be caught. It was thought better to invest limited resources in increasing the number of youngsters caught than in processing fully a much smaller number of cases. It was concluded that a greater risk of being apprehended (even though no punishment would follow) was enough to deter a high percentage of violators (Ekblom, 1987). The study of drunk driving in Madison reached a similar conclusion regarding that problem. Since the percentage of drinking drivers who are arrested is so low, and the criminal justice system can handle only a limited number of cases, it was reasoned that the police could have a significant deterrent effect by increasing the number of contacts with drinking drivers without expending the enormous resources required to take them through the system. Increased expectation of being caught was thought to be enough to deter many drivers from driving while intoxicated. Criteria were recommended for guiding police in determining who should be arrested and who should only be warned (Goldstein and Susmilch, 1982a).

The major concern of the police with this option is the fear of incurring liability for failing to make an arrest when evidence exists to support an arrest. (This concern is discussed earlier in this chapter.) Furthermore, warnings lose their effectiveness if there is no way of keeping a record of them. An admonishment that a repetition of the behavior will result in a sterner response relies on bluff for its effectiveness unless police assignment practices are such that the same officer is likely to encounter the same person engaged in the same behavior. To keep a record of warnings is not only cumbersome, it also raises difficult issues about the propriety of basing the use of subsequent, more severe actions on prior allegations that were not adjudicated or subject to any form of review.

Use of Arrest without the Intention to Prosecute Should the police, under any conditions, consider the use of arrest without a commitment to prosecution as an appropriate way to deal with a problem? If seen as an exceptional use of the criminal justice system—requiring great sensitivity and care—resorted to as a temporary measure if no other means are available, it may be both justifiable and the preferred response. But if resorted to often over a prolonged period of time as the primary response to a problem, it usually perpetuates the very troubles stemming from overdependence on the criminal justice system that problem-oriented policing is intended to eliminate. The conclusion that arrest without a commitment to prosecution is the best response to a problem is often the clearest indication we have of the need to craft a different response.

From a legal perspective, the police clearly have the authority to arrest if adequate evidence exists to support the arrest. Researchers who monitor intensive enforcement campaigns against street-level heroin dealers claim that the campaigns are not only an effective way to control the trafficking, but also can significantly reduce burglary and robbery rates (Kleiman, 1986, 1987; Zimmer, 1987). As a minimum, the areas in which the arrests are made are cleared of drug trade. Researchers also claim that arrest is the preferred method for handling spousal abuse in that it reduces subsequent abuse (Sherman and Berk, 1984). At the least, it separates the parties for a period of time.

As long as the police contend that their objective is to prosecute when an arrest is made, their choice of action is legally justifiable and may appear to be the preferred policy option. But in practice only a relatively small percentage of these arrests result in a prosecution, and an even smaller percentage result in a conviction. Police can take a formal position that they have carried out their job, and any failure to invoke the entire criminal justice system stems either from overloaded prosecutors and courts or from the reluctance of victims to cooperate in a prosecution.

But the frequency with which there is no prosecution is well known to the police. So in reality the commitment is not to prosecution but to the use of arrest as an end in itself. If used in a wholesale manner, programs of arrest without prosecution make both the citizenry and the police vulnerable. The delicate power of arrest, when exercised quickly and against large numbers of individuals, cannot be used in a discriminating manner. And with no scheduled judicial review—however perfunctory it may be when an arrest leads to a prosecution—the major control over the quality of arrests made by the police becomes inoperative. Without such review, programs in which arrest has been used as an end in itself tend to degenerate; they lead to sloppy practices in which individuals are taken into custody without adequate evidence. When this occurs, arrest becomes a program of summary punishment invoked by the police for violating whatever standards or rules they establish. In Chicago, for example, in an effort to control youth gangs, thousands of individuals were arrested and jailed pending court appearances, at which the cases against them were routinely dismissed because the police did not appear in court. Challenged in the federal courts, the city agreed to stop the practice and to submit to court monitoring of the corrective steps required (*Nelson* v. *City of Chicago,* 1983). Resort to "sweeps" as a way of coping with gang violence in Los Angeles has led to similar criticism (e.g., *The Wall Street Journal,* May 5, 1988).

The needs that led to the development of these practices are obvious and beg for a response. The police must have some means by which, as a minimum, they can disperse congregations of drug sellers and buyers who disrupt neighborhoods. They must have a way to manage large numbers of gang members when the evidence is clear that the gangs are engaged in violent activity. And they must have the authority to separate individuals engaged in combat. The difficult question is whether it is best to attempt to achieve these limited objectives through the use of just the front end of the criminal justice system. There is strong support for this in some quarters. How much of this support stems from the value of temporary jailing as a form of punishment? If this is the true objective, the practice probably cannot be justified on any grounds. If the support reflects a sincere desire to carry through a criminal prosecution, police must condition their involvement on the capacity of the rest of the system to carry out its functions. If support for the program has the limited objective of authorizing the police to intervene, then continued use, even as a temporary measure, requires elaborate steps to ensure that an adequate basis exists for each arrest; that due process is accorded all arrestees until released; and that the program is administered with appropriate concern for fairness and equality. Even if these steps are taken, it becomes important to launch an immediate search for an alternative that eliminates the need for intervention or crafts a form of authority that, for example, would authorize the police to disperse crowds or to separate combatants, and no more, preserving arrest for those situations in which prosecution is justified and achievable.

Attaching New Conditions to Probation or Parole When a convicted offender is set free under probation or parole, he or she may be prohibited from engaging in certain activities, associating with specified individuals, or frequenting designated locations. The conditions of probation or parole are established to increase the potential for a successful adjustment in the community and, of course, to reduce the likelihood of new criminal involvement. As a result of analyzing a problem, the police interest in convicted offenders may or may not coincide with that of the probation and parole officers. Thus, for example, police concerned with eliminating prostitution in a given area have a special interest in ensuring that convicted prostitutes not be allowed to return to the area. And police want to ensure that an individual convicted for harassment not be allowed to have contact with the person harassed. In both Newport News and Baltimore County, this led to the concept of "mapping"—arranging with the judge, as a condition of probation, to prohibit the offender from being present within a designated radius of the center of the activity for which the offender was arrested. Heralded as an extraordinarily effective means for dealing with problems such as street prostitution and the harassment of neighbors, it simply requires, in setting out the conditions of probation or parole, a consideration of community problems along with continuing concerns about the released offender. And, of course, it requires a systematic way in which officers on the street are notified of the conditions under which some ex-offenders are free in the community.

Using Civil Law to Control Public Nuisances, Offensive Behavior, and Conditions Contributing to Crime

Because most of what the police do in the use of the law involves arrest and prosecution, we tend to forget that the police and city government can initiate a number of other legal proceedings.

As an example, there is great variation in the use made by city governments of their authority over licensed premises, such as those selling alcoholic beverages, and even more variation in the role played by the police in enforcing the conditions to which licensees are held. Some agencies turn quickly, in dealing with a problem, to check these conditions; the thought simply does not occur to others. Since many police problems are associated with premises and occupations that are licensed by city government, an intensified police effort to deal with these problems often leads to the conclusion that fuller use can be made of existing controls. Police agencies that in the past have not been involved in seeking to revoke the license of a dispenser of alcoholic beverages, a peddler, a pawnshop operator, or a restaurant may find that a commitment to more rigorous enforcement of the conditions set forth in their respective licenses may be the most effective way in which to deal with a long-standing problem. (For an examination of efforts to control the drinking driver, for example, by controlling servers, see Mosher, 1983.)

More effective zoning, or the enforcement of existing zoning laws that have fallen into disuse, may hold the answer to a problem. Thus, for example, in a rural section of Baltimore County, efforts on the part of the police to deal with fear growing out of a crime led, in turn, to identification by the community of a problem of widespread concern—homeowners were using old vehicles as storage sheds. Police initiative in determining that this constituted a zoning ordinance violation led to solution of the problem. In large cities, zoning has been used occasionally to avoid the problems associated with a concentration of adult entertainment in an area by limiting the proximity of pornography stores and adult entertainment movies to each other (see Strom, 1977). Since zoning is the accepted way of resolving conflicts in the use of space, police are well advised at least to give conscious consideration to its applicability to problems of concern.

Police, in most states, have long had the authority to confiscate property used in the commission of a crime, and some have had the authority to confiscate the proceeds of criminal activity as well. But this authority was rarely used creatively or fully as part of a broader attack on a problem of which the crimes committed were but one aspect. Now, however, in attempting to cope with the enormous problem of drugs, the police, often with expanded and clarified legislative authority (usually in the form of acts to control organized crime), have turned increasingly to confiscation and forfeiture, seizing not only drugs, vehicles used in their transportation, and monetary assets, but property that facilitates or is intended for use in the commission of a crime. Also now commonly subject to seizure are the apartments and homes in which violations occur. With encouragement and financial support from the federal government, state and municipal police agencies have established "asset forfeiture" programs that are now an integral part of their response to the drug problem. (For details on these programs, see Stellwagen, 1985; Ferris, 1988; and Holmes, 1988. Developments in this area are so rapid that the Police Executive Research Forum and the Bureau of Justice Assistance of the U.S. Department of Justice publish a periodic newsletter, *Asset Forfeiture Bulletin*.)

Most states provide authority to city governments to abate some nuisances or to padlock premises on which repeated violations of the law occur. Because of lack of familiarity with these provisions and the absence of a tradition for using them, they often are not considered to be among the tools that the police have available to them. (See Potter, 1987, for a comprehensive analysis of their use in dealing with prostitution.) Their use may be the most satisfactory method for handling a difficult situation. Thus, for example, Baltimore County police employed the seldom-used abatement laws to have a structure that was the gathering place of a group of troublesome youth declared a nuisance and ordered removed, thereby eliminating the problem.

Injunctive relief is also underused by the police. Injunctive relief is the process of obtaining a judicial order to require a person to do, or more commonly to desist from doing, a particular act. In the context of problem-oriented policing, it has the great value of attempting to deal with a problem in a preventive way, before serious consequences can arise. Often a person (such as a threatening spouse) or persons (such as a striking labor union) may actually announce an intent to engage in criminal conduct or in a confrontation. In such situations, injunctions enable the police to take action before the act is committed.

The use of injunctive relief, commonly initiated by application for a temporary restraining order, recently has received much more attention because legislation has been enacted that authorizes the victims of spousal abuse to obtain injunctions to prevent an abusive spouse from returning to the family residence. The police may then arrest for violation of the injunction. This widespread use of injunctive relief, initiated in this case by a private party, should make police comfortable with the process and stimulate their thinking about other situations in which it might be the most appropriate response.

A recent example of just such creativity occurred in Los Angeles, where the city attorney's office obtained an unusual injunction ordering members of a drug-dealing street gang not to annoy, harass, or intimidate the residents of the gang's territory. Prosecutors contended that the gang was an "unincorporated association" whose members were individually liable for the actions of its members and, as such, constituted a nuisance. News accounts attributed the ineffectiveness of the move to lack of follow-through once the injunction was obtained (*The Wall Street Journal,* Mar. 30, 1988).

CHOOSING FROM AMONG ALTERNATIVES

Any single tailor-made response to a problem is likely to consist of a blend of alternatives. And that blend may not be the same from one city to another or, in dealing with street-level problems, from one beat to another within the same city. Much will depend on the results of the analysis, the factors considered in weighing the merit of alternatives, and, most important, the values attached to these factors. This process recognizes that solving problems is not a sterile exercise. Systematic analysis can lead to possible solutions, but community values must be considered in assessing the merits of these solutions. That is as it should be, given our commitment to a form of policing that is responsive to the interests and needs of the local community. The resulting experiences, and the opportunity to compare among experiences based on the varied combinations of responses that may be tried, is one of the major benefits that can be realized from our decentralized, locally oriented form of police organization. This richness can contribute significantly to advancing the quality of policing.

Officers and departments experimenting with problem-oriented policing typically settle on a multifaceted response involving several alternatives in dealing with a single problem. The different alternatives may be interdependent. More importance may be placed on one than the other.

Some may be specifically designed to achieve a short-term effect, while others may reflect long-term goals.

The manner in which this works can best be demonstrated by expanding on several examples used in this chapter to illustrate alternatives. By summarizing the original problem and the full combination of alternatives that were ultimately employed, one can demonstrate the use of multifaceted responses and the community values that influence the choices made.

One problem initially assigned to the Baltimore County COPE unit was defined as breaking and entering in an apartment complex. Upon analysis, it was concluded that the central problem was that long-established elderly residents feared new residents, who were younger and of a different racial mix. The COPE unit responded by arranging upgraded lighting; the construction and controlled use of a basketball court; rules for the compatible use of the swimming pool; some additional police patrol; organization of both the seniors and the youngsters for a discussion of the problem and the development of solutions; and, through another county agency, creation of an ambitious program to promote interaction among residents so that the elderly helped meet some of the needs of the young, and the young helped meet some of the needs of the elderly—with the concurrent objective of bringing them together as a single community. The choices reflected a number of value judgments, even though they were not formally articulated: a commitment on the part of the police and the larger community to reduce fear and thereby improve the quality of life; to stabilize neighborhoods; to reaffirm the equal rights of minorities in housing; and to promote harmonious relations among individuals of different races, ages, and backgrounds.

After analyzing the problem of panhandling, the Madison police took steps to ensure that panhandlers in fact did have access to food and shelter. They then reduced the rewards of panhandling by persuading the community not to contribute. They supported enactment of an ordinance that enabled them to take into custody those panhandlers who harassed citizens, and they cooperated with the local detoxification center in arranging operating policies that offered assistance to panhandlers—the vast majority of whom were alcoholics—but that did not facilitate their addiction to alcohol. The blend of responses reflected a compromise between the commitment of the community to humane treatment of those in need and the rights of citizens to use the streets without being subject to harassment. The department consciously rejected other alternatives that would have cleared the streets of panhandlers with less concern for their welfare, reflecting the department's assessment of community attitudes toward the problem.

In the New Briarfield project, the analysis of the Newport News police, which took them far beyond the initial concern with burglaries, resulted in a blend of short-term tactics to improve the situation and a longer-term plan. Immediate arrangements were made to clean up the project: to improve garbage collection; to remove abandoned cars, refrigerators, and other large debris; and to repair the streets. Concluding that it would be much too costly to press for remodeling the complex to bring it up to adequate standards, the cooperating city agencies jointly agreed that the ultimate objective should be to raze and replace the complex. In the interim, they arranged to find safer and better housing for some of the residents; to remove the 57 units that had been condemned; and to encourage HUD to foreclose on the owners and assume direct responsibility for managing the complex. The officer assigned to the area organized the residents to keep them informed of these measures and to elicit their involvement in preventing crime. Concern about maintenance sustained the organizing effort more than did the concern about crime. (For a full description of all of the elements in the police response, see Eck and Spelman et al., 1987, pp. 66–72.) The actions of the police and the city government of Newport News in responding to the New Briarfield problem reflected a concern about the quality of life of its poorest citizens; a judgment that the conduct of management in neglecting the housing was certainly as reprehensible as the petty burglaries that were being committed, if not more so; and a commitment to equal application of laws intended to provide a uniform minimum standard for housing.

Although the values reflected in the choice of alternatives will obviously vary from one community to another, within communities, and over time, the early experiments in problem-oriented policing have drawn attention to a fairly uniform set of factors that warrant consideration in making the choice from among available alternatives. Among them are the following:

- The potential that the response has to reduce the problem
- The specific impact that the response will have on the most serious aspect of the problem (or those social interests deemed most important)
- The extent to which the response is preventive in nature, thereby reducing recurrence or more acute consequences that are more difficult to handle
- The degree to which the response intrudes into the lives of individuals and depends on legal sanctions and the potential use of force
- The attitude of the different communities most likely to be affected by adoption
- The financial costs
- The availability of police authority and resources
- The legality and civility of the response, and the way in which it is likely to affect overall relationships with the police
- The ease with which the response can be implemented

Recognizing that different weights can be appropriately assigned to these factors, it is advantageous to discuss openly the importance attached to each of them in deciding how best to handle a problem. The fact that an otherwise desirable alternative is rejected primarily because of its cost, for example, may elicit ideas from others, not involved in the deliberations, of ways in which the cost can be greatly reduced.

The kinds of decisions involved in fashioning appropriate police responses reflect extremely important policy judgments, and many would argue that, under our system of government, they ought not to be made without direct community input. A strong commitment to consulting with the affected community is inherent in problem-oriented policing. But, as explored elsewhere (see, e.g., Goldstein, 1977, pp. 131–156), no easy way exists to achieve more direct citizen review of police policy making than that already established through the political processes by which police agencies are currently directed. This process, of course, is clear when alternatives require the approval of a mayor, city manager, city council, or legislature. It is less clear when the police administrator is the sole decision maker. But numerous opportunities exist for clarifying these processes so that a higher degree of accountability is achieved. This improved accountability, in my opinion, can best be achieved by having police administrators assume a greater responsibility for decisions that, either by design or by default, are already theirs to make. They are in the best position to weigh alternative responses to citywide problems. They are most likely to have the staff and resources required to conduct analyses, to implement policies, and to achieve conformity with them. Administrators are also in the best position to determine the latitude of decision making that can be delegated to officers on the street and the methods by which this decision making can be reviewed.

This assumes a fuller recognition of the important policy-making role of police administrators and the risks that such policy making entails. That is why, in the context of problem-oriented policing, so much emphasis is placed on equipping police administrators to carry out their role in a more intelligent, responsible manner. That is why not only police administrators, but the rank and file and all the levels of management in between must be involved in the careful analysis of facts, the consideration of community interests, the search for more effective responses, and, upon implementation, the constant evaluation of the effectiveness of these responses. And that is why so much emphasis is placed on the openness of the process—telling the community how the police intend to respond, the rationale for their response, and the criteria they will employ in implementing the response. Some police administrators will probably err in the way in which they handle this responsibility; they may exceed their authority or attempt to implement policies with which the community disagrees. But the mechanism—primarily openness—is there to hold them accountable for their actions. And ultimately, wider recognition of their responsibility will establish more clearly what is expected of them and contribute significantly toward eliciting higher standards of performance.

MEASURING THE EFFECTIVENESS OF ALTERNATIVE RESPONSES

Mindful that the desire to improve police effectiveness is the primary reason for becoming involved in the entire process of identifying and analyzing problems, searching for alternative responses, and implementing these responses, it is essential that procedures be developed to assess their value. At the outset, much work has to be done to clarify our thinking about what we mean when we use the term "effectiveness." We often grossly oversimplify by making bold claims for the value of a police strategy without any persuasive evidence. But we also err, at the other extreme, in creating the impression that one cannot make any assertions regarding relative effectiveness without exhaustive, costly study. This impression is reinforced by the academic debates that almost always follow publication of the results of a major experiment in policing in which reasonable efforts have been made to assure validity. Such cross-criticism, useful in the academic arena as a way to elicit conformity with high standards, tends to inhibit well-motivated, innovative people in the police field from making any claims about the value of their efforts.

Like many difficulties in policing, this one stems from a failure to address the specifics of police business. Were we to do so, we would find that some assessments of effectiveness are relatively easy to make; others are much more complex. When a *specific* response is related to a *specific* problem—especially when the problem is finite—the effectiveness of the response is often obvious. Judging effectiveness for other types of problems may be so complicated that not even an elaborate, controlled experiment—in which attempts are made to isolate the effect of what the police do from other influences—could produce meaningful results.

Opportunities exist to develop the middle ground by thinking through more carefully what is involved in making statements about police effectiveness. Ideally, evaluating the police response to each problem requires the following:

- A clear understanding of the problem
- Agreement over the specific interest(s) to be served in dealing with the problem, and their order of importance
- Agreement on the method to be used to determine the extent to which these interests (or goals) are reached

• A realistic assessment of what might be expected of the police (e.g., solving the problem versus improving the quality of the police management of it)

• Determination of the relative importance of short-term versus long-term impact

• A clear understanding of the legality and fairness of the response (recognizing that reducing a problem through improper use of authority is not only wrong, but likely to be counterproductive because of its effects on other aspects of police operations).

The contribution to this exercise of some of the earlier steps in the analysis of problems should be apparent, as should be the interdependence of these steps. Thus, for example, the task of establishing a standard for measuring effectiveness is greatly facilitated if, having clearly defined a problem, agreement then exists on the specific goals of the police in dealing with it.

For some problems, the identification and ordering of the various goals will provide explicit standards. Such could be the case, for example, in the preceding illustration relating to the police handling of a demonstration. Suppose a decision is made that the primary goal of the police is to ensure the rights of the demonstrators to express their views, and that a second goal is to prevent conflict and injuries. It would then be easy to assess the effectiveness of the police response. Were the demonstrators able to proceed? Did any physical clashes take place? Was anyone injured?

Even when agreement on the interest being served does not result in so clear a definition of the standard against which performance can be measured, identifying the primary interests greatly advances our ability to assess the value of the police response. For example, in addressing the enormous problem of drugs in large cities, it is futile to attempt to assess the value of a new response if the objective is vaguely defined as reducing the drug problem. But if, in analyzing the problem, priority is assigned to eliminating the blatant, open sale of drugs that creates a high level of fear in a community, some basis exists for beginning to measure police effectiveness. A reduction in the number of open sales and in the congregating on the streets of drug users and sellers, coupled with a reduction in the level of fear in the community, would indicate success (not, as some might claim, an increase in the number of arrests, though the making of arrests may be the means used to clean up the area).

Achieving greater clarity of the standard to be used in measuring effectiveness may require still further breakdown, given the magnitude and intractability of many of the problems the police handle. Thus, even after specific interests have been identified, one must be realistic about the degree to which they can be satisfied. That is why Eck and Spelman, in the Newport News project, identified five varying degrees of impact that the police might have on a problem, from totally eliminating it to (out of exasperation) removing the problem from police consideration (see Chapter 4). In the preceding example, police may not be able to eliminate all sales of drugs in a given area, but they may be able to reduce the numbers of sellers and buyers and the flagrant manner in which transactions are made. What this says is that pushing sales into alleys, side streets, and vestibules may, under some conditions, constitute progress.

The last several factors that should be considered in developing measures of effectiveness are also nicely illustrated by the same example. In the ultimate judgment about the effectiveness of the police in making the public way usable and in reducing fear, consideration should be given to the amount of time the improvement lasts and to the legality of police methods and their effect on the attitudes of both neighborhood residents and drug traffickers. If police practices result in the abuse or harassment of all those using the streets, the resulting lack of cooperation with the police in carrying out their other functions may detract substantially from whatever positive claim can be made for the practices.

From these examples, it should be clear that measuring effectiveness entails far more than counting the familiar variables that lend themselves to counting, such as numbers of arrests, numbers of reported crimes, and numbers of calls for assistance to the police. (For further exploration on measuring effectiveness relating to traditional crime categories, see Spelman, 1987.) By focusing on specific aspects of police business, new measures of effectiveness can be developed. If they more accurately measure what the police are attempting to achieve, great strides will have been made in evaluating police effectiveness even if the measurements are not as scientifically precise as we might ultimately like them to be.

CHAPTER **9**

CHANGES IN MANAGEMENT: CREATING A SUPPORTIVE ORGANIZATIONAL ENVIRONMENT

The management style of a police agency and that agency's collective concept of its function in the community are inextricably interrelated. Ideally harmonious, a police agency should be managed in a way that facilitates achieving its function, meeting the needs of both its "consumers" and its employees. Unfortunately, much more effort has been invested in managing police agencies than in thinking about the police function and, as a result, management has become an end in itself. Existing management styles have, in many instances, impeded efforts to alter and improve services provided to the community. They have failed to adjust to changing concepts of the police role.

Problem-oriented policing provides an opportunity to rethink the central issues in the management of police agencies in the context of how they affect the capacity of the police to meet public expectations. The concept has implications for every aspect of management. Success in its implementation requires major changes, but is more heavily dependent on some than on others.

REDEFINING THE ROLE FOR RANK-AND-FILE OFFICERS

Of all of the changes required, redefining the role of rank-and-file police officers is the most important and has the greatest implications for the future of policing. Many of the earlier efforts to reform the police concentrated on doing things about or to rank-and-file officers. Problem-oriented policing not only involves rank-and-file police officers in the change effort, it depends on their involvement. Beyond this, it has an enormous potential for increasing the return, in the form of productive, beneficial work, from the great investment made in police personnel.

When the need for greater concern with the substance of policing was first articulated (Goldstein, 1979), emphasis was placed on the value of tapping the expertise of police officers. But it was not apparent at the time that efforts to meet the need would have such striking, far-reaching implications for the role of rank-and-file officers. That this should be the case is a testimonial to the value of allowing ideas to grow and develop and, most especially, to the willingness of some police administrators to experiment with them and to build on them. (I am thinking here particularly of the foresight of the police leadership in Newport News, Baltimore County, and Madison, who saw the potential in applying the basic concept of problem-oriented policing at the operating level.) Upon witnessing some of the results of these experiments, it quickly became clear that an intensified effort to focus on the substance or end product of policing could become the vehicle for boldly solving, once and for all, some of the perplexing problems associated with the role of rank-and-file officers that have long stymied those concerned with the effective management of a police agency.

- Boredom and lack of challenge are associated with many aspects of policing. Charging officers with the responsibility to work on substantive problems—to use their time, talent, and imagination in doing so—will make their job much more stimulating.
- A working environment in which great stress is placed on controlling employees results in a lack of dignity for those at the bottom and often adversely affects productivity. This condition can be corrected by the new sense of importance, independence, and prestige that comes from a relationship with management built on mutual trust and on agreement that an officer has the freedom to think and act within broad boundaries.
- Dealing with problems that frequently recur causes officers to feel that they are accomplishing little. The opportunity to solve or mitigate recurring problems, to see more directly the benefits of their labors, and to enjoy positive feedback would make their job much more satisfying.
- A lack of opportunities for upward movement in a closed personnel system results in the vast majority of officers spending their careers at the lowest rank in the organization. The negative consequences of this arrangement can be reduced somewhat by making the job of the officer more rewarding.

• A conflict has existed between the drive to attract college graduates into policing (because of the broader and, sometimes, more humanistic perspective attributed to them) and a working environment that stifles some of the attributes cultivated by college education. Redefining the officer's role would make college education and police work more compatible, challenging the officer and enabling the agency to benefit from the greater opportunity the officer has to use his or her education.

• The concept of professionalism, as applied in policing, lacks important elements. This need can be filled by a more intensive, systematic interest on the part of police employees in the substantive problems with which the police are expected to deal, and by a commitment to refining the unique body of expertise possessed by practitioners regarding these problems.

This opportunity to fit together in a more complementary manner the various pieces in a puzzle that has long challenged the police field provides a much-needed framework for advancing the field. But implementation will not be easy. The plan sharpens fundamental differences in the way in which the police job has been perceived and will develop new pressures to make hard choices that have been avoided in superficial efforts to upgrade the police. The form in which these differences begin to surface is illustrated by an observation made in Newport News. Some officers reported that they were so stimulated by the challenge to work through problems that they "took them home with them"—thinking about them and actually working on them during their off-duty hours. Other officers, however, resisted becoming involved in problem-oriented policing, citing the opportunity that patrol work (as distinct from detective work) gave them to leave their job behind when their shift ended.

Both management and unions will be pressed to think through how the perquisites associated with the police officer's job in the past can be reconciled with the needs of a redefined job. Will the majority of rank-and-file officers be willing to alter long-fought-for contract provisions governing choice of assignments, overtime, salary-setting criteria, and relationships with superiors in order to accommodate the types of changes that are proposed? If the move to make fuller use of rank-and-file officers is accompanied by a move to involve them in decision making, still more complex questions are raised. How much of the initiative for change and decisions about the form of change should be left to the rank-and-file, and how much initiative and authority should be reserved for management? The adjustments required to realize the potential in making fuller use of rank-and-file officers are many in number and far-reaching, relating to practically every aspect of management—especially those selected for discussion in this chapter.

MANAGING THE USE OF TIME

The largest percentage of a police budget is invested in the salaries of rank-and-file police officers, and the return on that investment is largely dependent on the use these officers make of their time. Currently, the assumption is that much of that time, between handling calls for assistance, will be devoted to preventive patrol. A common initial reaction to problem-oriented policing is that the agency has no time available for it. A commentator on the experiments in London could not have been more blunt: "The Metropolitan Police has a full work load, and it cannot take on the process as an addition to its everyday work" (Hoare, Stewart, and Purcell, 1984, sec. 10.3.7). This type of reaction assumes that problem-oriented policing is an add-on. It fails to recognize that the concept raises fundamental questions about how police *currently* spend their time, both in responding to calls for assistance and in the intervals between such calls.

The reaction is especially understandable in some large-city police agencies, in which the number of assignments or positions to which the department is currently committed often exceeds the supply of available officers. As a result, on any one day, positions may be unfilled; beats may be uncovered. Special needs that arise for personnel are usually filled by drawing individuals from patrol. In a large city like New York, permanent assignments to a wide array of specialized units make first claim on the contingent of officers assigned to a precinct, so that as few as 14 percent of all precinct officers may be available for assignment to motorized patrols. Understandably, it borders on the absurd to suggest that this residue of officers—who spend much of their time rushing from one call to another—should take the time to analyze and develop creative responses to problems.

But the situation is quite different in most police agencies, in which the majority of police officers continue to be assigned to patrol. Even though some beats may not be filled, studies repeatedly find that officers have substantial time available between calls for assistance. In the Kansas City study, the most ambitious effort to analyze patrol time, it was found that 60 percent of the observed time of officers was uncommitted (Kelling et al., 1974). Informal local inquiries confirm that officers may be called on to respond to as few as two or three calls during an 8-hour shift. During much of their time in the field, therefore, officers are free to initiate activities on their own. They frequently are idle and perhaps even bored. But that does not mean that they take kindly to the suggestion that they use the time more productively. Officers may feel very possessive about the time they have between calls, assuming that it is theirs to use as they wish.

If one takes present-day policing as a given, complaints about the lack of time are understandable. But if one sees the move to problem-oriented policing as a broadly based, comprehensive realignment of priorities and methods of operating, time can be found. The time now wasted between handling calls for help and in the limited number of self-initiated activities of officers can be put to better use. The value of many of the specialized and permanent jobs (other than patrol) to which officers are currently assigned can be challenged, with reassignment to more useful work. Many hours can be saved by using different responses to problems. Alternatives to arrest, when feasible, can greatly reduce the inordinate amount of time commonly consumed in processing an arrest. Calls to the police can be screened more effectively and, where appropriate, handled by telephone or diverted to another unit of the department or to another agency. Police efforts to organize a community can result in citizens settling among themselves problems that they will otherwise look to the police to handle. And finally, more satisfactory police-initiated responses to problems that frequently recur can gradually reduce the demand for fire-brigade responses to incidents. (For a thoughtful exploration of how the need to respond to urgent calls can be reconciled with the need to make more time available to work on problems, see Larson, 1988. Larson builds on the experience he gained in evaluating the split-force experiment in Wilmington, Delaware [Tien, Simon, and Larson, 1978].)

A NEW LEADERSHIP STYLE

The need for changes in police leadership have long been apparent. Efforts to introduce more concern for substantive problems greatly intensify this need, requiring changes that are far more radical than anything that has been advocated in the past.

Three changes are especially important to the success of problem-oriented policing: (1) Police leaders must articulate the basic values with which they approach the police task and which influence their management techniques; (2) they must have a strong commitment to problem-solving as the core of policing, with all that it entails; and (3) more broadly, they must make fundamental changes in the most common type of relationship that exists between leadership and the rank and file in a police agency.

Articulating Values

At the outset, police administrators must do more to articulate the values they believe to be important in the provision of police services. From the 1930s on, the exemplar of a police leader was defined in neutral terms as an efficient, honest, apolitical manager, equipped to implement the professional model of policing. In an earlier work, this author stressed that good administration is not necessarily good leadership (Goldstein, 1977, pp. 225–231). Citing the classic writings on leadership by Philip Selznick (1957), I argued that leaders cannot be neutral: They must stand for something. They must have a set of values—a commitment, goals, and governing principles. Skolnick and Bayley (1986), in describing the importance of quality leadership to the success of recent community policing projects, also drew on Selznick's work in arguing that a chief must "build a sense of purpose into the structure of the enterprise" (p. 221).

How this sense of purpose is articulated will vary. Interestingly, the first such effort is not contemporary, but dates back to 1829. In that year, Sir Richard Mayne, who was then commissioner of the London Metropolitan Police, published a set of governing principles in the form of his "Primary Objects of the Police." This remarkable document has such enduring quality that much of it could be used, unaltered, to fill gaps in the guidance provided by police leadership in the United States in the 1980s. Sir Kenneth Newman, a recent commissioner of the London Metropolitan Police, undertook to update and elaborate on Mayne's principles, producing a 61-page publication addressed primarily to new recruits (1985). Some progress along these lines is being realized in this country. Lee Brown, the chief of police in Houston, having recognized the importance of articulating the values of the organization as a basis for effecting change, appointed a department task force to spell out those values thought important to the Houston police. He has since spoken and written about his concept of managing by values (Brown, 1984). As part of the Newport News project, the initial management committee appointed by Chief Darrel Stephens listed department values (Eck and Spelman et al., 1987, p. 39)—an exercise that was considered important in establishing a foundation for subsequent development of the project. Enlightened police leaders want to assert "up front" the principles that guide an agency in developing policies and in handling the endless array of unpredictable situations that arise on the streets to which no previously developed policy applies. (For an up-to-date summary of the use of values in managing change in policing, see Wasserman and Moore, 1988.)

The "principles" that show up in the value statements of police leaders typically include a strong commitment to protect the Constitutional rights of all citizens; to adhere to legal constraints on the use of police authority; to restrict the use of force, especially deadly force; and to use the least restrictive alternative in dealing with troublesome individuals. They increasingly hold the agency accountable to the citizenry for its actions. They support openness, consultation with the community regarding important policy decisions, and engaging the community to cope with community problems. They also commit the agency to the value of education, research, and, most recently, the active participation of employees in the development and implementation of policies and programs. And they often include a firm recommitment to dealing with serious crime.

A new set of commitments, by itself, is, of course, not enough. Of equal importance are the efforts that administrators make to articulate these commitments to those around them and to incorporate their values into the collective thinking of the department. Constant reiteration makes it clear that the administrator means what he says—which is important in a field in which officers are often given dual, conflicting messages. The strength of the message can be further reinforced by incorporating the philosophy into the criteria used in the promotion of personnel and the selection of new recruits; into each contact with the public and operating personnel; and into all decisions affecting the daily operation of the agency.

Understanding Problem-Oriented Policing and Conveying Its Meaning to Subordinates

Just as there is need on the part of all leadership within an agency for commitment to a set of basic values about policing, so there is need for a strong commitment to all that is entailed in problem-oriented policing. The early experiences, described in Chapter 5, demonstrated repeatedly that successes were directly linked to the commitment of top leadership, and that this commitment, in turn, was heavily dependent on how thoroughly these leaders understand the concept.

We often err by underestimating what is required to introduce new concepts into a police agency. New proposals are outlined or requirements set down without adequately conveying the rationale that led to them. A high percentage of police administrators in this country have not given much thought to the changes and issues raised in Chapters 2 and 3. They are not familiar with the recent literature and research on policing. And the same can be said for their immediate subordinates and those in the ranks of captain, lieutenant, and sergeant. It should not be surprising, therefore, when one hears of police administrators who announce that they have implemented problem-oriented policing but whose programs bear little relationship to the concept; or when an administrator with a full grasp of the concept experiences difficulty in eliciting needed help in its implementation.

To meet the need requires a "crash program" that takes individuals in leadership positions over ground that others who have kept abreast of developments in policing may already have covered. And recognizing that attitudes do not change simply in response to a series of seminars, developing broader understanding among leadership within a police agency requires reinforcement through all of the daily interaction that occurs among those in management positions.

Top leaders must constantly bolster their commitment to some basic underlying principles, such as the importance of greater interest in the substantive aspects of police work, of preventing incidents rather than just responding to them, and of working with the community. Building on acceptance of these principles, there are more specific steps that leaders—from the chief down through the sergeant—must take if their objective is to involve all rank and file. At the conclusion of their study of the implementation of problem-oriented policing in Newport News, Eck and Spelman identified four specific practices that police executives must adopt to get the entire agency involved:

1 Communicate to all department members why handling problems is more effective than handling incidents and why they should engage in problem-solving.
2 Provide incentives to those members who engage in problem-solving.
3 Reduce the barriers to officers engaging in the process, such as by working to make more time available and by eliminating administrative practices that squelch initiative and creativity.
4 Provide examples of what constitutes good problem-solving (Eck and Spelman et al., 1987, pp. 100–101).

It takes unique police chiefs and their immediate subordinates to assume this broadened leadership role. They must be comfortable in criticizing the past; confident in their grasp of the complexity of the police function; and open to new ideas. They must be willing to invest substantial time to studying the behavioral problems their agencies must handle, to searching for new responses to them, and to evaluating these responses. They must be prepared to abandon long-held notions about the nature of some problems when confronted with hard data that redefine them, and be open to challenges of the value of existing responses. And they must be willing to assume some of the risks entailed in departing from traditional policing.

Changing the Relationship between Employer and Employee

Top administrators can no longer—if they ever could—bring about major changes in operating philosophy through fiat. And serious limits exist on what can be achieved simply by reassigning personnel, changing the organizational structure, recruiting new personnel, and conducting training programs. Problem-oriented policing, with its strong commitment to engaging rank-and-file officers more fully in the operation of the police agency, greatly increases the likelihood that rank-and-file officers will support needed change, because they are an essential part of it.

This adds to the need for changes in traditional forms of leadership. Police leaders committed to problem-oriented policing must be prepared to adopt a flexible management style that gives much greater freedom to command officers, supervisors, and rank-and-file police officers. If they are to be effective in working on problems, officers must have sufficient freedom to make contacts in the community, to explore alternatives, to make some decisions for themselves, and even to make mistakes. In this type of atmosphere, a high value is placed on fostering creativity, on mutual respect and trust among co-workers, and on open communication regardless of rank. Supervisors, rather than devoting most of their time to controlling subordinates on behalf of top management, are encouraged to be facilitators, helping rank-and-file officers carry out their broadened roles.

These needs closely parallel the changes being advocated in leadership in the private sector and in other public agencies (see, e.g., Peters and Waterman, 1982; Kanter, 1983; Naisbitt and Aburdene, 1985; Peters and Austin, 1985; Deming, 1986). The movement has been characterized as a transformation in how one views the workplace. It is responsive to workers who express a need for personal growth, but it is designed as well to respond more directly to the needs of consumers, who are more demanding and more knowledgeable about the products they purchase. It reflects a major shift from the importance attached to technology and machines to people, with emphasis on the handling of information in decision making, on the ability to think, on encouraging creativity and innovation, on the development of human resources, and on engaging these resources to satisfy consumers. Though it is questionable if police are currently subject to as much pressure from consumers as are private corporations, the movement has direct relevance to the management of all public agencies, including the police, and is increasingly reflected in training programs for police executives and in changes in management being introduced in some police agencies (Brown, 1988a; Couper and Lobitz, 1988). Chief Couper, in particular, has become a strong advocate of adapting the private-sector experience to policing, fostering a concept he refers to as "quality leadership." He has launched an experimental program in the Madison police department that stresses the importance of teamwork; encourages employee involvement in key decisions; fosters mutual respect and trust, a customer orientation, creativity, and risk-taking; and redefines leaders as coaches and facilitators. The concept ties directly into problem-oriented policing because it helps create a supportive working environment and because it specifically commits leaders to problem-solving and to letting data, not emotions, drive their decisions.

DEVELOPING A NEW DIMENSION IN SUPERVISION

Issues relating to supervision are subsumed, to some degree, in the discussion of leadership. Supervisors, after all, are supposed to be leaders. All that is said about leadership applies equally to them. The influence of first-line supervisors, however, is so strong that their role warrants special attention. I refer here to sergeants and, to a great degree, lieutenants—job titles that themselves cause problems because, drawn from the military, they carry connotations of top-to-bottom management that are in conflict with the type of supervision envisaged in this model of policing.

The primary contact of officers with their agency is through their sergeant. However strongly the head of an agency may elicit a different style of policing, the quality of an officer's daily life is heavily dependent on how well the officer satisfies the expectations and demands of his or her immediate supervisor. Most officers do not see their sergeants as sources of guidance and direction, but rather as authority figures to be satisfied—e.g., by the number of traffic tickets issued, by the way in which forms are completed, and especially by the officer's ability to avoid citizen complaints (because the investigation of such complaints usually places a distasteful and burdensome task on a supervisor). Given this perspective, the less an officer sees of his or her immediate supervisor, the more pleasant is the job.

From my experience, changing the operating philosophy of rank-and-file officers is easier than altering a first-line supervisor's perspective of his or her job, because the work of a sergeant is greatly simplified by the traditional form of policing. The more routinized the work, the easier it is for the sergeant to check. The more restrictions placed on an officer (e.g., limitations on going outside a beat and on contact with drug users), the easier it is to recognize situations that suggest wrongdoing. The more emphasis placed on rank and the symbols of position, the easier it is for sergeants to rely on authority—rather than intellect and interpersonal skills—to carry out their duties. Given the ways they see their role, sergeants are usually appalled by descriptions of the freedom and independence suggested in problem-oriented policing for rank-and-file officers. They see the changes as making their jobs much more difficult. Very little in their experience equips them to supervise officers operating in the proposed mode. The concept can be very threatening to them—to their image of how well they can carry out their job. This understandably can create an enormous block to implementation, as the excitement and enthusiasm of rank-and-file officers are extinguished by sergeants who resist or lend little support to the concept.

As one would expect, administrators have turned to training in an effort to deal with this problem—to speed the adjustments required in the role of the first-line supervisor. But what does one try to convey in such training? What does it mean to be a facilitator and coach in the context of problem-oriented policing? The best answers are emerging from observations of those first-line supervisors who support the concept and who have played a critical role in contributing to the successes in the early experiments. What adjustments have they made in their supervisory methods?

They run interference for their subordinates. They shield them from peer pressure to revert to traditional policing. They arrange for them to have time to work on problems by freeing them from some tasks, providing substitutes, and authorizing flexible hours. They develop familiarity with an officer's beat and the incidents officers are required to handle so that, through frequent discussions, problems that lend themselves to analysis and more effective treatment will be identified. They encourage officers to think in terms of handling problems as the primary unit of work. The most successful encourage officers to plan their daily activities in much the same way as a school teacher develops a lesson plan, asking what problems they are working on and what they are doing about them. They provide officers with the freedom to make broad inquiries—to contact residents, officials, and data sources—and they offer suggestions on appropriate contacts. They confer with officers about the results of their inquiries and press them to explore a problem in sufficient depth by raising appropriate questions. They encourage officers to look beyond traditional responses. And, of course, when analyzing or responding to a problem requires the approval or involvement of other units of the agency, the supervisor has a special role to play as advocate in acquiring such approval or support. (For a description of some specific examples of supervisory support that surfaced in Newport News, see Eck and Spelman et al., 1987, pp. 104–105. For a summary of suggestions for how supervisors working in a community-oriented policing mode should develop the ability of their officers to deal with community problems, see New York City Police Department, 1988a. And for a helpful analysis of the problems that arise in shifting supervisory styles, see Weisburd, McElroy, and Hardyman, 1988.)

Currently, the most effective means we have to alter the attitude of first-line supervisors is to convince them that adopting a different style of supervision makes good sense in today's environment. What else might be done? In Madison, all officers have been notified that subsequent promotions will be based, in part, on the degree to which candidates reflect a commitment to newly defined supervisory and leadership styles. The suggestion has been made that change might be further expedited by allowing the rank and file to rate their supervisors, just as their supervisors rate them. In an agency fully committed to problem-oriented policing, with a more relaxed management style, such feedback from operating officers could enable supervisors to perfect their skills and contribute even more to improving the overall quality of policing.

DECENTRALIZATION TO ENABLE OFFICERS TO CAPITALIZE ON THEIR KNOWLEDGE OF THE COMMUNITY

The model organization that emerged from past preoccupation with efficiency and achieving maximum control over operating personnel was highly centralized. The number of precincts or districts was reduced, specialized units (task forces) were created, and all calls to the police were received, screened, and dispatched. A major objective was to provide uniform service throughout the jurisdiction, regardless of neighborhood characteristics. No special value was attached to who from among available officers was assigned to filling patrol positions. Officers were considered interchangeable.

The commitment to a highly centralized form of police organization was questioned, initially, in the critical analysis of policing that followed the urban riots of the 1960s. Relationships between the police and minority communities had always been stressful. It was now clear that the move to greater centralization had aggravated that situation. In providing a more impersonal form of policing, police were operating with less sensitivity to how their practices affected and were seen by different identifiable communities within their total jurisdiction.

Upon reflection, the move to centralize control and standardize procedures greatly undervalued the importance in policing of knowledge about the specific community being policed. It also undervalued the importance of the type of relationship maintained with the community (see Slovak, 1987). To rectify matters, it was obvious that the police first had to deal with the negatives—with practices and police behavior that generated hostility toward them. Beyond that, they needed to cultivate a positive relationship with residents: to enlist them in supporting their efforts. But in rethinking relationships, it became clear that the ability of the police to carry out their traditional function of fighting crime is heavily dependent on their familiarity with the area to which they are assigned—its streets and buildings; its people, their life-styles, and their culture. It is absurd to assume that a police officer without such familiarity can be other than minimally effective in identifying suspicious or criminal conduct in an area. Recognition of the broader role of the police, in maintaining public order and in providing a wide range of services, often requiring knowledge of subtle differences between beats and even city blocks, accentuates this need. Furthermore, there is a growing feeling in police circles that an officer who is familiar with an area and its people is less likely to resort to force to control a situation than one who, foreign to an area, is suddenly injected into a situation in which he or she must decide if force should be used.

Taken aback by the degree of alienation, and forced to reflect on the extent to which police work depends on a positive, continuing relationship with the community and on an accumulation of knowledge about the community, police agencies executed a dramatic about-face in their attitudes about centralization. It was reflected in the move to establish new precincts, ministations, and storefront offices. It led eventually to the more advanced forms of community policing in which the most important element is usually the permanent assignment of an officer to a neighborhood.

If any doubts remain about the importance of decentralized police operations, they should be eliminated upon recognizing that so much of policing consists of dealing with problems. And while some problems can be viewed as citywide and relatively uniform wherever they occur, most have a local character to them or may even be unique to a specific beat. It requires officers close to a community to identify them and to deal with them.

This need can best be met through the ultimate form of decentralization in which officers are assigned permanently, for a minimum of several years, to a specific area (a practice now commonly referred to as maintaining beat integrity). Such an arrangement enables an officer to get to know the problems of a community, the strengths and weaknesses of existing systems of control, and the various resources that are useful in solving problems. The officer is in a position to monitor new responses that are implemented. His or her effectiveness is greatly increased through interaction with citizens. (Much of the frustration in some of the early experiments stemmed from the reassignment of officers just when they had become deeply involved in working on local problems.)

The value of permanent assignments must be squared with the value attached to rotating shifts (e.g., weekly, monthly, or every 3 months) to provide 24-hour coverage. Although not as disruptive as the reassignment of an officer from one area to another, changes in the time during which a police officer works (compounded because not as many officers are needed on one shift as another) seriously detract from the potential to cement relationships between a police officer and those residing or doing business in the area he or she serves. The population of the area may differ at various times during the day, as may the problems. If maintaining permanent assignments to both an area *and* a time of day is not possible, considerable effort must be invested in communications among officers serving the same area to ensure continuity and consistency in dealing with any problems being addressed.

Like all needed changes in policing, permanent assignments have a potentially negative side that must be acknowledged. A police officer may become so detached from central controls that matters requiring coordination are mishandled. This is especially true if officers assigned to an area are not informed of incidents handled by other police in the area. More perplexing is the fear that alliances will develop between the community and the officer assigned to it that result either in the misuse of authority (in response, for example, to demands to get tough) or in corruption.

BROADENING RESEARCH AND PLANNING EFFORTS

Police agencies spend a shamefully small percentage of their total budget on analyzing their own operations, critiquing the effectiveness of their efforts, and thinking about the future. To set aside funds for this purpose in policing subjects an administrator to the simplistic charge of sacrificing immediate crime-fighting capacity for the somewhat questionable benefit to be derived from still another group of desk-bound employees. This reflects the widespread assumption that everyone knows what must be done to get the police job accomplished: that it is simply a matter of making the maximum number of officers available to do it.

"Research," as that term is used in the police field today, immediately brings to mind the major studies of nationwide significance that have been conducted over the past two decades. But if one inquires what research a given police agency is doing, one finds, as Weatheritt (1985, pp. 82–84) found in England, that almost all of it is concerned with improving internal management rather than improving police performance. Most police administrators continue to think of research as the work done by their planning and research units. These units originated in the 1950s to improve management within agencies (O. W. Wilson, 1952). They focused initially on developing plans for police coverage of special events, on streamlining internal procedures, and on allocating police personnel. In some departments they were given the responsibility for crime analysis. They subsequently became involved in forms management, in the design of communications systems, and, most recently, in the application of computers to police operations. Their focus today varies. In some agencies the planning and research unit has deteriorated into a clerical arm of the chief administrator's office, answering letters and questionnaires and handling a wide assortment of special projects. In the vast majority of departments, the unit remains concerned with improving the management of the agency—developing specifications for new equipment, plans for reorganization, and new procedures. Some planning and research units get more involved in the substantive aspects of police business because they continue to have the responsibility for crime analysis. Occasionally a unit, on its own initiative, has undertaken a study of a specific substantive problem, but such studies are the exception.

A whole new dimension must be added to prior research and planning activities. In a rough equivalent to the private sector, it calls for going beyond operational research concerned with efficient ways to produce a product. It extends to developing the ability to assess and control the quality of the product, to engage in market research, and to design new products. From the chief executive all the way down to rank-and-file officers, personnel ought to have available to them a research staff that has the time, talent, and independence to monitor and improve the effectiveness of the agency in handling the problems of the community. In larger departments, such a staff would itself conduct studies of those problems that occur throughout the city and lend themselves to a fairly uniform response, such as, for example, child abuse. For more localized problems taken on by command staff, supervisors, or rank-and-file officers, the staff should provide needed technical support. Given the skills and experience that would develop in analyzing substantive problems, a centralized planning and research unit could contribute a great deal by providing training to field personnel in problem-solving and by monitoring department-wide problem-solving efforts, alert to additional ways in which it might support these efforts.

Development of an expanded research component will require more than dollar support. One must anticipate these needs:

- Individuals with strong backgrounds in methodology are not commonly found among police personnel. Quality research requires such skills—especially the ability to identify hidden complexities and methodological flaws and biases in the use of data.
- Experience must be gained in applying basic research techniques to the study of problems handled by the police, so that useful, valid results can be obtained without unreasonable investment of time and resources. Only experienced researchers can dare to take shortcuts.
- Smaller agencies, however strong their commitment, are not likely to be able to invest sufficiently in research and development to maintain a staff exclusively assigned to this function. It will be necessary to pool resources at a regional or state level to provide such assistance.
- Sophisticated, elaborate controlled experiments to test the relative merits of different responses may be so costly and extend over so long a

period of time that they are possible only with state or federal assistance or funding from a private foundation. Such assistance may be justified, given the national significance of the study.

• Research staffs will inevitably be called on to evaluate the effectiveness of alternative responses. Considerable effort has gone into evaluative research in the past decade, but many of these efforts, for understandable reasons, have been rather crude. Much work remains to be done to develop techniques for evaluating police effectiveness.

In the early studies in Madison, we learned that, even in a fairly progressive and open police agency, many subtle, practical difficulties exist in conducting quality research. It is hard to engage in organizational self-criticism, knowing one must continue to work with the officers whose current efforts are criticized. Existing practices, when analyzed, can be embarrassing. The daily activities involved in conducting research may be viewed negatively in the police subculture as "goofing off" (Goldstein and Susmilch, 1982c, pp. 146–147). Clearly, it will take much effort to develop an internal capacity to conduct quality research.

REVISING THE CRITERIA FOR RECOGNIZING PERFORMANCE

Police agencies have long been notorious for urging rank-and-file officers to do one thing while rewarding them for doing something else. Officers have been schooled to place highest priority on preventing crime—on preventing minor incidents from escalating into more serious problems. But the systems for rewarding officers continue to reflect the traditional expectations of both the community and the police administration. They place a high value on crimes solved, arrests made, traffic tickets issued, and especially heroic actions carried out in the face of personal danger.

More striking is the tenacity with which the field adheres to these criteria even after making a substantial commitment to a new form of policing. In an awards ceremony for officers working under a community policing concept, for example, half of the awards went to officers who located and apprehended persons wanted for serious crimes or who performed an especially heroic act that saved a life. In the internal newsletters exchanged among officers in another community policing project, most of the commendations reflected the same attachment to traditional policing. It seems clear that even administrators and police officers involved in novel programs want to legitimize their "off-beat" efforts in the eyes of the larger agency and the community by heralding actions that fit the old criteria.

To succeed, problem-oriented policing requires that officers be rewarded for solving problems—for identifying them, analyzing them, and developing creative, innovative responses that eliminate or reduce them. This requires both the development of appropriate measures of successful performance and a clearer definition of the rewards to which officers can aspire.

We have not yet figured out how to measure the effectiveness of an officer in handling problems on his or her beat. The old adage, "one knows one when one sees one," seems to describe aptly the officer who is good at problem-solving, but translating that criterion into language and factors that can be used by supervisory and command officers is difficult. (Among those who have struggled most with this need is the staff of the Vera Institute of Justice engaged in evaluating the problem-solving performance of CPOP officers.) Clearly, it will be necessary to place a high value on qualitative assessments rather than quantitative data. Administrators use traditional criteria, such as numbers of arrests, clearances, and calls handled, because these data are easy to compile and seem more objective to both unions and individual officers. In an effort to explore alternatives, Mastrofski (1983) examines the potential of using knowledge of a patrol beat as a measure of performance. This effort is relevant, since knowledge of a beat is one of the prime means for identifying problems in need of solution. In Newport News, first-line supervisors motivated subordinates to implement the concept by emphasizing in their evaluations of performance the degree to which officers were incorporating problem-solving into their work. In still another approach, administrators have announced that promotions will go to those who are committed to problem-oriented policing.

Incentives to officers to improve the quality of their performance are limited in the police field. Salaries are fixed. Few opportunities exist for promotion, and they are often strongly influenced by factors beyond the control of the administrator. Bonuses are rarely used in municipal government. Medals, ribbons, plaques, and citations have some value, but are more appropriate for a paramilitary system than the type of organizational environment in which problem-oriented policing will thrive.

Against this rather bleak background, problem-oriented policing creates the opportunity for many intrinsic rewards. An officer can derive satisfaction from dealing with and solving problems. In addition to a personal sense of accomplishment, the officer will receive positive feedback from his or her department and from members of the community who benefit from the officer's actions. This phenomenon began to show up in some of the early community-policing projects. Changes associated with decentralization—greater autonomy, increased responsibility, increased contact with citizens in nonadversarial conditions, and participation in decision making—all increased officer satisfaction on the job (e.g., Murphy and Muir, 1984, pp. 176–177; Friedmann, 1986, p. 72; Skolnick and Bayley, 1988b, p. 34; Wycoff, 1988, pp. 103-120). When officers are encouraged to work under these same conditions with the additional mandate and authority to deal with problems, they consistently report to observers that they derive much satisfaction from their work (e.g., Farrell, 1986, p. 78; Taft, 1986, p. 24).

A number of other factors contribute to job satisfaction in problem-oriented policing. Officers are apparently much more frustrated than is generally recognized when they must respond repeatedly to similar incidents and are not in a position to do something that will reduce or eliminate future calls. They are also more frustrated than is commonly recognized when their involvement in a matter is terminated before the matter is resolved. They appreciate the opportunity to work a problem through from beginning to end. And they appreciate, of course, the acknowledgment that they have something to contribute in the form of their accumulated expertise, their imagination and creativity, and their problem-solving ability. Although this increase in job satisfaction is significant, it does not diminish the need to continue to develop more formal rewards that acknowledge accomplishments in the context of problem-oriented policing and that elicit support for newly emerging styles of policing.

RECRUITMENT AND SELECTION

Police agencies should, in their recruitment of new personnel, attempt to hire those whose abilities and skills make them best suited to functioning in a problem-oriented milieu. This requires greater emphasis, in the screening of applicants, on subjective criteria such as attitudes toward the job, expectations of what policing is about, and personality traits. But many police agencies have been required to use more easily measurable objective criteria in the screening process to reduce the potential for discrimination. Can these seemingly conflicting needs be resolved?

For many years, efforts to update the criteria for recruiting and selecting new officers lagged behind the growing consensus about the characteristics and skills that were most likely to result in high-quality performance on the job. (For a summary assessment, see President's Commission on Law Enforcement and Administration of Justice, 1967.) In some jurisdictions, great progress has been realized in closing this gap. Progress, however, has required that police administrators correct simplistic public images of what it takes to be a police officer; that they overcome the resistance of independent civil service agencies and personnel administrators who lack direct familiarity with the complexity of the police task; and that they overcome, too, the attitudes of veteran officers involved in recruitment and screening, who have a tendency to search for applicants who subscribe to traditional values (Gray, 1975).

At the same time, it has become essential that police hire a greater number of minorities and women. Those agencies that have shown progress in meeting affirmative action goals usually enjoy greater latitude in the screening of applicants. But police agencies in many cities (especially the larger ones) that have lagged behind have faced court challenges contending that the standards for appointment and the examinations were racially or gender biased and were not related with sufficient specificity to the requirements of the job. Absent validated criteria as to what constitutes a good officer in accordance with the most advanced notions of policing, the criteria employed in screening have therefore frequently been reduced to the most elementary requirements of the job. Thus, in departments subject to such suits, the need to ensure objectivity in screening reduces the latitude of administrators to consider subjective criteria.

Under the best circumstances, judicially mandated or supervised hiring to achieve racial and gender balance is not likely to be a finely tuned instrument for hiring officers with the best aptitudes for and attitudes about policing. But it is important to recognize that such hiring practices are last-resort mechanisms, invoked only after an agency has failed to take sufficient initiative on its own. In the bigger picture, it is more important that a police agency's composition reflect the community policed. But beyond this, the addition of minorities and women to police agencies will greatly influence the police subculture. It contributes to creating a more diversified atmosphere in which past practices are more subject to challenge. Thus, an increase in the numbers of minorities and women may do as much to open police departments to needed change as any subjective screening mechanisms that we are now capable of devising.

Having demonstrated its commitment to affirmative action, an agency can build into the screening process consideration of criteria that support problem-oriented policing. It should, for example, give higher priority to applicants who demonstrate an ability to function independently; who enjoy and are adept at solving problems; who are creative and imaginative; who can make good judgments in choosing from among a range of available alternatives; and who, in a general way, have the intellectual capacity to do more thinking about police work. As police gradually learn more about the problems they must handle and the best ways to handle them, an even sounder basis emerges for defining the criteria for employing new officers. From the limited experience to date, it is already clear that administrators would be well advised to look for applicants who have the potential to become skilled in such areas as mediating conflict, dispensing information, and organizing communities. It may eventually be possible to validate the connection between such skills and the ability to perform well in a police agency, enabling administrators to set forth with much greater confidence the selection criteria that best reflect the complexity of the job.

TRAINING

Introduction of so dramatic a change in the concept of policing has major implications for the content and form of training programs, both for recruits and for those who are already in police service. The change creates three specific needs: (1) to convey a clear understanding of the overall concept of problem-oriented policing as a way of thinking about the police function; (2) to equip officers to identify and analyze problems and to develop effective responses to them; and (3) to convey knowledge to officers about the most common substantive problems that they are expected to handle and to alert them to the issues involved.

The first need—eliciting support and understanding for a philosophy of policing—cannot be met by any single class or specific element in the curriculum. The commitment to problem-oriented policing would be expected to pervade all aspects of the organization and be reflected in all aspects of police training. Nevertheless, at some stage a concentrated period of time should be devoted to the concept and how it has evolved. As noted in the discussion of leadership needs, those who are at the forefront of change in policing tend to forget that relatively few operating officers have worked their way through all the mental gymnastics that make problem-oriented policing such a natural next step.

Both the Baltimore County and Newport News police departments have reported significant accomplishments in training officers to identify and analyze problems and to develop new responses (Eck and Spelman et al., 1987; Higdon and Huber, 1987). This is no small achievement, given that officers first must be drawn into an entirely new mind-set before they can be schooled in the specifics of, for example, defining problems, identifying sources of relevant information, collecting data, and subjecting them to appropriate analysis. If these steps are taught in a mechanical fashion, without adequate attention to the overall concept of which they are a part, indications are that they are not effective. An effort is under way to develop special materials for the training of CPOP officers in New York City in problem-solving (New York City Police Department, 1988b). As these materials become available, along with techniques from Newport News and Baltimore County, the potential for increasing the quality and effectiveness of training will be raised.

Although the best current police training programs already include some units in the curriculum that are problem-specific (e.g., sexual assault, spousal abuse, drunk driving), most police training remains generic. It teaches the law, department regulations, and skills (e.g., interrogation, fingerprinting, gathering evidence, conducting investigations, defense tactics) without much attention to how these might apply to specific problems. That is one major reason why recruit training has so often been criticized as having no relevance to the job. It does not deal realistically with the specific problems police are expected to handle and the methods for dealing with them.

If the police gradually develop a body of knowledge regarding each of the problems they treat and develop tailor-made responses to them, a vast amount of rich material will be added to what is already available, but untapped, for training. A training program that is supportive of problem-oriented policing should have a substantial number of units devoted to the problems that police are commonly called on to handle. The units should convey the best available information about the substantive problem, examine issues that arise in responding to the problem, and acquaint officers with carefully-thought-through responses. This type of emphasis affords an opportunity to make training programs more relevant, credible, and effective. The generic subjects and skills, which must be covered, can be taught better in relation to substantive problems, just as the diversity and sensitivity of the police function, the complexity of relating to individuals under frequently adverse conditions, and the limits on police authority can be conveyed best in the context of a specific problem. Officers should have the opportunity, for example, to reflect on the use of police authority to stop and question people both in the context of apprehending persons fleeing from the scene of a homicide and in the context of controlling street prostitution.

DEVELOPING NEW SOURCES OF INFORMATION AND NEW KNOWLEDGE

In pushing for the development of tailor-made responses, the importance of understanding the local character of a problem has been emphasized. Yet many of the problems handled by police departments are common from one neighborhood to another and from one city to another. And it follows that a response that works well in Los Angeles may work equally well in Boston with some minor modifications. A critical need exists, therefore, to develop new arrangements for facilitating the exchange of information, though it remains for the local police agency, in consultation with the community, to determine the applicability of a response to a given problem in that community.

Networking within and among Police Agencies

One of the benefits to be expected from having so many independent police agencies is a richness of different approaches to dealing with common problems. That is often cited as one of the great advantages of our federal system and decentralized government. Until recently, however, a police agency would rarely reach out to determine how another agency handled problems of similar form. Yet the knowledge and experience acquired by some police can be of great benefit to others.

- In a meeting of officers from different units of a large city department, officers from one precinct described their struggle with the problem of street peddlers. Those from another unit not only recognized the problem; they had experienced it in a much more acute form. They described how they handled it; where necessary legal guidance could be obtained; and who, in city government, was most helpful in working through to a solution.
- In a meeting of police from nine cities in three different states, an officer presented a case study on how his agency dealt with the nuisance and dangers created by drivers who congregated to demonstrate their souped-up vehicles. Representatives of each of the departments then volunteered their own responses to the same problem, placing a wide range of attractive, imaginative alternatives on the table.
- An officer undertook a study of the police response to noise in a college community. As a result of calls made to a number of police agencies serving similar communities, he acquired ideas for alternative responses from which to choose in deciding on how best to improve the local response.
- An officer working on problems in a large city department developed a method to deter the theft of expensive radio equipment from vehicles owned by the residents of an exclusive neighborhood. A description of his program has been passed on by word of mouth, resulting in his receiving inquiries personally addressed to him from distant police agencies.

Currently, no comprehensive, institutional system collects, assesses, and shares the experiences of different agencies in dealing with common community problems. Often, as noted in the first example, exchanges do not occur even within the same police agency.

But some major advances are being made. Primarily through the support of the National Institute of Justice, police agencies now have available to them a number of reports presenting program options regarding a substantive problem. Until recently, almost all of this exchange reflected the dominant police interest in the internal management of a police agency. In a welcome shift, the amount of material focusing on substantive problems has been increasing rapidly—material relating, for example, to arson (Hammett, 1987); domestic violence (Goolkasian, 1986); the mentally ill, public inebriates, the homeless (Finn and Sullivan, 1987); and the demand for drugs (DeJong, 1987).

Also noteworthy is the work done by the Police Executive Research Forum (PERF) in bringing together materials on the police responses to spousal abuse (Loving, 1980) and the chronically mentally ill (Murphy, 1986). PERF has also begun publishing a modest but helpful newsletter, *Problem Solving Quarterly,* which fosters exchanges of information and experiences regarding problem-oriented policing—including in each issue case studies of specific problems, most of which were handled at the street level (Police Executive Research Forum, 1988).

The Police Foundation has produced material on the police response to child sexual abuse (Besharov, 1987). The International Association of Chiefs of Police (IACP) has received a grant to create a center for the collection, development, and dissemination of police department policies (Vaughn, 1987), but how much of their focus will be on substantive, as distinct from management, problems is not yet clear. The IACP's major publication, *The Police Chief,* occasionally carries an article that provides an in-depth description of the police response to a given problem. Excellent examples are two recent articles on responses to teenage cruising (Bell and Burke, 1989; Patterson and Barbour, 1989). In England, the *Home Office Research Bulletin,* with increasing frequency, is reporting on experiments in dealing with specific behavioral problems. (See, for example, its publications on burglary in schools and the problem of drinking and disorder in the center of a city [Hope, 1985]; and on vandalism [S. Wilson, 1978; Clarke, 1980b; Winchester and Jackson, 1982].) A summary of police research in England for 1986 and 1987 listed many studies completed or under way on specific aspects of police business (Police Foundation, 1987).

In addition to benefiting from national studies, police managers will want to turn for facts, ideas, and insights to similar communities that have experienced similar problems. (Doing so is now expedited through the use of computer conferencing systems such as METAPOL, established by the Police Executive Research Forum.) Initially, of course, they will find that most other communities have little to offer. But the process of inquiry alone, supplemented by the sharing of results, could be a major stimulant for such analysis. (Police, like other bureaucracies, do not like to be unable to answer appropriate questions.) Problem-oriented policing could stimulate a massive exchange of local studies and experiences that would be of enormous value in improving the quality of local responses to specific problems.

With the increased exchange of information, a greater interest should naturally develop in the evaluation of experiences, since descriptions of responses inevitably lead to questions about their effectiveness. The most valued descriptions of programs will be of those that have been soundly evaluated.

Professional Journals

Professionals have traditionally used professional journals and conferences to disseminate new knowledge. They report to their peers, and the quality of what they have to report is controlled by the review of their peers.

The number of professional journals that include material relating to policing has mushroomed in the past two decades. Unfortunately, most of the articles in them are written by academics and are addressed to academics. And like the articles that appear in the publications of various police associations, they reflect a preoccupation with the running of a police agency. Many of them are written in a dense style, difficult for practitioners—as well as others—to follow. The police field is in desperate need of one or more professional journals dedicated to disseminating knowledge acquired about specific problems police must handle and about the effectiveness of their responses. Journals of this nature could become an indispensable source of information for police administrators throughout the country.

Professional conferences are another means of sharing information on substantive problems. The type of forum established by the National Institute of Justice in its annual state-of-the-art conference or by the Police Executive Research Forum in its annual meetings could be adapted easily to serve this need.

A Research Agenda for State and Federal Agencies, Academics, and Research Organizations

Some needs, in a total program of research, can be met only with the support of state and federal government and with the involvement of academic personnel and others outside police agencies.

Increased concern with substantive problems will identify the need for carefully controlled experiments to test the value of different types of responses. Because these are costly and difficult, even the largest agencies cannot undertake them. Moreover, the need to ensure the independence of investigators, to ensure unbiased results, and the significance that such studies would have for many police agencies warrant their financing by federal or state government.

The closest we have come to such experiments was in testing the value of arrest as a response to spousal violence (Sherman and Berk, 1984). The original study illustrates both the value and the difficulties of conducting such research. It separated out for careful attention one of the most common, critically important substantive problems that police handle, and it attempted to learn about the effectiveness of alternative responses. Until relatively recently, spousal abuse was not even separately identified by the police. But the results of the study were promoted in ways unjustified by its limited nature (Binder and Meeker, 1988). This is understandable, given the intense interest that developed in the problem of spousal abuse. If such research were more routine, it would be possible to condition the police to treat the results more cautiously until replication addresses concerns raised by the original effort.

The need to acquire more knowledge about the problems that police handle and the value of alternative responses is so vast that state and federal agencies committed to helping the police, by focusing on substantive problems, could put together productive agendas for their research programs for the next several decades.

In addition to the need for financial support, the need for certain types of expertise will require police agencies to obtain outside assistance, even if they develop a substantial internal research capacity. Detailed exploration of some problems will require individuals with specialized knowledge about the problem (e.g., psychologists regarding certain forms of violence; accountants regarding certain forms of computer crime) or with specialized knowledge about a potential response (e.g., the mental health system, the design of buildings and public facilities, the drafting of legislation). Illustrative is a recent statewide study in Wisconsin of the response to child sexual abuse, which examines programs in three different counties. It draws on the combined knowledge and experience of social workers, prosecutors, defense counsel, judges, and the police and was appropriately coordinated from a university base (Jones, 1986). Often, the decision to locate a research effort outside a police agency will be dictated primarily by the need for independence or expertise in research methodology (e.g., Clifton, 1987).

GETTING GOING: SPECIAL UNIT OR DEPARTMENT-WIDE IMPLEMENTATION?

The needed adjustments in management that have been highlighted in this chapter are part of a coherent scheme for supporting problem-oriented policing. But change of such magnitude requires time. One cannot wait for ideal conditions; one must take satisfaction in any actions that move police toward a greater concern with substantive problems. This has long posed a strategic question for those anxious to hasten change in policing. Is it best to introduce innovations throughout a police agency; or to introduce them initially in a small unit, with the ultimate objective of extending them to the rest of the agency? The question arises anew with regard to problem-oriented policing.

Behind this question is the realization that the speed of change is probably most dependent on the attitudes of officers toward the change. Attitudes cannot be altered mechanically. Many officers, whether experienced and set in their ways or new and recruited with certain expectations about policing, find it difficult to alter how they think about their job. If one sets out to effect changes that depend for their success on a change in attitude of all members of a police agency, the task is enormous; many people must be reached, and the effort is bound to be diluted by those who are either passive or—as is likely to be true especially of middle management—actively resist and perhaps even attempt to sabotage the efforts. Undertaken in this manner, planned change requires a long time frame, consistent and persistent efforts, facilitated by a gradual turnover in personnel. It is hard to sustain.

For the police administrator operating on a much shorter time frame, the temptation is great to expedite change by undertaking it in much smaller units in which like-minded officers and supervisors (perhaps even volunteers) who are committed to the goals of the proposed change are concentrated. This avoids some of the major impediments to change. It is like undertaking change in an incubator, under the most favorable conditions, protected from the negative influences of the larger organization. Unquestionably, with this approach, much more can be accomplished in a shorter period of time with clear-cut results that are visible for all to see.

But the long-range effects may have serious consequences for the organization. Skimmed of the officers who are supportive of change, the balance of the organization may harden its commitment to traditional policing—making it even more difficult to effect change in the total organization. Tensions may develop between officers in the new unit and those who continue to function as in the past. These tensions will be increased if the officers working in the new unit are perceived as not doing "real" police work—especially if their assignment results in increased work loads for those who are left to meet the daily, routine demands made on the agency. (Officers in CPOP in New York City, who are insulated from the pressures of daily calls made to the police, are sometimes referred to by other officers as "the untouchables." In Baltimore County, officers in COPE are referred to by regularly assigned officers as "cops on pension early.") In its most acute form, this kind of division—whether for problem-oriented policing or some other initiative associated with community-oriented policing—could lead to abandoning the concept. Against this background, the Newport News experience argues persuasively for the more ambitious department-wide approach, despite the difficulties and slower pace that must be anticipated.

Out of the debate over the relative merits of these two approaches, four observations emerge of value in making the hard choice about how best to proceed. In first contemplating a movement into problem-oriented policing (or, for that matter, any change in police operations), the readiness of the agency for change should be assessed. If a critical mass exists in support of the change, if some middle managers are supportive, and if the union of rank-and-file officers is at least open to the idea, the potential for succeeding through a department-wide effort is greatly increased. If, on the other hand, the organization is rigid, middle management is resistant and of one mind, and identifying a substantial number of rank-and-file officers who would be receptive is difficult, it would be foolish to attempt to initiate the project for the entire department.

Second, a compromise between the two extreme models may be possible. Madison's experimental police district was staffed by volunteers who exercised their choice through the system of priorities for job assignments established by their union. Although this led to the involvement of many officers committed to the experiment, it also resulted in more of a cross section, since other officers opted for involvement for unrelated reasons, such as the shift they would work or the area of the city to which they would be assigned. Although hand-picking all participants might have achieved greater immediate impetus for the effort, the cooperation of the police union, the reduced schism between those in and out of the experiment, and the potential that less committed officers would become advocates for the new style of policing in the larger department provided offsetting advantages. Furthermore, by having officers participate who brought different attitudes to it, the project came closer to being a true experiment.

Third, the negative consequences that commonly result from creating an incubator unit may be mitigated if, from the outset, participants integrate the work of the unit with the rest of the department. If the geographic areas in which officers work overlap, officers in the special units are required to develop relationships with officers who are regularly assigned to the area: keeping them informed and showing how their work might be of value to the patrol officer. (Observations of the early experiments indicate that frequently no communication occurs between officers from different units serving the same neighborhood.)

It is also commonly proposed that a system of personnel transfer be developed so that, after several years, officers with experience in the unit can apply its approach outside—and perhaps reduce cynicism in the department as a whole. At the same time, additional officers from patrol can be afforded an opportunity to work in the unit. But for this to succeed, the experience within the unit must be a positive one, and supervisors outside the unit must be sufficiently informed and committed to encourage officers to use what they have learned. Observations of some of the early experiments reveal that the investment made by the officers in the special units is often wasted when they are transferred back to regular patrol; that their superiors do not have a good grasp of the goals of the special unit, or do not believe in those goals, or simply do not believe that the strategies have any relevance outside the special unit. And if the special unit involves permanent assignment of officers to specific neighborhoods, a fixed system of mandatory transfer after a specified number of years may be dysfunctional, abruptly terminating a relationship with a neighborhood that a police officer has worked hard to cultivate just as it is beginning to produce the desired results.

These drawbacks lead to the fourth and final observation—that the likelihood of realizing the benefits of a segregated project can perhaps best be realized, and the negative consequences minimized, if there is a commitment, from the outset, to expanding the project (either in numbers or in area), assuming it succeeds. In this manner, a steadily increasing percentage of department resources would be committed to working in the new mode. The need to keep officers in the areas to which they are assigned could be accommodated. And with each expansion, the opportunity would be created to build on prior experiences, avoiding the mistakes that were made and experimenting with the latest ideas. Assuming that such an approach is spread over a sufficiently long period of time, depending on the magnitude of change and the size of the agency, it has the added advantage of benefiting from normal attrition and changes in recruitment standards, promotion criteria, and the content of training programs.

CHAPTER **10**

REFLECTIONS ON IMPLEMENTATION EFFORTS

Since we know, given the current state of policing, that changes in management of the magnitude described in Chapter 9 are difficult to implement in many communities, does this mean that these agencies are precluded from making any use of problem-oriented policing? Does this limit progress to a small number of agencies? More specifically, does this render problem-oriented policing a "pie-in-the-sky" idea, sound in concept but not likely to be implemented?

First of all, one must avoid stereotyping the vast majority of police agencies as having a single management style or being at any single stage of development. The range is broad, and it has increased in the past decade. Some police departments have not changed their operating philosophy and some of their procedures for 30 or 40 years. Others are at the cutting edge of advancement, with talented personnel in key positions and rank-and-file officers with great potential, all of whom are hungry for more effective ways in which to operate. It makes no sense to pose, as the acid test of a new idea, the ability to apply it universally to all police agencies.

Progress in policing does not require that each police agency go through a standard metamorphosis, like butterflies. Opportunities exist to take shortcuts to more advanced stages. If there is any indication of readiness for change, in the attitudes of the community, department leadership, and the rank and file, one can develop a concern for substantive problems even though the full benefits of doing so might not be realized for some time.

Any movement toward increased concern with substantive problems is better than none at all. A traditionally oriented police agency that openly recognizes the work of a police officer in dealing imaginatively with one or more problems on the officer's beat has demonstrated some progress. A police agency that studies spousal abuse and implements a new department-wide policy for responding to the problem is ahead of the department that does nothing, even though the new policy may not be fully implemented at the operating level. The department that makes a commitment to researching substantive problems at the administrative level—and goes no further in problem-oriented policing—nevertheless is more advanced than the department that limits its research to revising records systems, designing equipment, and reallocating personnel. And the department that creates a special unit in which officers are empowered to deal with problems directly is obviously much further along than the department that has made no effort to engage operating personnel, even though the special unit may create tensions with officers who are committed to traditional policing.

It is encouraging that, in recent months, there has been a rapid increase in the number of police agencies that claim to have adopted some form of problem-oriented policing. This is due primarily to the publicity received by the early experiments reported on in Chapter 5, and to the many endorsements of these efforts. Problem-oriented policing is now linked with community policing as the avant-garde programs for improving the quality of police service. In one of several descriptions of these developments in popular journals, Wilson and Kelling, who authored the original "Broken Windows" article that was so influential (1982), observe:

> The sort of police work practiced in Newport News is an effort to fix the broken windows. Similar projects are under way in cities all over America. This pattern constitutes the beginnings of the most significant redefinition of police work in the past half century (Wilson and Kelling, 1989).

Not all students of policing would make so firm and optimistic a statement. (For the views of several skeptics regarding the changes most commonly associated with community policing, see Greene and Mastrofski, 1988. For comments on the relative merits of the potential in community policing vis-à-vis problem-oriented policing, see Skolnick and Bayley, 1988a, pp. 17–19.)

Tracking an idea as it spreads in policing is not easy. I have, myself, learned about local efforts to implement problem-oriented policing from limited observations in the field, attending conferences, participating in training sessions, conversing with colleagues, reading police journals and department newsletters, and seeing the coverage of the national and local media. Because of my association with the concept, I have also learned a great deal from key personnel engaged in some form of implementation in a number of agencies. But a cardinal rule in studying change in the police is that one cannot make any assessment of actual change without the benefit of on-site, in-depth inquiry, such as a study of the type conducted in Newport News. It is, therefore, impossible to summarize what is occurring based on such sources, and it would be foolhardy to try. But the feedback one gets from such varied and multiple contacts nevertheless has some value.

While the slightest progress toward focusing on substantive matters is commendable, concern about dilution of the concept is justified. Some accounts of claimed implementation of problem-oriented policing contain very little that reflects any engagement with substantive problems and little understanding of the overall concept. Among police agencies, some have an uncanny knack for placing new labels on old practices—for claiming change without changing. I have seen elaborate but totally unrealistic schedules for "full implementation" that seem more appropriate to a military exercise than to implementing a complex, necessarily long-term plan for organizational change requiring a radical shift in the way in which employees view their job and carry it out.

But against the background of these concerns are the many police agencies, units within police departments, and individual officers who have gone far beyond superficial change and are already realizing some of the projected benefits. While they have not, by any means, implemented all elements of the concept, they are very much on track. They demonstrate an excellent grasp of the full dimensions of the concept, recognize the interrelationships between and among various elements, and see clearly the long-range nature of the commitment and its implications for policing. They seem challenged—often enthusiastic—in adapting to a new way of operating.

One can, I believe, easily trace these more successful efforts to obvious factors such as the quality of leadership in a police agency, the support of the community, and the political environment—factors that Skolnick and Bayley identified in their analysis of efforts to implement community policing in six cities (1986). It is my impression, however, that beyond these factors, progress is most heavily dependent on the degree to which the agency or involved police officers have understood some of the fundamental lessons learned about policing in the past several decades. I have repeatedly found that the greatest barrier in opening the minds of police officers to problem-oriented policing is that they continue to cling to notions of policing that have been abandoned by more progressive police agencies and officers. Where most progress has been made in implementing problem-oriented policing, one finds that it is taken for granted that:

- Policing consists of dealing with a wide range of quite different problems, not just crime.
- These problems are interrelated, and the priority given them must be reassessed rather than ranked in traditional ways.
- Each problem requires a different response, not a generic response that is applied equally to all problems.
- Use of the criminal law is but one means of responding to a problem; it is not the only means.
- Police can accomplish much in working to prevent problems rather than simply responding efficiently to an endless number of incidents that are merely the manifestations of problems.
- Developing an effective response to a problem requires prior analysis rather than simply invoking traditional practices.
- The capacity of the police is extremely limited, despite the impression of omnipotence that the police cultivate and others believe.
- The police role is more akin to that of facilitators, enabling and encouraging the community to maintain its norms governing behavior, rather than the agency that assumes total responsibility for doing so.

Acceptance of these realities about policing is much more significant than a lay person might recognize. It sweeps the slate clean of assumptions and constraining frameworks that have had an enormous, powerful, and, I would argue, negative influence on police work. With a clean slate, problem-oriented policing invites the police, the community, and elected officials to adopt a fresh, more forthright agreement about what the police do, how they do it, and their potential for success. It is this "new honesty," in my opinion, that—more than any other feature—accounts for the unusual enthusiasm commonly expressed for problem-oriented policing by police officers, community members, and elected officials, even when the interests of these groups are in conflict. They find it refreshing to operate in a new type of environment that recognizes the reality of police work; that substitutes candid, open discussion for bluff and secrecy; that introduces more logic into deciding on policies and practices; and that makes greater use of common sense in developing the police response. They seem relieved to drop the misconceptions and unrealistic expectations of the past.

At the heart of this more honest approach to policing is the realization that the objective in attempting to bring about change is not simply to improve the police, but rather to solve community problems. All parties find that to be a welcome, productive shift in focus. The police are much more willing to join with others in solving community problems than in dwelling on the real or perceived shortcomings in their organization or methods of operating. And the community and elected officials are eager to address more directly the problems of concern to them rather than place their faith in proposals to improve the police, which may or may not have an impact on the community's problems. To move from an analysis of problems to solutions and only then to designing the organization to implement those solutions (rather than vice versa) makes good common sense. But as Voltaire wrote in 1764, "Common sense is not so common."

REFERENCES

American Bar Association (1973). *The Urban Police Function,* Approved draft. Chicago: American Bar Association.

Asbury, Kathryn E. (1988). "Social Control in a Local Community: The Role of the Apartment Superintendent," *Journal of Research in Crime and Delinquency,* **25:**411–425.

Balles, Joseph A. (1986). "A Problem-Oriented Approach to Police Service of the Citizen Noise Complaint." Madison, Wis.: University of Wisconsin Law School. Photocopy.

Bard, Morton (1970). *Training Police as Specialists in Family Crisis Intervention.* Washington, D.C.: U.S. Government Printing Office.

Bayley, David H. (1976). *Forces of Order: Police Behavior in Japan and the United States.* Berkeley and Los Angeles, Calif.: University of California Press.

Behan, Cornelius J. (1986). "Fighting Fear in Baltimore County: The COPE Project," *FBI Law Enforcement Bulletin,* **55** (Nov.):12–15.

Bell, John, and Barbara Burke (1989). "Cruising Cooper Street," *The Police Chief,* **56** (Jan.):26.

Besharov, Douglas J. (1987). *Child Abuse: A Police Guide.* Washington, D.C.: Police Foundation and American Bar Association.

Binder, Arnold, and James W. Meeker (1988). "Experiments as Reforms," *Journal of Criminal Justice,* **16:**347–358.

Bittner, Egon (1967). "The Police on Skid-Row: A Study of Peace Keeping," *American Sociological Review,* **32:**699–715.

Bittner, Egon (1970). *The Functions of the Police in Modern Society: A Review of Background Factors, Current Practices, and Possible Role Models.* Chevy Chase, Md.: National Institute of Mental Health.

Blanchard, Janelle (1973). "Proposal for a Model Residential Building Security Code," in U.S. Department of Justice, *Deterrence of Crime in and around Residences.* Washington, D.C.: U.S. Government Printing Office.

Braiden, Christopher (1986). "Bank Robberies and Stolen Bikes: Thoughts of a Street Cop," *Canadian Police College Journal,* **10:**1–30.

Brown, Lee P. (1984). "A Police Department and Its Values," *The Police Chief,* **51** (Oct.):24–25.

Brown, Lee P. (1985). "A Future Direction for Police Operations," *The Police Chief,* **52** (June):21–24.

Brown, Lee P. (1988a). "Excellence in Policing: Models for High-Performance Police Organizations," *The Police Chief,* **55** (Apr.):68.

Brown, Lee P. (1988b). "Strategies for Dealing with Crack Houses," *FBI Law Enforcement Bulletin,* **57** (June):4–7.

Brown, Lee P., and Mary Ann Wycoff (1987). "Policing Houston: Reducing Fear and Improving Service," *Crime & Delinquency,* **33:**71–89.

Bugg, William H. (1988). Memorandum to Inspector Edward McLaughlin, Philadelphia Police Department, Mar. 15.

Cahn, Michael F., and James M. Tien (1981). *An Alternative Approach in Police Response: Wilmington Management of Demand Program.* Washington, D.C.: U.S. Government Printing Office.

Clarke, R. V. G. (1980a). "'Situational' Crime Prevention: Theory and Practice," *British Journal of Criminology,* **20:**136–147.

Clarke, R. V. G. (ed.) (1980b). *Tackling Vandalism,* Home Office Research Study No. 47. London: Her Majesty's Stationery Office.

Clarke, R. V. G. (1983). "Situational Crime Prevention: Its Theoretical Basis and Practical Scope," in *Crime and Justice: An Annual Review of Research,* vol. 4, Michael Tonry and Norval Morris (eds.). Chicago: University of Chicago Press, pp. 225–256.

Clarke, R. V. G., and P. Mayhew (eds.) (1980). *Designing Out Crime.* London: Her Majesty's Stationery Office.

Clifton, Wayland, Jr. (1987). "Convenience Store Robberies in Gainesville, Florida: An Intervention Strategy by the Gainesville Police Department." Gainesville, Florida, Police Department. Photocopy.

Cohen, Bernard (1980). *Deviant Street Networks: Prostitution in New York City.* Lexington, Mass.: Lexington Books.

Cordner, Gary W. (1985). *The Baltimore County Citizen Oriented Police Enforcement (COPE) Project: Final Evaluation,* Final Report to the Florence V. Burden Foundation. Baltimore: Criminal Justice Department, University of Baltimore.

Cordner, Gary W. (1986). "Fear of Crime and the Police: An Evaluation of a Fear-Reduction Strategy," *Journal of Police Science and Administration,* **14:**223–233.

Cordner, Gary W. (1988). "A Problem-Oriented Approach to Community-Oriented Policing," in *Community Policing: Rhetoric or Reality?* Jack R. Greene and Stephen D. Mastrofski (eds.). New York: Praeger, pp. 135–152.

Couper, David C., and Sabine H. Lobitz (1988). "Quality Leadership: The First Step towards Quality Policing," *The Police Chief,* **55** (Apr.):79.

Cowart, Ronald (1986). "The Dallas Refugee Affairs Liaison Office," *Police Manager,* **2**:7.

Davis, Kenneth Culp (1969). *Discretionary Justice: A Preliminary Inquiry.* Baton Rouge, La.: Louisiana State University Press.

Davis, Kenneth Culp (1974). "An Approach to Legal Control of the Police," *Texas Law Review,* **52**:703–725.

Davis, Kenneth Culp (1975). *Police Discretion.* St. Paul, Minn.: West Publishing Co.

DeJong, William (1987). *Arresting the Demand for Drugs: Police and School Partnerships to Prevent Drug Abuse.* National Institute of Justice, Issues and Practices. Washington, D.C.: U.S. Department of Justice.

Deming, W. Edwards (1986). *Out of the Crisis.* Cambridge, Mass.: MIT Center for Advanced Engineering Study.

Eck, John E. (1979). *Managing Case Assignments: The Burglary Investigation Decision Model Replication.* Washington, D.C.: Police Executive Research Forum.

Eck, John E. (1982). *Solving Crimes: The Investigation of Burglary and Robbery.* Washington, D.C.: Police Executive Research Forum.

Eck, John E. (1984). *Using Research: A Primer for Law Enforcement Managers.* Washington, D.C.: Police Executive Research Forum.

Eck, John E., and William Spelman (1987). "Who Ya Gonna Call? The Police as Problem-Busters," *Crime & Delinquency,* **33**:31–52.

Eck, John E., William Spelman, Diane Hill, Darrel W. Stephens, John R. Stedman, and Gerard R. Murphy (1987). *Problem Solving: Problem-Oriented Policing in Newport News.* Washington, D.C.: Police Executive Research Forum.

Ekblom, Paul (1987). *Reducing Shoptheft,* Crime Prevention Unit. London: Home Office Research and Planning Unit.

Engstad, Peter, and John L. Evans (1980). "Responsibility, Competence and Police Effectiveness in Crime Control," in *The Effectiveness of Policing,* R. V. G. Clarke and J. M. Hough (eds.). London: Gower, pp. 139–162.

Farmer, Michael T. (ed.) (1981). *Differential Police Response Strategies.* Washington, D.C.: Police Executive Research Forum.

Farrell, Michael J. (1986). "C.P.O.P. (Community Patrol Officer Program)," Interim Progress Report No. 2. New York City Police Department and Vera Institute of Justice. May. Photocopy.

Feins, Judith D. (1983). *Partnerships for Neighborhood Crime Prevention.* Washington, D.C.: National Institute of Justice.

Ferris, Janet E. (1988). "Establishing Asset Forfeiture Programs, A Guide for State and Local Prosecutors." Washington, D.C.: Bureau of Justice Assistance Project on Asset Forfeiture Training and Police Executive Research Forum.

Finn, Peter, and Monique Sullivan (1987). *Police Response to Special Populations.* National Institute of Justice, Issues and Practices. Washington, D.C.: U.S. Department of Justice.

Force, Robert (1972). "Decriminalization of Breach of the Peace Statutes: A Nonpenal Approach to Order Maintenance," *Tulane Law Review,* **46:**367–493.

Fosdick, Raymond B. (1915). *European Police Systems,* 1969 reprint. Montclair, N.J.: Patterson Smith.

Fowler, Floyd J., Jr., and Thomas W. Mangione (1986). "A Three-Pronged Effort to Reduce Crime and Fear of Crime: The Hartford Experiment," in *Community Crime Prevention: Does It Work?* Dennis P. Rosenbaum (ed.). Beverly Hills, Calif.: Sage, pp. 87–108.

Friedmann, Robert R. (1986). "Transformation of Role for Israeli Police Officers," *Police Studies,* **9:**68–77.

Fuld, Leonhard F. (1909). *Police Administration: A Critical Study of Police Organizations in the United States and Abroad,* 1971 reprint. Montclair, N.J.: Patterson Smith.

Gay, William G., and Robert A. Bowers (1985). *Targeting Law Enforcement Resources: The Career Criminal Focus.* National Institute of Justice, Issues and Practices. Washington, D.C.: U.S. Department of Justice.

Gay, William G., Thomas M. Beall, and Robert A. Bowers (1984). *A Four-Site Assessment of the Integrated Criminal Apprehension Program.* Washington, D.C.: University City Science Center.

Goldstein, Herman (1963). "Police Discretion: The Ideal versus the Real," *Public Administration Review,* **23:**140–148.

Goldstein, Herman (1967). "Police Policy Formulation: A Proposal for Improving Police Performance," *Michigan Law Review,* **65:**1123–1146.

Goldstein, Herman (1977). *Policing a Free Society.* Cambridge, Mass.: Ballinger.

Goldstein, Herman. (1979). "Improving Policing: A Problem-Oriented Approach," *Crime and Delinquency,* **25:**236–258.

Goldstein, Herman, and Charles E. Susmilch (1981). "The Problem-Oriented Approach to Improving Police Service: A Description of the Project and an Elaboration of the Concept," vol. 1 of the Project on Development of a Problem-Oriented Approach to Improving Police Service. Madison, Wis.: University of Wisconsin Law School. Photocopy.

Goldstein, Herman, and Charles E. Susmilch (1982a). "The Drinking-Driver in Madison: A Study of the Problem and the Community's Response," vol. 2 of the Project on Development of a Problem-Oriented Approach to Improving Police Service. Madison, Wis.: University of Wisconsin Law School. Photocopy.

Goldstein, Herman, and Charles E. Susmilch (1982b). "The Repeat Sexual Offender in Madison: A Memorandum on the Problem and the Community's Response," vol. 3 of the Project on Development of a Problem-Oriented Approach to Improving Police Service. Madison, Wis.: University of Wisconsin Law School. Photocopy.

Goldstein, Herman, and Charles E. Susmilch (1982c). "Experimenting with the Problem-Oriented Approach to Improving Police Service: A Report and Some Reflections on Two Case Studies," vol. 4 of the Project on Development of a Problem-Oriented Approach to Improving Police Service. Madison, Wis.: University of Wisconsin Law School. Photocopy.

Goolkasian, Gail A. (1986). *Confronting Domestic Violence.* National Institute of Justice, Issues and Practice. Washington, D.C.: U.S. Department of Justice.

Gray, Thomas C. (1975). "Selecting for a Police Subculture," in *Police in America,* Jerome H. Skolnick and Thomas C. Gray (eds.). Boston: Little, Brown, pp. 45–56.

Greenberg, Bernard, Oliver S. Yu, and Karen Lang (1973). *Enhancement of the Investigative Function, vol. 1, Analysis and Conclusions,* Final Report, Phase 1. Springfield, Va.: National Technical Information Service.

Greene, Jack R., and Stephen Mastrofski (eds.) (1988). *Community Policing: Rhetoric or Reality?* New York: Praeger.

Greenwood, Peter W., Joan Petersilia, and Jan Chaiken (1977). *The Criminal Investigation Process,* Lexington, Mass.: D.C. Heath.

Gregory v. *City of Chicago* (1969). 394 U.S. 111, 118.

Hammett, Theodore M. (1987). *Toward Comprehensive Anti-Arson Programs.* National Institute of Justice, Issues and Practices. Washington, D.C.: U.S. Department of Justice.

Harring, Sidney (1983). *Policing a Class Society.* New Brunswick, N.J.: Rutgers University Press.

Higdon, Richard Kirk, and Phillip G. Huber (1987). *How to Fight Fear: The Citizen Oriented Police Enforcement Program Package.* Washington, D.C.: Police Executive Research Forum.

Hoare, M. A., G. Stewart, and C. M. Purcell (1984). *The Problem Oriented Approach: Four Pilot Studies.* London: Metropolitan Police, Management Services Department.

Holmes, Cameron H. (1988). *Strategic Forfeiture: Targeting Drug Traffickers' Assets.* Washington, D.C.: Police Executive Research Forum.

Hope, Tim (1985). *Implementing Crime Prevention Measures,* Home Office Research Study No. 86. London: Her Majesty's Stationery Office.

Hough, J. M. (1980–1981). "Designing Out Crime," *Police Research Bulletin,* **35–36:**28–31.

Humphreys, Laud (1975). *Tearoom Trade: Impersonal Sex in Public Places.* Chicago: Aldine, Enlargement of 1972 ed.

Irwin v. *Ware* (1984). 392 Mass. 745, 467 N.E. 2d 1292.

Jacobs, Jane (1962). *The Death and Life of Great American Cities.* New York: Vintage.

Jeffrey, C. R. (1977). *Crime Prevention through Environmental Design.* Beverly Hills, Calif.: Sage.

Jones, Ronni (1986). *Punish the Offender, Protect the Victim, Treat the Family: A Guide for Communities Interested in Breaking the Cycle of Child Sexual Abuse.* Madison, Wis.: University of Wisconsin Law School.

Kansas City, Missouri, Police Department (1974). *Directed Patrol: A Concept in Community Specific, Crime Specific, Service Specific Policing.* Kansas City, Mo.: K.C.M.P.D.

Kansas City, Missouri, Police Department (1978). *Response Time Analysis,* vol. 2. Washington, D.C.: U.S. Government Printing Office.

Kanter, Rosabeth Moss (1983). *The Change Masters: Innovation and Entrepreneurship in the American Corporation.* New York: Simon & Schuster.

Karchmer, Clifford (1985). *Neighborhood Based Arson Control: Collected Papers.* Washington, D.C.: Battelle Human Affairs Research Centers and Citizens Committee for Fire Protection.

Kelling, George L. (1985a). "Neighborhoods and Police," Working paper 85-05-02, Program in Criminal Justice Policy and Management. Cambridge, Mass.: John F. Kennedy School of Government, Harvard University.

Kelling, George L. (1985b). "Order Maintenance, the Quality of Urban Life, and Police: A Line of Argument," in *Police Leadership in America: Crisis and Opportunity,* William A. Geller (ed.). Chicago: American Bar Foundation and Praeger Publishers, pp. 296–308.

Kelling, George L. (1988). *Police and Communities: The Quiet Revolution.* National Institute of Justice, Perspectives on Policing. Washington, D.C.: National Institute of Justice, U.S. Department of Justice, and Harvard University.

Kelling, George L., and Mark H. Moore (1988). *The Evolving Strategy of Policing.* National Institute of Justice, Perspectives on Policing. Washington, D.C.: National Institute of Justice, U.S. Department of Justice, and Harvard University.

Kelling, George L., Tony Pate, Duane Dieckman, and Charles E. Brown (1974). *The Kansas City Preventive Patrol Experiment: A Summary Report.* Washington, D.C.: Police Foundation.

Kennedy, David M. (1986). "Neighborhood Policing in Los Angeles," Case No. C16-86-7170 in the Case Program of the John F. Kennedy School of Government, Harvard University, Cambridge, Mass.

Kleiman, Mark A. R. (1986). "Bringing Back Street-Level Heroin Enforcement," Working paper 86-01-08, Program in Criminal Justice Policy and Management. Cambridge, Mass.: John F. Kennedy School of Government, Harvard University.

Kleiman, Mark A. R. (1987). "Crackdowns: The Effects of Intensive Enforcement on Retail Heroin Dealing," Working paper 87-01-11, Program in Criminal Justice Policy and Management. Cambridge, Mass.: John F. Kennedy School of Government, Harvard University.

Klockars, Carl B. (1985). "Order Maintenance, the Quality of Urban Life, and Police: A Different Line of Argument," in *Police Leadership in America: Crisis and Opportunity,* William A. Geller (ed.). Chicago: American Bar Foundation and Praeger Publishers, pp. 309–321.

Klockars, Carl B. (1986). "Street Justice: Some Micro-Moral Reservations: Comment on Sykes," *Justice Quarterly,* **3**:513–516.

Krantz, Sheldon, Bernard Gilman, Charles G. Benda, Carol Rogoff Hallstrom, and Eric J. Nadworny (1979). *Police Policymaking: The Boston Experience.* Lexington, Mass.: D.C. Heath.

LaFave, Wayne R. (1965). *Arrest: The Decision to Take a Suspect into Custody,* Frank J. Remington (ed.). Boston: Little, Brown.

Larson, Richard C. (1988). "Rapid Response and Community Policing: Are They Really in Conflict?" Paper based on presentation to Seventh Meeting of the Executive Session, Community Policing, Harvard University, Kennedy School of Government, Cambridge, Mass., Sept. Photocopy.

Lavrakas, Paul J. (1985). "Citizen Self-Help and Neighborhood Crime Prevention Policy," in *American Violence and Public Policy,* Lynn A. Curtis (ed.). New Haven, Conn.: Yale University Press, pp. 87–115.

Lavrakas, Paul J. (1986). "Evaluating Police-Community Anticrime Newsletters: The Evanston, Houston, and Newark Field Studies," in *Community Crime Prevention: Does It Work?*, Dennis P. Rosenbaum (ed.). Beverly Hills, Calif.: Sage, pp. 269–291.

Lindsey, William H., Ronald Cochran, Bruce Quint, and Mario Rivera (1985). "The Oasis Technique: A Method of Controlling Crime and Improving the Quality of Life," in *Police Leadership in America: Crisis and Opportunity*, William A. Geller (ed.). Chicago: American Bar Foundation and Praeger Publishers, pp. 322–331.

Loree, Donald J. (1988). "Innovation and Change in a Regional Police Force," *Canadian Police College Journal*, **12**:205–239.

Loving, Nancy (1980). *Responding to Spouse Abuse and Wife Beating: A Guide for Police*. Washington, D.C.: Police Executive Research Forum.

McClure, James (1986). *Cop World: Inside an American Police Force*. New York: Dell Publishing Co.

McEwen, J. Thomas, Edward F. Connors, III, and Marcia I. Cohen (1984). *Evaluation of the Differential Police Response Field Test*. Alexandria, Va.: Research Management Associates.

Maguire, M. (1982). *Burglary in a Dwelling: The Offence, the Offender and the Victim*. London: Heinemann.

Manning, Peter K. (1977). *Police Work: The Social Organization of Policing*. Cambridge, Mass.: MIT Press.

Martin, Susan E., and Lawrence K. Sherman (1986). *Catching Career Criminals: The Washington, D.C., Repeat Offender Project*. Washington, D.C.: Police Foundation.

Mastrofski, Stephen (1983). "Police Knowledge of the Patrol Beat: A Performance Measure," in *Police at Work: Policy Issues and Analysis*, Richard R. Bennett (ed.). Beverly Hills, Calif.: Sage, pp. 45–64.

Mastrofski, Stephen (1986). "Police Agency Accreditation: The Prospects of Reform," *American Journal of Police*, **5**:45–81.

Metropolitan Police (1984). *Oxford Street: Shopper as Victim*, Interim Report 15-4-84. London: The Metropolitan Police.

Moore, Mark H., and Robert C. Trojanowicz (1988). *Policing and the Fear of Crime*. National Institute of Justice, Perspectives on Policing. Washington, D.C.: National Institute of Justice, U.S. Department of Justice, and Harvard University.

Moore, Mark H., Susan R. Estrich, Daniel McGillis, and William Spelman (1984). *Dangerous Offenders: The Elusive Target of Justice*. Cambridge, Mass.: Harvard University Press.

Moore, Mark H., Robert C. Trojanowicz, and George L. Kelling (1988). *Crime and Policing*. National Institute of Justice, Perspectives on Policing. Washington, D.C.: National Institute of Justice, U.S. Department of Justice, and Harvard University.

Mosher, James F. (1983). "Server Intervention: A New Approach for Preventing Drinking Driving," *Accident Analysis & Prevention*, **15**:483–497.

Muir, William Ker, Jr. (1977). *Police: Streetcorner Politicians*. Chicago and London: University of Chicago Press.

Murphy, Chris, and Graham Muir (1984). "Community Based Policing: A Review of the Critical Issues," Working paper. Ottawa: Royal Canadian Mounted Police and Programs Branch of the Ministry Secretariat.

Murphy, Gerard R. (1986). *Special Care: Improving the Police Response to the Mentally Disabled.* Washington, D.C.: Police Executive Research Forum.

Naisbitt, John, and Patricia Aburdene (1985). *Re-inventing the Corporation.* New York: Warner Books.

National Advisory Commission on the Causes and Prevention of Violence, Task Force on Law and Law Enforcement (1969). *Law and Order Reconsidered.* Washington, D.C.: U.S. Government Printing Office.

National Advisory Commission on Civil Disorders (1968). *Report of the National Advisory Commission on Civil Disorders.* Washington, D.C.: U.S. Government Printing Office.

National Advisory Commission on Criminal Justice Standards and Goals (1973). *Police.* Washington, D.C.: U.S. Government Printing Office.

National Press Club press conference (1988). "Research Monies," a letter to the President and Congress supporting action on research and program evaluation, Washington, D.C., July 25.

Nelson v. *City of Chicago* (1983). Consent decree, no. 83-C-1168 (N.D. Ill., E. Div., July 7).

Newman, Kenneth (1984). Memorandum to Metropolitan Police Colleagues, New Scotland Yard, London, Nov. 19.

Newman, Kenneth (1985). *The Principles of Policing and Guidance for Professional Behavior.* London: The Metropolitan Police.

Newman, Oscar (1972). *Defensible Space: Crime Prevention through Urban Design.* New York: Macmillan.

New York City Police Department (1985). "The Community Patrol Officer Program." New York: N.Y.P.D. Photocopy.

New York City Police Department (1987a). "The Community Patrol Officer Program: Implementation Guide." New York: N.Y.P.D. Photocopy.

New York City Police Department (1987b). "The Community Patrol Officer Program: Orientation Guide." New York: N.Y.P.D. Photocopy.

New York City Police Department (1988a). "The Community Patrol Officer Program: Supervisory Guide." New York: N.Y.P.D. Photocopy.

New York City Police Department (1988b). "Problem Solving and the Community Patrol Officer Program." New York: N.Y.P.D. Photocopy.

The New York Times (1985). "Police to Round Up Homeless When Cold Grips New York," Jan. 23, p. 1; "Seat-Belt Law Is Used to Battle Prostitution," Mar. 8, p. 2.

The New York Times (1988). "Graffiti Seems to Be Fading from New York Walls," May 6, p. 12.

Ostrom, Elinor, Roger B. Parks, Gordon P. Whitaker, and Steven L. Percy (1978). "The Public Service Production Process: A Framework for Analyzing Police Services," *Police Studies Journal,* **7**:381–389.

Palenski, Joseph E. (1984). "The Use of Mediation by Police," *Mediation Quarterly,* **5**:31–38.

Parnas, Raymond I. (1967). The Police Response to the Domestic Disturbance," *Wisconsin Law Review,* 914–955.

Pate, Antony M., Paul J. Lavrakas, Mary Ann Wycoff, Wesley G. Skogan, and Lawrence W. Sherman (1985). "Neighborhood Police Newsletters: Experiments in Newark and Houston, Executive Summary," Final Draft Report to the National Institute of Justice, Washington, D.C. Photocopy.

Pate, Antony M., Mary Ann Wycoff, Wesley G. Skogan, and Lawrence W. Sherman (1986). *Reducing Fear of Crime in Houston and Newark: A Summary Report.* Washington, D.C.: Police Foundation and National Institute of Justice.

Patterson, John, and Gary R. Barbour (1989). "Cruise Control in Lakewood," *The Police Chief,* **56** (Jan.):32.

People v. *Bright* (1988). 526 N.Y.S. 2d 66, 520 N.E. 2d 1355.

Peters, Thomas J., and Nancy Austin (1985). *A Passion for Excellence.* New York: Random House.

Peters, Thomas J., and Robert H. Waterman (1982). *In Search of Excellence.* New York: Harper & Row.

Pierce, Glen, S. A. Spaar, and L. R. Briggs, IV (1984). *The Character of Police Work: Implications for the Delivery of Police Services.* Boston: Northeastern University.

Police Executive Research Forum (1988). *Problem Solving Quarterly,* **1** (Winter).

Police Executive Research Forum (1989). *Taking a Problem-Oriented Approach to Drug Enforcement.* Bureau of Justice Assistance. Washington, D.C.: U.S. Department of Justice.

Police Foundation (1981). *The Newark Foot Patrol Experiment.* Washington, D.C.: Police Foundation.

Police Foundation (1987). *Register of Policing Research 1986–87.* London: Police Foundation.

Potter, Ira L. (1987). "*Arcara v. Cloud Books, Inc.:* Locking Out Prostitution," *Hastings Constitutional Law Quarterly,* **15:**181–192.

Poyner, Barry (1980). *A Study of Street Attacks and Their Environmental Settings.* London: The Tavistock Institute of Human Relations.

Poyner, Barry (1983). *Design against Crime: Beyond Defensible Space.* London: Butterworth.

Poyner, Barry, and Ruth Woodall (1987). *Preventing Shoplifting: A Study in Oxford Street.* London: Police Foundation.

President's Commission on Campus Unrest (1970). *The Report of the President's Commission on Campus Unrest.* Washington, D.C.: U.S. Government Printing Office.

President's Commission on Law Enforcement and Administration of Justice (1967). *The Challenge of Crime in a Free Society.* Washington, D.C.: U.S. Government Printing Office.

Punch, Maurice (1979). *Policing the Inner City.* London: Macmillan.

Ramsay, Malcolm (1982). "City-centre Crime: The Scope for Situational Prevention," Research and Planning, Unit Paper 10. London: Home Office.

Reiner, Robert (1985). *The Politics of the Police.* Sussex, England, and New York: Wheatsheaf Books and St. Martin's Press.

Reiss, Albert J., Jr. (1971). *The Police and the Public*. New Haven, Conn.: Yale University Press.

Reiss, Albert J., Jr. (1985) *Policing a City's Central District: The Oakland Story*. Washington, D.C.: National Institute of Justice.

Reiss, Albert J., Jr., and Michael Tonry (eds.) (1986). *Communities and Police*. Chicago: University of Chicago Press.

Reppetto, Thomas A. (1974). *Residential Crime*. Cambridge, Mass.: Ballinger.

Reuss-Ianni, Elizabeth, and Francis A. J. Ianni (1983). "Street Cops and Management Cops: The Two Cultures of Policing," in *Control in the Police Organization,* Maurice Punch (ed.). Cambridge, Mass.: MIT Press, pp. 251–274.

Rosenbaum, Dennis P. (1987). "The Theory and Research behind Neighborhood Watch: Is It a Sound Fear and Crime Reduction Strategy?" *Crime & Delinquency,* **33:**103–134.

Rosenbaum, Dennis P., Dan A. Lewis, and Jane A. Grant (1986). "Neighborhood-Based Crime Prevention: Assessing the Efficacy of Community Organizing in Chicago," in *Community Crime Prevention: Does It Work?*, Dennis P. Rosenbaum (ed.). Beverly Hills, Calif.: Sage, pp. 109–133.

Rubinstein, Jonathan (1973). *City Police*. New York: Farrar, Straus and Giroux.

Scarr, Harry A. (1973). *Patterns of Burglary,* 2d ed. Washington, D.C.: U.S. Government Printing Office.

Selznick, Philip (1957). *Leadership in Administration*. New York: Row, Peterson.

Sherman, Lawrence W. (1987). Repeat Calls to Police in Minneapolis. Washington, D.C.: Crime Control Institute.

Sherman, Lawrence W., and Richard A. Berk (1984). "The Specific Deterrent Effects of Arrest for Domestic Assault," *American Sociological Review,* **49:**261–272.

Skogan, Wesley G. (1988). "Community Organizations and Crime," In *Crime and Justice: A Review of Research,* vol. 10, Michael Tonry and Norval Morris (eds.). Chicago and London: University of Chicago Press, pp. 39–78.

Skolnick, Jerome H. (1966). *Justice without Trial: Law Enforcement in Democratic Society*. New York: John Wiley & Sons.

Skolnick, Jerome H., and David H. Bayley (1986). *The New Blue Line: Police Innovation in Six American Cities*. New York: The Free Press.

Skolnick, Jerome H., and David H. Bayley (1988a). *Community Policing: Issues and Practices around the World*. National Institute of Justice, Issues and Practices. Washington, D.C.: U.S. Department of Justice.

Skolnick, Jerome H., and David H. Bayley (1988b). "Theme and Variation in Community Policing," in *Crime and Justice: A Review of Research,* vol. 10, Michael Tonry and Norval Morris (eds.). Chicago and London: University of Chicago Press, pp. 1–37.

Slovak, Jeffrey S. (1987). "Police Organization and Policing Environment: Case Study of a Disjuncture," *Sociological Focus,* **20:**77–94.

Smith, Bruce (1940). *Police Systems in the United States*. New York: Harper & Row.

Spelman, William (1987). *Beyond Bean Counting: New Approaches for Managing Crime Data*. Washington, D.C.: Police Executive Research Forum.

Spelman, William, and Dale K. Brown (1984). *Calling the Police: Citizen Reporting of Serious Crime*. Washington, D.C.: U.S. Government Printing Office.

Spelman, William, and John E. Eck (1987a). "Newport News Tests Problem-Oriented Policing," *NIJ Reports,* Jan.–Feb., pp. 2–8.

Spelman, William, and John E. Eck (1987b). "Problem-Oriented Policing," *Research in Brief.* Washington, D.C.: National Institute of Justice, Jan.

Stellwagen, Lindsey D. (1985). "Use of Forfeiture Sanctions in Drug Cases," *Research in Brief.* Washington, D.C.: National Institute of Justice, July.

Stone, J., and F. Taylor (1977). *Vandalism in Schools.* London: The Save the Children Fund.

Strom, Fredric A. (1977). *Zoning Control of Sex Businesses: The Zoning Approach to Controlling Adult Entertainment.* New York: Boardman.

Sykes, Gary W. (1986). "Street Justice: A Moral Defense of Order Maintenance Policing," *Justice Quarterly,* **3**:497–512.

Sykes, Richard E., and Edward E. Brent (1983). *Policing: A Social Behaviorist Perspective.* New Brunswick, N.J.: Rutgers University Press.

Taft, Philip B., Jr. (1986). *Fighting Fear: The Baltimore County C.O.P.E. Project.* Washington, D.C.: Police Executive Research Forum. Pamphlet.

Thurman v. *City of Torrington* (1984). 595 F. Supp. 1521 (D. Conn.).

Tien, James M., James W. Simon, and Richard C. Larson (1978). *An Alternative Approach in Police Patrol: The Wilmington Split-Force Experiment.* Washington, D.C.: U.S. Government Printing Office.

Tiffany, Lawrence P., Donald M. McIntyre, Jr., and Daniel L. Rotenberg (1967). *Detection of Crime: Stopping and Questioning, Search and Seizure, Encouragement and Entrapment,* Frank J. Remington (ed.). Boston: Little, Brown.

Trojanowicz, Robert (n.d.). *An Evaluation of the Neighborhood Foot Patrol Program in Flint, Michigan.* East Lansing, Mich.: Michigan State University.

Trojanowicz, Robert, Marilyn Steele, and Susan Trojanowicz (1986). *Community Policing: A Taxpayer's Perspective,* Community Policing Series No. 7. East Lansing, Mich.: National Neighborhood Foot Patrol Center. Pamphlet.

Tumin, Zachary (1986). "Community-Based Policing: The Houston Experience," Working Paper #C87-01, Program in Criminal Justice Policy and Management. Cambridge, Mass.: John F. Kennedy School of Government, Harvard University.

U.S. Department of Commerce (1969). *Statistical Abstract of the United States.* Washington, D.C.: U.S. Government Printing Office.

U.S. Department of Justice, National Institute of Justice (1987). Third National Policing State of the Art Conference, Phoenix, Ariz., June 10–13.

Van Maanen, John (1974). "Working the Street: A Developmental View of Police Behavior," in *The Potential for Reform of Criminal Justice,* Herbert Jacob (ed.). Beverly Hills, Calif.: Sage, pp. 83–130.

Vaughn, Jerald R. (1987). "Executive Director's Report: Law Enforcement Policy Resource Center Established," *The Police Chief,* **54** (Oct.):8.

Vera Institute of Justice (1987). *A Proposal to Strengthen the Planning and Problem-Solving Capacity of CPOP Units.* New York: Photocopy. Mar.

Vollmer, August (1936). *The Police and Modern Society,* 1971 reprint. Montclair, N.J.: Patterson Smith.

Walker, Samuel (1977). *A Critical History of Police Reform: The Emergence of Professionalism*. Lexington, Mass.: Lexington Books.

Walker, Samuel (1986). "Controlling the Cops: A Legislative Approach to Police Rulemaking," *University of Detroit Law Review,* **63**:361–391.

The Wall Street Journal (1984). "The Need to Police Domestic Violence," by Lawrence W. Sherman and Anthony V. Bouza, May 22.

The Wall Street Journal (1988). "Los Angeles Seeks Ultimate Weapon in Gang War," Mar. 30; "Los Angeles Can't Win Drug War by Cracking Whip," May 5.

Ward, Benjamin (1985). *The Community Patrol Officer Program*. New York: New York City Police Department.

Wasserman, Robert, and Mark H. Moore (1988). *Values in Policing*. National Institute of Justice, Perspectives on Policing. Washington, D.C.: National Institute of Justice, U.S. Department of Justice, and Harvard University.

Weatheritt, Mollie (1985). "Policing Research and Policing Policy," *Policing,* **1**:77–86.

Weatheritt, Mollie (1986). *Innovations in Policing*. London: Croom Helm.

Weisburd, David, Jerome McElroy, and Patricia Hardyman (1988). "Challenges to Supervision in Community Policing: Observations on a Pilot Project," *American Journal of Police,* **7**:29–50.

Westley, William A. (1970). *Violence and the Police: A Sociological Study of Law, Custom, and Morality*. Cambridge, Mass.: MIT Press.

Whitaker, Catherine J. (1986). "Crime Prevention Measures," Special Report. Washington, D.C.: U.S. Department of Justice, Bureau of Justice Statistics, Mar.

Wilson, James Q. (1968). *Varieties of Police Behavior: The Management of Law and Order in Eight Communities*. Cambridge, Mass.: Harvard University Press.

Wilson, James Q., and George L. Kelling (1982). "Broken Windows: The Police and Neighborhood Safety," *The Atlantic Monthly,* Mar., pp. 29–38.

Wilson, James Q., and George L. Kelling (1989). "Making Neighborhoods Safe," *The Atlantic Monthly,* Feb., pp. 46–52.

Wilson, O. W. (1950). *Police Administration,* 1st ed. New York: McGraw-Hill.

Wilson, O. W. (1952). *Police Planning*. Springfield, Ill.: Charles C Thomas.

Wilson, O. W. (1963). *Police Administration,* 2d ed. New York: McGraw-Hill.

Wilson, S. (1978). "Vandalism and 'Defensible Space' on London Housing Estates," in *Tackling Vandalism,* Home Office Research Study No. 47, R. V. G. Clarke (ed.). London: Her Majesty's Stationery Office.

Winchester, S., and H. Jackson (1982). *Residential Burglary: The Limits of Prevention,* Home Office Research Study No. 74. London: Her Majesty's Stationery Office.

Wycoff, Mary Ann (1986). "The Dallas Storefront: One Observer's Perspective," *Police Manager,* **2**:8–9.

Wycoff, Mary Ann (1988). "The Benefits of Community Policing: Evidence and Conjecture," in *Community Policing: Rhetoric or Reality?*, Jack R. Greene and Stephen Mastrofski (eds.). New York: Praeger, pp. 103–120.

Wycoff, Mary Ann, Wesley G. Skogan, Antony M. Pate, and Lawrence W. Sherman (1985). "Police as Community Organizers: The Houston Field Test: Executive Summary," Final draft report from the Police Foundation to the National Institute of Justice. Washington, D.C.: Photocopy.

Zeisel, J. (1976). *Stopping School Property Damage: Design and Administrative Guidelines to Reduce School Vandalism.* Arlington, Va.: American Association of School Administration.

Zimmer, L. (1987). "Operation Pressure Point: The Disruption of Street-Level Drug Trade on New York's Lower East Side," Occasional Papers from the Center for Research in Crime and Justice, New York University School of Law, New York.

INDEX

Abandoned cars, 119
(*See also* Traffic law enforcement)
Abatement laws, 140
Abuse:
child, 107, 170, 172
spousal, 18, 44, 114, 137, 140, 141, 171–172
Accountability of police, 10, 11, 27–28, 46–48, 144–145, 153
Advocacy role, 47
Affirmative action, 166
American Bar Foundation, 8
Analysis, 60, 65–66, 76, 82–101
adequacy of, 98–101
in Baltimore County, 52–53, 62, 63, 69, 90
of calls, 20–21, 152
crime, 37–38, 55, 72, 80–81
of drug problem, 63–64
Analysis (*Cont.*):
level of, 144
operating/street, 61–63, 69, 81, 86, 90, 94
top-, 61–63, 81, 89
in London, 55, 62
in Madison, Wis., 51–52, 62
monitoring of, 90
in Newport News, Va., 62, 63, 69, 83–84, 90, 94
research methods in, 89–90
of response, 21, 44–47, 49, 94–98
use of information in, 82–89
assessment/evaluation of, 88–89
distortion of, 91
from offenders, 80, 87
from police files, 86, 91–93
from rank and file, 93–94, 97–98
from victims, 80, 86

Arrest, 39, 43, 132
alternatives to, 136, 152
custody without, 130, 131, 142
for drug trafficking, 44, 137
for gang control, 44, 137–138
without intent to prosecute, 44, 136–138
intervention without, 135–136
objectives of, 9, 137
for spousal abuse, 44, 137, 171–172
Arson, 18
Assault (*see* Sexual assault)
Asset forfeiture programs, 140
Athletic leagues, 24, 103
Auto theft, 75
(*See also* Traffic law enforcement)

Baltimore County, Md.:
abatement laws in, 140
Citizen Oriented Police Enforcement (COPE) program in, 52–53, 65, 75, 77, 173
as conflict resolution, 112–113
fear as focus of, 115
housing complex problems as focus of, 113, 142
neighborhood surveys by, 118
community concerns in, 71
community police relations in, 60
harassment response in, 135
mapping in, 139
problem-oriented policing in, 60, 66
analysis in, 52–53, 62, 63, 69, 90
problem redefined in, 77
Baltimore County, Md., problem-oriented policing in (*Cont.*):
rank and file's role in, 61, 69, 149
training in, 167
traditional response prohibited in, 102
zoning laws enforced in, 139
Bard, Morton, 112
Bayley, David H., 24, 153, 178
Beat officer, 24, 153, 178
conflict resolution by, 113
discretion of, 94
informal practices of, 112
integrity of, 160
knowledge of, 83–84, 164
mediation skills of, 112
(*See also* Rank and file)
Beat patrol, 18, 24, 60
in Flint, Mich., 57–58
in New York City, 58
as primary work unit, 32–33
(*See also* Rank and file)
Behan, Cornelius, 52
Behavior:
community curbs on, 15, 22
as incident-cluster theme, 67
as problem characteristic, 67
Bittner, Egon, 8, 95
Blockwatch programs, 23
Braiden, Chris, 59–60
Brown, Lee P., 59, 153
Burglaries, 44–45
ordinances to prevent, 127

Calls:
analyzed/screened, 20–21, 152
differential/alternative response to, 20–21, 152
on noise, 92–93
priority of, 12, 14, 19, 20

Canada, community-based policing in, 59–61, 70, 71
Cars, abandoned, 119
Chahley, Leroy, 60
Chicago, gangs in, 137–138
Child abuse, 107, 170, 172
Children, missing, 18, 99
Citizen Oriented Police Enforcement (COPE) (*see* Baltimore County, Md., Citizen Oriented Police Enforcement program in)
Commission on Accreditation for Law Enforcement Agencies, 13
Community:
  as behavior curb, 15, 22
  crime prevention by, 23
  decision-making by, 47–48
  defined, 25
  as information source, 86–87
  initiatives by, 24
  problem identified by, 34–35, 40, 41, 63–64, 70–71, 99, 134, 135
  role of, in policing, 21–27
  as untapped resource, 21, 45
Community Mobilization Project, 58–60, 74
Community-oriented policing, 21–27, 32, 45, 52, 57–61, 163, 164, 178
  in Baltimore County (*see* Baltimore County, Md., Citizen Oriented Police Enforcement program in)
  in Canada, 59–61, 70, 71
  in Flint, Mich., 57–58, 60, 61
  in Houston, Tex., 59
  in Japan, 118
  in Los Angeles, Calif., 58–60, 74
Community-oriented policing (*Cont.*):
  in Newport News, Va., 60
  in New York City, N.Y., 58, 60
  rank-and-file used in, 28–29
Community Patrol Officer Program (*see* New York City, N.Y., Community Patrol Officer Program in)
Community-police relations, 3, 4, 10, 14, 22–27, 30, 48, 57–61, 70–71, 152
  awareness of police limitations in, 117–119
  consultation in, 144, 153
  control of police in, 45, 47
  decision-making shared in, 25, 26
  information conveyed in, 114–119
  input on responses in, 26, 119–121, 144
  police knowledge of, 83–84, 159–160, 164
  police supported by, 117
  police serve, 16, 17
  wide versus narrow focus of, 24–26
Confiscation of assets, 140
Conflict, xii–xiii
  management/resolution, 10, 112–113
  over public space, 77, 112, 118, 139–140
  racial, 7, 9, 10, 22–23, 109, 120
Controls on police:
  external, 1, 17, 28, 44, 45, 47
  internal, 7, 27–28
Convenience store robberies, 80–81, 87, 88, 128

COPE (*see* Baltimore County, Md., Citizen Oriented Police Enforcement program in)
Corruption, 6, 161
Couper, David, 52, 156
CPOP (*see* New York City, N.Y., Community Patrol Officer Program in)
Crackdowns, 132
Crime:
analysis of, 37–38, 55, 72, 80–81
community controls on, 23
environment, effects on, 23, 47, 124–126
police role in, 10, 11
(*See also* Arrest; Response)
prevention of, 23, 61, 103–104, 127
Criminal justice system, 2, 43
alternatives to, in response, 11, 44–45, 130, 131–132
better use of, 130, 131–139
misuse of, 43–44
selective enforcement of, 132–133
Criminals, 39
"career," 104
(*See also* Offenders, repeat)
Custody without arrest, 130, 131, 142

Decentralization of management, 159–161, 164
Decision-making, 144
community shares in, 25, 26, 47–48
by rank-and-file, 150
Decoy operations, 18, 132
Deinstitutionalization of mentally ill, 46, 52, 105
Demonstrations, response to, 9, 101
(*See also* Conflict, racial)
Differential-response program, 56
Discretion, 6, 9, 11, 27, 40, 43, 47, 95, 96
misused, 94
narrowed, 129
Domestic disturbances, 91, 112
(*See also* Spousal abuse)
Drinking:
and disorder, 89–90
and driving, 35, 51, 85, 87, 89, 90, 91, 96–97, 136
in public, 105, 130
Drug trafficking, 124
alternative response to, 146, 147
analysis of, 63–64
arrest for, 44, 137
confiscation of proceeds from, 140
as conflict problem, 112
police resources overwhelmed by, xi, xiii, 2

Eck, John E., 12–13, 20, 36, 72–73, 147, 155
Edmonton, Alberta, Canada, 21, 59–61
Effectiveness, 35–36, 162
evaluated, 49, 145–147, 164
of response, 129, 145–147, 164
Enforcement:
via crackdown, 132
of other agencies' laws, 133–134, 139–140
as police role, 2, 18, 40, 133
prevention as alternative to, 103
selective, 132–133

Enforcement (*Cont.*):
traffic, proactive, 18
of traffic laws, 18, 133
of zoning laws, 139–140
Enticement, 135
Environment, effects on crime, 23, 47, 124–126
Exhibitionists, 101

Facilitators, police as, 122
Fear:
of elderly, 45, 119–120
police dealing with, 10, 11, 52–53, 155
of rape, 115, 120
Flint, Mich.:
Flint Neighborhood Foot Patrol Program, 57
police and other agencies in, 107
problem-oriented policing in, 57–58, 60, 61
Force, Robert, 20, 131
Forfeiture of assets, 140
Fosdick, Raymond B., 6, 7
Fuld, Leonard F., 6, 7

Gainesville, Fl., convenience store robberies in, 80–81, 87, 88, 128
Gangs, 44, 54, 69, 85, 134, 137–138, 141
Gates, Daryl F., 58
Graffiti, 126–128

Harassment, 44, 135, 138–139, 141
Harvard, John F. Kennedy School of Government at, 24
Hoare, M. A., 54
Home Office Research Bulletin, 170
Homeless, police response to, 18, 130–131
Hope, Tim, 89–90
Housing complexes:
in Baltimore County, Md., 113, 142
burglaries in, 44–45
conflict resolution in, 113
fear in, 45, 119–120
in Newport News, Va., 99, 113, 134, 142–143
racial conflict in, 120
in St. Louis, Mo., 126
services to, 109–110
as territory, 68
Houston, Tex., 59, 71

Identification (*see* Problem identification)
Incident:
categorized, 38–39
clustered, 33–35, 66–67, 72
Incident-driven policing, 20
Incident-handling, 8, 9, 32–33
Information, 82–89
from community, 86–87
conveyed, as response, 114–119
distorted, 91
evaluated/assessed, 88–89
via networking/professional organizations, 168–170, 171
from offenders, 80, 87
from police files, 85–86, 91–93
rank-and-file as source of, 83–84, 86, 93–94, 97–98, 149, 164
retrieval of, 87–88, 92–93
from victims, 89, 86
Injunctions, 140–141

Integrated Criminal Apprehension Program (ICAP), 37
Interests, multiple, 99–100, 146
International Association of Chiefs of Police (IACP), 7, 170
Irwin v. *Ware,* 129

Jacobs, Jane, 103
Japan, 118
Job satisfaction, 164–165

Kansas City, Mo., 83
  Preventive Patrol Experiment in, 12–13, 23, 61, 151
Kelling, George L., 23, 112, 124, 177
Kennedy, David M., 74

Larson, Richard C., 21, 152
Law Enforcement Assistance Administration, 10, 37
Law Enforcement Code of Ethics, 7
Liability for nonaction, 47, 96, 129, 136
Lindsay, John, 19
Loitering statutes, 134, 135
London, England:
  crime prevention programs in, 103
  drinking and disorder, study of, 89–90
  gangs in, 54, 69, 85
  Home Office in, 89–90, 103, 125, 136
  Metropolitan Police, 5–6
    analysis by, 55, 62
  motor vehicle crime in, 54, 69
London, England (*Cont.*):
  problem-oriented policing in, 53–55, 62, 84, 125
  research in, 85, 170
  shoplifting studies in, 125, 136
  street prostitution in, 54, 69
  theft from shoppers study of, 54, 69, 86, 92
Los Angeles, Calif.:
  Community Mobilization Project (CMP) in, 58, 59, 60, 74
  injunctions against gangs in, 141

Madison, Wis.:
  drinking driver study of, 51, 85, 87, 89, 90, 96–97, 136
  mentally ill, study of, 52, 105
  panhandling, study of, 52, 135, 142
  police department in, 51, 52
    coordination with other agencies, 108, 109
    management style of, 156–157
    promotion criteria of, 158–159
  problem-oriented policing in:
    analysis of, 51–52, 62
    identification of problem, 76, 79
    information gathered, 87
    rank-and-file used, 149
  sexual offense, study of, 51–52, 76, 108
  street prostitution in, 52
Management, 148–175
  analysis by, 61, 62–63, 81, 89
  centralized, 159
  decentralized, 159–161, 164
  dispatcher's role in, 21
  efficiency of, 7, 14–18
  employer-employee relations in, 155–157

Management (*Cont.*):
as end in itself, 14–18, 148
information exchanged by, 168–170
participative, 28
permanent assignments versus rotating shifts, 160–161
preoccupation with, 15–18, 27, 28
problem identification by, 72–73
for problem-oriented policing, 154–156, 173–180
promotion criteria of, 158–159
recruitment by, 165–167
reform of, 6–7, 35–36, 55–56
research and planning by, 161–163
style of, 152–157, 176
supervision by, 157–159
of time use, 151–152
on training needs, 167–168
values articulated by, 152–154
(*See also* Professional model)
Mapping, 139
Mastrofski, Stephen, 164
Mayne, Sir Richard, 153
Mediation skills, 111–114
Medical field, police compared to, 15–17, 106
Mentally ill:
deinstitutionalization of, 46, 52, 105
response to, 18, 130, 170
METAPOL, 170
Minneapolis, Minn., 72
Minorities, 159
(*See also* Conflict, racial)
Missing children, 18, 99
Mott Foundation, 57
Muir, Graham, 70, 71
Murphy, Chris, 70, 71
National Advisory Commission on the Causes and Prevention of Violence, 9
National Advisory Commission on Civil Disorders, 9
National Advisory Commission on Criminal Justice Standards and Goals, 9
National Criminal Justice Reference Service, 85
National Institute of Justice (NIJ), 51, 56, 63, 169, 171
Neutrality of police, 113–114
Newman, Sir Kenneth, 53–55, 153
Newman, Oscar, 103
Newport News, Va.:
conflict resolution in, 113
housing complex, study of, 99, 113, 134, 142–143
mapping as response in, 139
performance evaluation in, 164
police and other agencies in, 127
problem-oriented policing in, 55–57, 155, 173, 177, 178
analysis in, 62, 63, 69, 83–84, 90, 94
information gained in, 87
problem identification in, 65, 66, 74, 76–79
rank-and-file used in, 61, 69, 149, 150
training in, 167
values in, 153
theft from autos in, 127
New York City, N.Y.:
community concerns in, 71
Community Patrol Officer Program (CPOP) in, 58, 60, 73, 74, 88, 95, 164, 173
new personnel for, 61
training in, 167

New York City, N.Y. (*Cont.*):
street prostitution response in, 43–44
subway graffiti removed in, 126–128
911, 19
Noise:
calls on, 92–93
as problem, 71, 81, 112
response to, 40, 128

Oakland, Calif., 99–100, 135
Oasis project, 125
Offenders:
crime analysis identification of, 37
information from, 80, 87
problem focuses on, 105
repeat, 52, 76, 104, 105
response based on, 104–106
Operating level (*see* Beat officer; Beat patrol; Rank-and-file)
Ordinances, 128, 139–140, 142
burglary-prevention, 127
misused, 134, 135
loitering, 134, 135
for street order, 134

Panhandling, 52, 117, 135, 142
Parnas, Raymond, 8
Parole, 138–139
Patrol:
beat (*see* Beat officer; Beat patrol; Rank-and-file)
in Kansas City, Mo., 12–13, 61, 151
motorized, 12–13, 18, 19
random, 12–13
Philadelphia, Pa., 81
Police:
abuse by, 6, 45, 122, 130
accountability of, 10, 11, 27–28, 46–48, 144–145, 153
as advocates, 47
as anomaly, xii
authority of, xii, 6, 11, 45, 122, 128–131
and community (*see* Community-police relations)
conflict resolution by, 112–113
controls:
external, 1, 17, 28, 44, 45, 47
internal, 7, 27–28
credibility of, 134
detectives, 12
as facilitators, 122
fear of, 23, 24
frustrations of, 14–15, 20, 30, 165
hostility to, 22–23
image versus practice of, 8–9
job satisfaction of, 164–165
liability of, 47, 96, 129, 136
medical field compared to, 15–17, 106
as neutral and unbiased, 113–114
numbers of, 21
and other agencies, 106–110, 172
as palliators, 16
and politics, 6, 10, 50
as problem-solvers, 57–58, 73
as professionals, 150
(*See also* Professional model)
on racial equality, 7
research on, 8–13, 85, 89, 161–163, 170

Police (*Cont.*):
subculture of, 29–30, 163, 166
traditional, 178–179
work of (end product), 2, 3, 15, 16
workload, 20–21
(*See also* Policing)
Policing (*see* Community-oriented policing; Police; Problem-oriented policing)
Police Executive Research Forum (PERF), 52, 55, 56, 62, 63, 170, 171
Police Foundation, 10, 170
Portland, Oreg., 127
Poyner, Barry, 125
President's Commission on Campus Unrest, 9
President's Commission on Law Enforcement and Administration of Justice, 9
Prevention:
of crime, 23, 61, 103–104, 127
response as, 14, 143
Proactive role, 21, 32, 45–47, 52, 59, 60, 132
decoy operations as, 18, 132
in problem identification, 46
sting operations as, 132
traffic enforcement as, 18
Probation, 138–139
Problem(s):
analysis of (*see* Analysis)
characteristics of, 34, 36–37, 67–68
disaggregated, 38–40
eliminated or reduced, 36
identification of (*see* Problem identification)
labeling of, 38–40
local (area-specific), 53, 69, 168
multiple interest in, 40–41
Problem(s) (*Cont.*):
offender-focused, 105
redefined, 76–77
response to (*see* Response)
selection among, 77–79
as work unit, 35
Problem identification, 46, 65–79, 81
behavior as focus of, 67
by community, 34–35, 40, 41, 63–64, 70–71, 99, 134, 135
conflict as basis of, 112
incident-clustering leads to, 33–35, 66–67, 72
by management, 72–73
in Newport News, Va., 65, 66, 74, 76–79
persons as focus of, 68
by rank-and-file, 73–75, 83–84, 164
territory as focus of, 67–68
time as focus of, 68
Problem-oriented policing:
analysis in (*see* Analysis)
in Baltimore County, Md. (*see* Baltimore County, Md., problem-oriented policing in)
barriers to, 54–55
community-based (*see* Community-oriented policing)
defined, 3, 32
early experiments in, 51–64
in Flint, Mich., 57–58, 60, 61
implemented, 3, 66, 172–175
in London, 53–55, 62, 84, 125
management in (*see* Management, for problem-oriented policing)
in Newport News (*see* Newport News, Va., problem-oriented policing in)

Problem-oriented policing (*Cont.*):
  as open process, 141–145
  in Philadelphia, Pa., 81
  problem identification for (*see* Problem identification)
  problem-solving as goal for, 56–58
  rank-and-file in (*see* Rank-and-file)
  response in (*see* Response)
  risk in, 48–49
  time needed for, 151
  training in, 65, 167–168
Problem Solving Quarterly, 170
Professional model, 6–8, 17, 19
  and community relations, 22
  crime analysis as important part of, 37
  departure from, 55–56
  on incident-handling, 33
  negative aspects of, 10
  on police role, 112
  reevaluated, 12–13
Professionalism, 17, 150
Prostitution (*see* Street prostitution)
Purcell, C. M., 54

Racial conflicts, 7, 9, 10, 22–23, 109, 120
Rank-and-file:
  analysis by, 61–63, 69, 81, 86, 90, 94
  better use of, 15, 27–29, 32, 56, 61–62
  community-oriented policing based on, 28–29
  decision-making by, 150
  knowledge of, 83–84, 86, 93–94, 97–98, 149, 164
Rank-and-file (*Cont.*):
  problem identification by, 42, 73–75, 83–84, 164
  problems/frustrations of, 149–150
  role of, redefined, 148–150, 157–159
  and supervisors, 157–159
  time use by, 151
Reactive role, 6, 18–21, 32, 33, 132
  motorized patrol as, 18, 19
Reform, 6–7, 9–10, 35–36, 55–56
  change in perspective as, 2
  crisis as factor of, 50
  goals of, 1
  lack of coherent plan, 30–31
  limits on, 15, 29–31
  rank-and-file on, 29, 30
Reiss, Albert, 8, 18
Repeat-offender programs, 104
Research on policing, 8–13, 85, 89, 161–163, 170
Response, 36, 55, 65, 78, 102–147
  accountability of, 144–145
  alternative, 20–21, 103–147, 152
  analysis of, 21, 44–47, 49, 94–98
  arrest as, 37, 136–138, 171–172
  asset forfeiture as, 140
  to burglaries, 44–45
  to calls, 19, 20–21, 152
  to child abuse, 170
  civil law system used in, 139–141
  community input on, 26, 119–121, 144
  community mobilization as, 119–121
  conflict-resolution as, 112–113
  criminal justice system used in, 11, 43–44, 45, 129, 130, 131–139